Mass Authorship and the

Rise of Self-Publishing

IMPRESSIONS ≡

Studies in the Art, Culture, and Future of Books

Matthew P. Brown, series editor

University of Iowa

Mass Authorship and the

Rise of Self-Publishing

Timothy Laquintano

UNIVERSITY OF IOWA PRESS

IOWA CITY

University of Iowa Press, Iowa City 52242
Copyright © 2016 by the University of Iowa Press
www.uiowapress.org
Printed in the United States of America
Design by Sara T. Sauers

The University of Iowa Press is a member of Green Press
Initiative and is committed to preserving natural resources.

Printed on acid-free paper

Library of Congress Cataloging-in-Publication Data
Names: Laquintano, Timothy, author.
Title: Mass authorship and the rise of self-publishing / Timothy Laquintano.
Description: Iowa City : University of Iowa Press, 2016. |
Series: Impressions: Studies in the art, culture, and future of books |
Includes bibliographical references.
Identifiers: LCCN 2016004609 (print) | LCCN 2016016925 (ebook) |
ISBN 9781609384456 (pbk) | ISBN 9781609384463 (ebk)
Subjects: LCSH: Self-publishing. | Authorship. | Books and reading. |
Literature and society. | BISAC: LANGUAGE ARTS & DISCIPLINES / Publishing.
Classification: LCC Z285.5 .L37 2016 (print) | LCC Z285.5 (ebook) |
DDC 070.5/93—dc23
LC record available at https://lccn.loc.gov/2016004609

for Alexander and Matthew

Contents

Acknowledgments

DESPITE THE MANY hours I have spent writing alone, this book has been a collaborative effort. I am indebted to those who have supported my writing, my education, and this project. First, the incomparable Deborah Brandt let me believe I was a competent scholar long enough for me to become a competent scholar. She offered an incredible amount of time and energy to support my work at the University of Wisconsin, and she continued to read drafts and offer insightful feedback on this book well into her retirement. She is an exemplary scholar-teacher. Other Wisconsin faculty offered insightful feedback and support in my graduate education and in the work that would eventually form the basis for this book, including Michael Bernard-Donals, Greg Downey, David Fleming, Rob Howard, Brad Hughes, Marty Nystrand, and Morris Young. Fellow Badgers from the University of Wisconsin kept me sane while I was working on the dissertation and the manuscript, including Scot Barnett, Rik Hunter, Adam Koehler, Corey Mead, Annette Vee, and Kate Vieira.

In addition to the Wisconsin influence, faculty at other institutions have offered me key support along the way. Christiane Donahue, Charles Bazerman, and Christina Haas provided keen feedback at the Dartmouth Summer Seminar, and Professors Michael West and Tyler Hoffman have both offered astute counsel on the trajectory of my education. Annette Vee, Kate Vieira, and Lee Nickoson read drafts of the chapters as they were being produced. My writing colleagues at Lafayette College, Patricia

Donahue and Bianca Falbo, made sure I had time to write by helping me manage campus life. Chris Phillips was always willing to have conversations about the history of the book, and Paul Cefalu offered helpful and timely publishing advice. Lafayette's Academic Research Committee provided research funds and support for this project. These research funds also supported the work of Sam Griffith, a research assistant to whom I am thankful for helping me research Wattpad during the summer of 2011.

I owe special gratitude to the staff at the University of Iowa Press, especially Matthew Brown and Catherine Cocks for their guidance. Susan Hill Newton did a wonderful job ushering the text through production, and Judith Antonelli offered a sharp eye while copyediting. I also owe thanks to two anonymous reviewers who offered wonderful suggestions for revision.

Thanks to David and the two Christine Laquintanos, who supported me in various ways and entertained my children while I worked on holidays. Jill Belli offered crucial moral and professional support throughout the difficult final stages of the project. My deepest appreciation goes to Alexander and Matthew, whose constant demand for things like food and shelter encouraged me to keep working, and whose smiles made the entire process seem slightly less lonely.

Permissions

PARTS OF THIS manuscript have appeared in previous publications. A portion of chapter 1 appeared in "The Legacy of the Vanity Press and Digital Transitions" in the *Journal of Electronic Publishing* 16, no. 1 (2013): n.p. Parts of chapter 6 originally appeared in "Online Book Reviews and Emerging Generic Conventions: A Study of Authorship, Publishing, and Peer Review," in *International Advances in Writing Research*, ed. Charles Bazerman et al. (Fort Collins, CO: WAC Clearinghouse and Parlor Press, 2012), 521–38. Scattered across the manuscript are small parts of "Sustained Authorship: Ebooks, Value, and Participatory Culture," which appeared in *Written Communication* 27, no. 4 (Fall 2010): 469–93. Finally, the first half of chapter 5 appeared in "Digital Writing and the Flow of Intellectual Property," which was first published in *Computers and Composition* 23, no. 3 (Fall 2010): 193–201. Special thanks to the *Journal of Electronic Publishing,* Charles Bazerman, Elsevier, and Sage Publishing for allowing me to reprint the material.

Introduction

IN A 1996 ESSAY, published when bathtubs held a curiously prominent role in debates about reading, the eminent Italian author Umberto Eco expressed his hope that email would have happy consequences for the future of books:

> People can communicate directly without the intervention of publishing houses. A great many people do not want to publish; they simply want to communicate with each other. The fact that in the future they will do it by E-mail or over the Internet will be a great boon for books and for the culture and the market of the book. Look at a bookstore. There are too many books. I receive too many books every week. If the computer network succeeds in reducing the quantity of published books, this would be a paramount cultural improvement.[1]

Eco's meditation on information technologies is one part prediction and one part reiteration of the perennial fantasy authors and publishers have had of solving the "problem" of book abundance. Writing when poor resolution made screen reading unpleasant, Eco hoped that communication that didn't have to be in a book to satisfy its author's goals would migrate elsewhere, to other communicative forms made possible by information technologies.[2] This would leave only content that had a natural affinity with the codex to exist as a print book—the kind of thing one could comfortably read in a bathtub.

1

Two decades later a mutated version of Eco's prediction is still circulating: commentators speculate that eventually many books will be audience-tested digitally, and then only the most durable or popular will move into brick-and-mortar stores in print runs, thereby reducing the number of printed books. Imposing a divide between print and electronic formats, Eco did not anticipate the rapid integration of the ebook into what Raffaele Simone calls "the brachylogy" of the book. This is the process by which we homogenize vastly diverse texts using the shorthand expression *book*, which indicates both the physical container of the medium and the content inside.[3] Although ebooks have containers with different physical properties than print books, they have been subsumed into this brachylogy because they have been called *books* by authors, readers, and publishers. This integration, along with widespread access to self-publishing technologies, has resulted in a vast increase in the output of books, a "hyperabundance" of books.[4]

Hyperabundance may be grim news to Eco, but it would not have surprised Edward Uhlan, a twentieth-century American subsidy publisher, a self-described "rogue of publishers' row" who tried for years to shake the "vanity publisher" label that dogged his career. Uhlan knew, as many publishing professionals who dealt with mountains of submissions at the time knew, that since at least the late nineteenth century the number of writers with manuscripts has dwarfed the number of books that could be published.[5] A great number of people *do* want to publish books. The so-called slush pile has vexed royalty publishers for more than 150 years, but Uhlan delighted in the writing of the masses, partly because it signaled profit for him but also because he had respect for it. He considered it an expected consequence of mass schooling: "Once writers were a class apart, distinguished by ink-stained fingers, unkempt hair, and a predilection for drinking cheap wine in cellars. Mass education has changed all that; scratch any man on the street, and you will find a little printer's ink oozing out."[6]

That ink is now digital text, and at the twentieth anniversary of Eco expressing his hope that information technologies might reduce the number of books, there are millions of books being published by the "[wo] man on the street" using digital technologies. Smashwords, a company that helps self-published authors distribute ebooks, recently noted on its website that it has helped writers publish close to fourteen billion words since it began in 2008.[7] Bowker reported that in 2013, self-published authors produced close to half a million books.[8] Notably, this does not include books published without International Standard Book Numbers (ISBNs), like many published through Amazon, nor does it include ebooks published on websites like Wattpad. Wattpad is an ebook website where writers can serialize and publish their writing for free through a mobile application, and its writers and readers have collectively spent billions of minutes per month on the site.[9]

Volume alone says little about the diversity of self-publishing, and this diversity often confounds the distinction between professional and amateur. Self-publishing tends to occupy the space between everyday personal writing and mass-produced corporate culture while also re-verberating in those areas. Self-published authors distribute their work for self-edification and for self-amusement, and they often write books to make meaning in and of their lives. They write popular fiction, memoirs, how-to guides, poetry, travel books, humor books, and more. Most recreational self-published authors reach audiences of tens or hundreds, but some reach audiences of tens of thousands or more. As output has grown, recreation has yielded to a growing professionalism, and some self-published authors have begun earning a living from their writing and identify with the independent, or "indie," author movement. Others self-publish to build an audience and marshal their following into a tra-ditional publishing contract. Some authors now traverse publishing and self-publishing in a hybrid model, and, mostly unthinkable even a decade ago, some literary authors have now begun self-publishing in order to augment their salaries, experiment with economically risky literary forms, or make out-of-print works available to readers.

Self-publishing, in other words, represents plural activities that have expanded rapidly in the wake of digital technologies. It has moved from the fringe of the publishing industry to become a small and fluid part of its core. A 2015 economic study found that since mid-2012, self-published titles have become a "consequential" part of the publishing industry, ac-counting for just over 10 percent of bestselling titles.[10] Although its future as an industry is somewhat fragile, self-publishing has become a durable part of the cultural milieu, with the potential to introduce a long-term shift into how we understand author-publisher-reader relations. It is not synonymous with the future of the book, but it has become an important component of how books are produced and circulated, and the discourse that surrounds it lays bare some of the deepest conflicts and anxieties surrounding media transition and the future of the book.

Rethinking Self-Publishing

In the publishing industry and in the popular press, there have been two dominant ways of understanding self-publishing and its copious output. The first position celebrates the freedom of digital publishing and the fall of New York gatekeepers who suppressed different kinds of writing because they were conservative by nature and had been corrupted by the market. The second position laments the fall of gatekeepers because accessible publishing presents an existential threat to the culture of the book. It has created a flood of amateurish books that should be ignored or dismissed because they do not adhere to professional standards. The first position presumes a weakening of the publisher, the second a weakening of the professional author, whose work is likely to be lost in the flood.

Umberto Eco's rumination on the glut of books shows how similar themes surface in academic discussions about the effect of digital technologies on the book. Publishing commentary and academic commentary often share similar language about technology, similar assumptions about the relationship between writers and readers, and a similar anxiety about the weakening of respected cultural institutions that have coalesced around the book. Eco published his desire to see fewer books during the days of hypertext theory. In that period, scholars interested in electronic writing made strong claims about the effect that digital technologies would have on authorship and the future of the book. Hypertext theorists argued that digital texts had two properties—they could be easily manipulated and easily circulated—that would weaken the status and power of the author (or blow the author's ashes out to sea, as his or her death was thought to have happened long ago, anyway). Critics speculated that the properties of digital technologies would decenter or marginalize the author and perhaps even encourage texts to circulate in a frictionless Foucauldian state without the cultural baggage of the author's name impeding the circulation and recomposition of texts. In other words, the most extreme predictions foresaw books circulating in the way many contemporary memes circulate (and morph) through social media.

In 2008 Matthew Kirschenbaum issued a sharp corrective to hypertext theory when he demonstrated that many hypertext claims focused exclusively on how texts behaved at the level of the graphical user interface. He noted that the theories failed to account for the ways other parts of the computer (such as storage) conditioned how digital texts were produced, circulated, and maintained.[11] Likewise, dramatic claims about the effect that digital technologies would have on authorship largely failed to take into account what people actually do with digital technologies once they sit down to use them—how they resist, manipulate, and exploit their affordances. Richard Grusin detected this problem with hypertext theory as early as 1994 when he called for ethnographic accounts of digital writers to combat what he saw as strains of "technological determinism" that had led to the strong claims about the "democratization" of writing and authorship.[12]

In the first decade of the new millennium, strong claims about Web 2.0 followed strong claims about hypertext. If hypertext theory foresaw the author's power slip away with easily manipulated texts, theories of Web 2.0 foresaw the publisher's power slip away with the spread of ubiquitous publishing that happened through platforms for participation energized by peer-to-peer production. In the discourse of Web 2.0, users ousted traditional gatekeepers by circumventing the industrial middleman to reach readers directly, a process referred to as *disintermediation*. In this narrative the power of the publisher recedes. Clay Shirky, for example, speculated that the spread of networked computing technologies would have extreme consequences for traditional publishers. He argued that the intellectual labor required to produce long-form writing would still be necessary, but in large part the cadre of professionals required to make a text public—configured in the manner of the twentieth-century publishing firm—would face growing obsolescence.[13]

Because the book has been such a revered communications medium, the debates of the last two decades—in academia, the publishing industry, and the popular press—have often become excessive, embedded with fear and loathing about the potential death of the book, the author, or the publisher. Instead of assuming hybridity and blending, the debates have pitted print and the digital against each other, and every new set of quarterly statistics on book sales whizzes through the blogosphere, becoming a referendum on the impending victory of the ebook or the heroic durability of the print book.

Mass Authorship takes a more measured approach, providing a grounded perspective on the contemporary relationship of writers to publishers, digital tools, and readers. It draws on eight years of Internet research and interviews with eighty-one self-published authors in four different groups of writers to study the interrelationship of writing, publishing, and reading during a time of transition, when it has become possible to publish books inexpensively and rapidly without the capital investment that was necessary in the twentieth century. It concentrates on the value that participants produce as they create and circulate ebooks, as well as the problems they face in systems in which representative stakeholders from the royalty system (such as professional agents, publishers, and reviewers) can be absent: How do authors and readers of nonfiction texts establish the credibility that royalty publishers have traditionally lent to published books? If, in the royalty system, "being published" was a mark of distinction that contributed to the writer's professional identity, how do writers reconfigure that identity in the absence of publishers? How do self-published authors amass an audience and acquire attention when, it sometimes seems, there are more writers than readers?

By concentrating on how these everyday authors conceptualize and execute their work, *Mass Authorship* avoids the argument of supersessionism, which concludes that self-publishing and ebooks are going to render publishers obsolete—a worry that dates back to at least the eighteenth century.[14] Indeed, very few self-published authors I interviewed, even those who had sold hundreds of thousands of books, thought that professional book publishers would soon be obsolete. Publishers provide considerable value to book production, they have stringent copyright laws protecting their backlists, and they largely control access to brick-and-mortar distribution. In contrast to the position that publishers will soon become obsolete, this book argues that multiple viable models of publishing have emerged to compete and complement one another; these multiple models force us to consider publishing both as a professional practice and as a literacy practice accessible to everyday people, creating multiple zones of activity that will continue to interact in blended ways with points of symbiosis and antagonism.

This line of thinking leads me to argue that two common ways of understanding self-publishing have significant limitations, and this is crucial because both ways of understanding have influenced how we think about digital writing and publishing at large. Indeed, my argument recasts the popular but weak debates about the flood and the gates.

First, I reconsider the position that self-publishing represents a flood of books that pose a threat to the culture of the book, especially because they don't adhere to the standards of the professional book industry. Some self-published books do adhere to these standards, but many don't. However, this position deploys notions of books, publishing, and authorship that are too heavily invested in the homogenizing professional standardization indicative of serious book culture, which is heavily invested in a "read-only" conception of the book—that is, a conception of the book as a finished entity, produced by capital and regulated by expertise.

Second, I rethink the viewpoint that self-publishing is free of gatekeeping. Related to yet distinct from the flood threat, arguments about the decline of gatekeepers are too heavily invested in a simplified theory of publishing and a strict hierarchy of value. This viewpoint obscures the realities of the new intermediaries. Rather than experiencing the decline of the gatekeeper, self-publishing writers actually contend with various kinds of refashioned intermediaries, from actual corporate entities such as Amazon to virtual constructs in the minds of the authors. Deploying either of the conventional frameworks makes it difficult to understand how and why people self-publish.

Instead, *Mass Authorship* provides a route to moving beyond flood metaphors and thus to understanding the hyperabundance that results when everyday people acquire access to widespread publishing technologies. Equally important, *Mass Authorship* encourages us to move past the puffery about disintermediation as a way to understand self-publishing (or any digital publishing). When writers circumvent publishers, they do indeed need to fill the vacuum of labor left by the absence of a publishing company, but this vacuum does not remain empty in a disintermediated state in which writer and reader communicate directly (although it does sometimes seem that way). Rather, self-publishing is intensely mediated:

the work of the authors is distributed across the digital platforms of giant corporations and small start-ups, through an emerging cottage industry of support services, and through the authors' mediated engagement with the peer-to-peer energy of readers in participatory culture. *Mass Authorship* provides a detailed analysis of the ways that authors orchestrate publishing activities as they use digital tools and ad hoc configurations of labor to fill the vacuum left by publishers.

The initial vacuum left by the disappearance of agents and publishers is not simply about labor, however. It is also about a corresponding loss of identity and the writer's opportunity to become an "author." In the twentieth century the commercial royalty publisher dominated the world of books. This model helped naturalize the assumption that writers would find a publisher for their work. With only a few minor exceptions, finding a publisher was a preliminary move to becoming an author, and except in extraordinarily rare cases, one could not be an author without having a publisher. Thus writers, both professional and amateur, used the idea of the publisher to orient themselves to their writing, its value, and their profession. Now, in the absence of such publishers, writers must refashion their identity and deploy alternate mechanisms to become authors and identify as such. This is not simply because writers can now make their texts publicly available without a publisher, but because everyone else can, too. For the time being, even in the environment of self-publication, the publisher has not disappeared but rather shapes the experience of self-publishing in powerful ways. With very important exceptions that I will document, the power, prestige, and standards that publishers have developed throughout the history of professional print culture have been partly reinscribed in digital spaces as differentiating processes that are considered necessary amid the sheer magnitude of aspiring writers now publishing books.

The Analytic Framework: Five Concepts

Because of the contemporary play between settled and new meanings for writer and publisher, I propose understanding the digital book culture made possible by self-publishing through an analytic framework comprising five interrelated concepts. These five concepts concentrate on the emergence of accessible publishing; on the contemporary relationships among writers, publishers, books, and readers; and on the copious output of self-publishing.

First, self-publishing is entailed in *shifting systems of mediation*, a more fine-tuned portrait of a refashioned gatekeeping. Partly through recounting the variety of vetting by nonpublishers throughout the history of the book and partly through an ideological critique of the term's misleading nature, I argue that *disintermediation* should be replaced, conceptually, with this layered approach to shifting systems.

Second, I construe *publishing as a literacy practice*, an umbrella that indicates the sociocultural activity that develops under conditions in which ordinary people have the ability to publish their writing using digital infrastructures. In this process, issues formerly relegated to book-culture professionals become infused into everyday experience in mundane (and exceptional) ways.

The third concept is *mass authorship*, which indicates both the growing class of writers who self-publish books and the way their experiences and identities are shaped by the ideological legacy of more exclusive forms of individual authorship.

The fourth concept is *the book as a read-write medium*, by which I mean both the material qualities of ebooks that differ from print and an attitude among laypeople and nonprofessional writers that leads them to feel authorized to write books and capable of doing so.

Finally, the fifth aspect of the framework highlights the role of *networked participants* (as opposed to "readers") with the capacity to publish and induce network effects that shape the trajectories and circulation patterns of both traditionally published and self-published books and create mediated book cultures. Let's look at each concept in turn.

Shifting Systems of Mediation

If we move away from disintermediation and the decline of gatekeeping, how are we to comprehend the impact of self-publishing? The first concept of my analytic framework, shifting systems of mediation, creates an alternative understanding that enables us to rely less heavily on those two ideas. The notion of disintermediation has influenced theories of publishing, empirical work about self-publishing, and considerations of new publishing technologies.[15] Indeed, I myself have used it in the past to discuss the ability of digital authors to interact with readers and circumvent publishers. The term has some value to indicate, in digital environments, the partial (or in some cases full) displacement of entrenched industrial intermediaries, gatekeepers who have had significant influence on the production of culture. However, the focus on gatekeepers reduces the emergence of multiple models of publishing, which coexist and are intertwined in complex ways, to the two competing interpretations described above: celebrating freedom from gatekeepers and lamenting the flood that results. These positions have stalemated and have little power to explain contemporary publishing environments.

In contrast, I will build on Evgeny Morozov's work, which opens a route around the stalemate. He has argued persuasively that digital systems are not disintermediated. In a gruff and scathing critique, Morozov claims that Silicon Valley stakeholders manufacture the ideology of "solutionism" and the Internet. This discourse champions new computing technologies and their rapid adoption, and it seeks to rationalize all social problems, naively assuming that such problems can be solved without traditional experts. All one needs are the right "data," the right platform, and the right networked citizen to solve the problem through crowdsourcing.[16]

The term *disintermediation* sits squarely in this ideology, since it has been deployed to frame print, and the expertise of print publishers, as passé. Morozov argues that there are two problems with the term. First, it's an abomination of the English language, the ugliest word in existence. Second, and more important, the term is deceptive. Rather than accepting the notion of the displacement of industrial intermediaries for direct digital connections, Morozov argues that we now see new intermediaries, corporations and entities that enable digital communications and that operate with an infrastructure and influence that are not always visible to the users who depend on them.[17]

Laura J. Miller comes to a similar conclusion in her discussion of self-publishing, noting that self-published authors face a future of relying heavily on corporate retailers that mediate their relationship with readers.[18] *Mass Authorship* makes the influence of these new intermediaries visible in a way that clearly shows the pressure they exert on the culture of ebooks. This includes the corporations that Miller and Morozov concentrate on, but *Mass Authorship* also considers less visible forms of mediation, such as algorithms and the intellectual property climates that condition the contemporary work of writing.

Another problem with disintermediation and its correspondent concept of gatekeeping is that gatekeeping is a deceptive metaphor for publishing. It suggests a model in which a manuscript is submitted to a publisher, who deems it worthy of publication and then manages the production of the text and sees it through to a ready and waiting reading public. Publishers have been profoundly influential gatekeepers by vetting the information in manuscripts, standardizing production and design, and investing capital to produce and distribute books. But even in the age of print, publishers were joined by a number of entities that enabled a book to circulate and amass a reading public. Scholarship in the history of the book shows that peer reviewers, book reviewers, booksellers who recommended books to customers, award committees, professors with syllabi, school boards, prize committees, fellow readers, and librarians all had gatekeeping functions and roles to play in how a text became public. Indeed, if publishers had really been stringent or homogeneous gatekeepers in the age of print, we probably wouldn't have had centuries of cultural critics lamenting trashy reading.

This insight, combined with the multiple trajectories that books now take to become public, suggests that publishing must be understood more capaciously as a widespread popular practice that exists alongside, and influences, professional practice. *Mass Authorship* thus deploys a notion of publishing that extends beyond the work of publishers to account for the activities that help books circulate. It considers the latent and active forces, activities, networks, and actors that enable a book to amass a reading public, and this includes micropublics, which have been relatively absent in the considerations of contemporary book culture. This approach is necessary when digital systems and feedback loops are recursive, messy, fast, and often publicly negotiated, as they are in self-publishing. This approach also suggests that the millions of self-published books now sitting in digital databases exist more as publicly accessible books than as published books. They exist largely as latent potential. In my understanding, books unengaged by readers haven't circumvented gatekeepers; they want for gatekeepers.

Publishing as a Literacy Practice

The second concept of my five-part framework is publishing as a literacy practice. Although Clay Shirky has been hyperbolic in his assessment of traditional publishing, he has made a keen insight about digital technologies: they have made publishing a literacy practice, by which he means an accessible activity that has moved from a group of specialists to become embedded in society and widely available to the citizenry.[19] Shirky spends more time thinking about how everyday publishing can be deployed for organizing political movements than for publishing books. So here I will fill out Shirky's idea in relation to books and writing. I define publishing as a literacy practice that develops under conditions in which ordinary people have the ability to publish their writing using digital infrastructures. This extends beyond the work of authors and includes the experiences of readers who participate in the publishing process by making their own writing public (e.g., through reviews and discussion). In this sense, publishing as a literacy practice and publishing as a professional field can coexist and have multiple points of contact.

My understanding of a literacy practice comes from the field of writing studies (sometimes also called composition and rhetoric).[20] I often use Paul Prior's term "literate activity" as a way of understanding contemporary meaning-making practices that often flow across media (e.g., screens, books, papers) and modes of communication (e.g., oral, written, visual, gestural). Prior argues that the production of writing is situated deeply in the environment among overlapping activity systems, which are composed of human and nonhuman actors, genres, modalities, semiotic resources, dynamics of mediation, technologies, and materials; all of these are developed in multiple times and spaces and converge to make written communication possible. In this view, writing is a goal-oriented, embodied, distributed act that requires writers to recruit cognitive and material tools to execute their activity.[21]

Charles Bazerman and David Russell have described an activity approach in this manner:

> Writing is alive when it is being written, read, remembered, contemplated, followed—when it is part of human activity. Otherwise it is

dead on the page, devoid of meaning, devoid of influence, worthless. The signs on the page serve to mediate between people, activate their thoughts, direct their attention, coordinate their actions, provide the means of relationship. It is in the context of their activities that people consider texts and give meaning to texts. And it is in the organization of activities that people find the needs, stances, interactions, and tasks that orient their attention toward the texts they write and read. So to study text production, text reception, text meaning, and text value apart from their animating activities is to miss the core of text's being.[22]

In this framework the book has no value except when understood in the systems of human activity that give it meaning. Multiple systems converge on any given context of literacy, sometimes introducing or reinforcing values, sometimes creating contradictions and tensions. The intense focus on human activity illustrates some of the incredibly minute and mundane interactions that can nevertheless shape a reader's approach to a text or a writer's approach to writing it.[23]

Let's explore how thinking about publishing as a literacy practice differs from thinking about publishing as a professional practice by probing a question that, in both academic commentary and industry commentary, has never been far from the discussions of self-publishing: Are self-published books any good? This question tends to be asked with a standard of quality in mind that derives from professional publishing. John B. Thompson explains, "For most trade publishers, the 'value' of a particular book or book project is understood in one of two ways: its sales or sales potential, that is, its capacity to generate economic capital; and its quality, which can be understood in various ways but includes its potential for winning various forms of recognition such as prizes and glowing reviews, or in other words, its capacity to generate symbolic capital. These are the only criteria—there simply are no other."[24]

In considerations of self-publishing, these two standards often tacitly underpin the debate, and this has enabled self-publishing detractors to dismiss much of the output. Using this standard to ascertain the value of self-published books certainly has relevance for professional publishers thinking about the future of their business models, but deploying a professional standard presents obstacles for understanding how and why people engage in publishing as a literate practice that provides meaning in their lives.

The first problem with using Thompson's standards is that professional publishing continues to reify the book as a discrete work; the autonomous book is embedded in the standard largely because of economic necessity. In the decades after the publication of Michel Foucault's "What Is an Author?", scholars spent substantial amounts of energy critiquing the viability and coherence of the autonomous work, emphasizing intertextuality and the way texts rely on others for their meaning. Although intertextuality makes the autonomous work a theoretically suspect construct, publishing still relies on a discrete unit for marketing and sales (which is now being challenged by subscription and serialization models). Moreover, to gain awards and recognition, a book has to be materially delineated from others; its intertextuality must be obfuscated in order for it to be considered new and original. Thus, even if the autonomy of the book is problematic in theoretical terms, it is still largely endemic to the way the entire publishing industry is structured. Professional publishing thus operates much like authorship in the humanities, where, despite decades of theoretical critiques of individual authorship, we continue to rely on the concept for economic and professional evaluation and advancement.[25]

The focus on this economic and material unit, the individual book, continues to disguise key insights about writing and reading made in the past decades. Echoing the language of rhetoric scholar Casey Boyle, I would say that Thompson's standard from publishing concentrates more on what a book is, whereas an approach to publishing as a literacy practice would be more concerned with what a book does, or perhaps more important, what people do with a book.[26] Writing studies scholars have been reluctant to grant the kind of autonomy to the individual book that is embedded in the economics of publishing. Instead they highlight how the book acts, and is acted upon, in media ecologies where people move through different media and modes of communication and where the book might take on multiple and plural forms of significance that run contrary to the author's intention.

This is not radically different from some of the key insights of post-structuralism, but like many current trends of thought in the humanities, research on literate activity has placed a much heavier role on embodied interaction and the material environment in the production of meaning-making practices. It takes the position that reifying the work itself has tended to artificially separate the book from other texts (as in poststructuralism), but it also concentrates on how an emphasis on the work has artificially separated the writing inside a book from the material environment, the technologies we rely on to make sense of it, and the modes of communication that enable its production and circulation: talk, visuals, embodied gestures, and so on. This may seem like an excessively arcane point, but if we think about publishing as literacy instead of as a profession, it is no longer necessary to concentrate on the book as a primary unit of analysis. In Prior's terms, books are only "focal texts" embedded in larger semiotic systems that are usually just as important, if not more so, than the text itself, and focal texts are no more autonomous from streams of discourse than "the spray thrown up by white water in a river."[27] For multiple reasons, professional publishers could not afford to conceptualize books in this manner.

Although the book is the core economic unit in publishing, an understanding of it as only a focal text minimizes focus on the object and shifts attention to the systems and practices in which it is situated. This means that the complexity of literacy practices surrounding a book is never reducible to, or determined by, the complexity of the linguistic code in a book. A "bad" book, which would be worthless by a particular professional standard, can nonetheless be complex, not necessarily because of the linguistic code inside but because of the densely textured systems involved in its production, circulation, reception, and effects. This is why understanding self-publishing as a literacy practice cannot happen solely through an analysis of the content of self-published books: the text inside does not determine the activity in which it is embedded, and the text does not determine how it will be interpreted, used, or appropriated.

Of course the text still matters, and *Mass Authorship* will spend considerable time demonstrating how publishing practices respond to the information inside a text, but it will never assume that the linguistic code in a book determines the book's activity or interpretations. This is an assumption that writing studies shares with certain traditions of cultural studies or reception studies, but whereas cultural studies has been more concerned with the uptake and appropriation of mass culture, writing studies has a longer tradition of focusing more intently on processes of written production.

The approach I have been summarizing has allowed scholars to think of the ways that textual value itself is context-sensitive and deeply situated, which encourages us to understand how communities of readers and writers develop their own standards for whether a communicative practice is worthwhile. The self-published books I studied ranged from forty pages to five hundred pages, with content that spanned everything from probability theory to fictional high school dating dynamics to gritty recollections of sex work. Some texts circulated only as PDF documents, a fact that might make some book professionals loath to call them books. But they were valued as books. Ryan Fee, for example, published a poker strategy guide as a PDF document at the age of nineteen. As released, it probably would not have passed muster if submitted for consideration with a traditional publisher. An editor would have pointed to issues with organization and undefined jargon and would probably have raised eyebrows when encountering phrases like "in the event that you bet and get raised on a card that sucks for you." This lack of standardized English has been a point of focus in laments about the poor quality of self-published books, and Fee's book would not have registered on Thompson's standards of value.

Writing studies, however, has long pointed out that writers are perfectly capable of creating shared meaning without a dutiful allegiance to standardized English. Fee was writing for his audience, not for professionally tuned sensibilities. His substantial readership (probably in the tens of thousands) called his manuscript a book when they discussed it and deferred to him as an expert author, thereby integrating a PDF file into the book's brachylogy. Beginning poker players pored over it, studied it, and discussed it online. Readers tolerated the nonstandard grammar because they valued the content. Because he released it for free, the book spread widely and was eventually translated by teams of volunteers into several other languages. If we studied the text, we would find little to value from the perspective of professional publishing. If we studied the practices that have surrounded it, however, we would see that by a number of measures (readership, length and ease of accessibility, number of translations) Fee's book has been far more successful than many professionally produced print books in the twentieth century, even though it lacked a number of their characteristics.

Thus, to understand publishing as a literacy practice is to understand that the question "Are the books any good?" is mostly a red herring that will not bring one closer to understanding the kinds of meaning people create in their lives by writing and publishing books. But because systems of literate practice travel and overlap, the purpose is also not to introduce a purely relative or subjective understanding of a book or its quality. This understanding is communally generated. And as I will show in chapter 3, even lay readers widely agree on some of the formal and technical characteristics of a "good" book, and those standards—along with standards of English—have surfaced in multiple configurations in the experiences of self-published authors. In fact, a number of readers blasted Fee for his grammar because they imposed expectations for what counts as a book onto his text, and these expectations are inherited from a long history of engagement with texts produced according to standards of professional publishers who have invested substantial capital and expertise to achieve them.

Mass Authorship

The third concept in my framework considers mass authorship instead of individual authorship. In his study of American copyright, Siva Vaidhyanathan argues that in the past decades scholars have studied multiple models of authorship, but there have been two particularly important lines of inquiry that depart from other definitions of an author.[28] One line studies (and deconstructs) the more elite Author with a capital *A*. This is the Romantic Author, the author as a cultural beacon, the author celebrated by critics. Also called the *modern author* or the *individual author*, this is the kind of author that poststructuralism has questioned as theoretically suspect: a genius creator rooted in exaggerated notions of originality and individuality. This author is scarce and is often tacitly male, and his work has to be made visible by protecting the world from a flood of "bad" books. This is the author that Michel Foucault contended is less a flesh-and-blood human than a function, a way of talking about and classifying literary culture and analysis. The discourse that circulates around this kind of author, Foucault writes, "must be received in a certain mode" and "in a given culture, must receive a certain status."[29]

The other line employs a more capacious notion of authorship. Vaidhyanathan follows this direction in his study, and it begins with a more agent-centered definition of an author as an ordinary creator of cultural goods.[30] Far more mundane than the Romantic Author, this approach is germane when digital technologies have made many forms of cultural production and distribution more accessible and when ordinary creators now experience tensions with copyright law, which has long helped define the contours of authorship. Rather than allowing Vaidhyanathan to mount theoretical critiques of the Romantic Author, this line enables his view of a more pertinent analysis for the current situation: "A seventeen-year-old mixing rap music in her garage," he writes, "does not care whether the romantic author is dead or alive. She cares whether she is going to get sued if she borrows a three-second string of a long-forgotten disco song."[31]

In my study of self-publishing book writers, I began with an inclusive definition of an author: a writer who has made his or her book publicly accessible. But as the study progressed, I found the notion of the Romantic Author to be tightly entrenched in everyday experience. In contrast to Vaidhyanathan's deejay, many of the writers I interviewed cared a great deal about whether the Romantic Author was alive. At the core of mass authorship is the idea that many of the values and ideologies of professional book culture, which is responsible for producing and protecting the Romantic Author, bear down on and organize the experience of ordinary creators when they turn to books as a mode of written production. This is similar to how the historical legacies of reading and writing—their association with capitalism, religion, and democracy—bear down on ordinary literacy practices, including the ways people access literacy, the opportunities it grants them, and the values that are assigned to different forms of it.[32]

The powerful legacies of book authorship are what differentiate the practices I theorize in this book from other instantiations of the online digital cultures that they nevertheless resemble. Print standards, values, and expectations have been developed over hundreds of years; they are absorbed through Western education, and writers bring these values and expectations to the Internet. *Mass Authorship* explores how authors exploit network effects, peer production, and new technologies to publish writing yet at the same time collectively shape their practices around issues of central importance to dominant forms of print authorship. Authors create localized procedures to control intellectual property. They obfuscate the source of collaborative labor to preserve individuality and textual ownership, and they develop standards for originality and textual quality.

The blend of accessible publishing and emerging practices with persisting legacies creates the backdrop to the rise of mass authorship. As I noted above, by mass authorship I mean both the growing class of writers who self-publish books and the way their experiences and identities are shaped by the ideological legacy of more exclusive forms of individual authorship. Mass authorship represents a third line of inquiry that synthesizes the two established lines of inquiry. This comes from a data-driven grounded approach to defining authorship that is neither agent-centered nor discourse-centered but is ultimately distributed—an approach that studies the meshing of the established discourses of an author with communally generated definitions, the self-identification of writers with authorship, online performances, and the affordances and uses of networked technologies and objects. These combine to make and remake cultures of mass authorship. As a phenomenon, mass authorship is distributed, in the sense that it is widely available to the population but also in the sense that the technological and cultural processes that make it possible are highly distributed through the activity of many actors and their use of tools and technologies.

The Book as a Read-Write Medium

If prestigious versions of authorship inflect the experience of ordinary writers, something similar can be said about book publishing. Ted Striphas examines the cultural work that enables "the book" to occupy a contradictory and culturally loaded position. On the one hand, the book has been at the edge of a nineteenth- and twentieth-century economic transition to a system in which economic vitality "increasingly hinged on working people's consumption of abundant, mass-produced goods." This mass production turned the book into a mundane and ubiquitous social artifact. On the other hand, Striphas argues, the work of culture continued to elevate and nurture "the book" as a "sacred" and "hallowed" object.[33]

One reason the book has maintained this status is that it has largely been understood as a read-only medium. Drawing on computer terminology, Lawrence Lessig distinguishes between "read-only" media and "read-write" media: read-only media require intensive capital investment to produce, extensive professional know-how, and sometimes permission from cultural gatekeepers. Read-write media are less expensive and more accessible, and they invite robust cultures of participation. For Lessig, corporate dominance of the culture industry throughout the twentieth century stifled amateur cultures of production, which became ingrained in how we understand certain media.[34] Because of its status as a hallowed object, the book has been the read-only writing media of the twentieth century par excellence, to the point that it hasn't been unknown for book professionals to pathologize as delusional the authors who tried to write and publish without some sort of third-party authorization.[35]

The book's read-only standing has been predicated on the circumstance that although books have become ubiquitous, opportunities to become a published author remained relatively scarce until the rise of mass publishing afforded by the Internet, an opportunity still in flux and in its infancy.[36] This read-only status has been the linchpin in complaints about abundance: the threat of "too many books" presents a problem for the two most visible participants of a read-only medium: the scarce author (whose work is obscured), and the reader (who might not find the most enlightening books if there are too many choices). Deborah Brandt argues that many Western institutions that promote mass literacy have been built on the assumption that "readers were presumed to be many and writers were presumed to be few," and she claims that this assumption has been upset as we have moved into an economy that demands mass writing as a mode of economic production.[37] Similarly, our understanding of book publishing and authorship has been grounded in the assumption that readers will be many and authors will be few. This assumption has been upset as we have moved into an era of accessible book publishing.

One consequence of the book having been so professionalized is that attempts to understand its digital transition have placed a heavy emphasis on the way people relate to books as readers and little emphasis on how they relate to books as potential writers, publishers, readers, reviewers, or curators.[38] Thus one aim of this book is to reorient our understanding of contemporary books away from an understanding of them solely as read-only objects and toward a more capacious understanding of them as read-write objects. A read-write understanding does not introduce a simply binary that implies the book was once a widespread form of consumption now morphing into a widespread act of production. As research on reading has shown, book consumption can be its own kind of production, its own kind of rewriting.[39]

A read-write understanding builds on Jay Bolter's point that digital writing media enable a blurring of reading and writing activities.[40] Yet it also calls attention to the circumstances motivating the significant output of self-publishing and how writers are working among them, including a deep shift to what Brandt calls a writing-based literacy. In this new arena, writing challenges the dominance that reading has traditionally held over it. Other circumstances include the empowering, utopic, democratic discourses surrounding social media that make sharing writing more acceptable. Publishing technologies are increasingly accessible. Emergent models of publishing challenge the grip of entrenched ones. And writers have the ability to use the Internet to find communities of readers. These conditions have led to a growing attitude among laypeople and nonprofessional writers that they are authorized to write books and are capable of finishing the projects. As *Mass Authorship* makes clear, a read-write understanding registers the book as a popular writing medium accessible to ordinary authors, but this does not mean that authorship becomes completely homogenized. More prestigious and scarce versions of books and authorship can survive in a context of ubiquitous publishing.

Networked Participants

The fifth concept in my analytic framework consists of reconceptualizing the audience from readers to networked participants. This phenomenon has been extremely well documented in media studies. Henry Jenkins has described the rise of participatory culture, in which digital tools enable people to produce as well as consume popular culture, a production fueled by peer-to-peer production. Yochai Benkler has shown how the rise of networked peer production enables participants to contribute small amounts of time to generate commons-based production, which has been partly responsible for producing collaborative informational goods like

Wikipedia or citizen journalism projects.[41] Although this kind of labor has not been particularly suitable for producing the kind of book that the reader expects a consistent voice throughout, it is the engine for much of the publishing activity in the cultures of reading and writing that *Mass Authorship* focuses on.

Scholarship focusing on participatory culture has been somewhat guilty of prematurely celebrating the way networked technologies may empower people. In the years after the explosive growth of social media sites, celebration of the amateur's ability to engage in commons-based production, and celebration of the new power of the "crowd," reached its zenith. Scholars argued that networked participants had the potential to remake culture, democracy, and freedom in radical ways. But the initial optimism about the potential of participatory culture has been tempered and qualified in a number of ways. Historical work has shown that digital participatory media has precedent and is not a radical break from the past.[42] Mounting evidence suggests that contemporary participation might be more limited than thought, since a small percentage of users are often responsible for producing most of the content on social media sites.[43] Corporations have worked to corral, centralize, and exploit amateur production, and participating in social media introduces a number of privacy concerns and possibilities for censorship and surveillance.

Although it would be a mistake to understand the rise of networked culture as a blanket shift from passive consumption to active production, and an even greater mistake to homogeneously characterize it as empowering ordinary people, contemporary cultures of peer-to-peer production do have some significant differences from audiences in the age of print. Participants have access to collaborative writing tools that exist on different scales of size and speed than in print systems. These tools include the capacity to make writing public, and their distributed nature means they are capable of inducing network effects. Digital texts operate on a different set of economics of reproduction than print texts do and can be more easily reproduced or distributed for free. Analytics and algorithms mediate cultures of reading and writing and provide new data sets that recursively shape activity. These tools will not necessarily lead to changes in some sort of technologically determined way—indeed, *Mass Authorship* highlights profound continuities from print to digital.

But it will become clear throughout this book that readers as participants and the peer-to-peer production they are capable of play a crucial role in self-publishing processes.

Defining Self-Publishing

Self-publishing has been so diverse—and of late so volatile—that no single study can provide a comprehensive understanding of it. In this section I discuss some key terms and definitions, then I explain the four studies that ground the claims in this book and how the parameters of those studies limit the scope of the argument. Although government, religious, and author-subsidized publishing produced books throughout the twentieth century, royalty publishing so dominated the commercial publishing industry that Jana Bradley and her colleagues refer to it as "traditional" publishing in their attempt to survey the rise of "nontraditional" publishing in the twenty-first century.[44] This binary only represents a starting point, and the label "traditional" publishing has the unfortunate consequence of homogenizing diverse print practices. The designation collapses the distinctions among corporate trade publishers, independent publishers, and academic publishers, and this collapse might incense independent publishers, who defined themselves *against* the corporate publishing ethos of the late twentieth century.[45]

Nevertheless, I use the term *traditional* sparingly in this book to describe twentieth-century publishers who operated on the royalty model because my participants used the term, and because I think it signifies that there are traditions, beliefs, and values about publishing and authorship associated with the royalty model that inflect the contemporary moment. For Bradley and colleagues, nontraditional publishing includes digital reprints of public-domain books, low-value spam ebooks, and self-publishing. Self-publishing is thus only one facet of the changes in book publishing.

The term *self-publishing* encompasses a range of practices and configurations of labor. Just like the term *individual author*, the word *self* masks the extensively collaborative process of self-publishing and the multiple trajectories a book can take to reach readers when it is self-published. I use *self-publishing* loosely to refer to writing and publishing experiences that include a number of characteristics. First, although the authors may have produced their writing as books through diverse configurations of labor and technology, they have done so without the direct capital investment of a third party associated with the book industry. I say *direct* because many of the proprietary digital distribution systems that enable these writers to self-publish have been capital-intensive, and these systems wield considerable influence over the work of self-publishing authors and in the overall trajectory of self-publishing's place in book culture, as I discuss in chapter 4. Second, although self-publishing authors often delegate the tasks and responsibilities of book production (editing, design, and formatting), they are responsible for acting as the general manager of their publishing process, which gives them a measure of control that authors relinquish in the royalty model. Finally, although print-on-demand technologies have allowed authors to publish print books inexpensively, ebooks dominate the self-publishing experience. Contemporary self-publishing is largely electronic self-publishing.

Self-published authors often fall into specific goal-oriented groups, which include the following:

- Hobbyists who post their fiction or nonfiction writing to web communities
- Nonfiction niche writers who write texts valuable enough to sell on the Internet but who could never find traditional publishers because their works are too specialized and thus not financially viable for brick-and-mortar retail distribution
- Entrepreneurs who carry on the tradition of writers who use books as a kind of business card
- Recreational writers who share their work with family and friends
- Traditionally published authors who move to self-publishing for financial reasons or for creative control
- Self-published authors who want to develop as writers and build an audience and move into traditional publishing
- Hybrid authors who move back and forth between traditional publishing and self-publishing
- Self-published authors who network in the growing movement of indie authors and hope to make a living from writing

- Academics who self-publish textbooks, popular books, and in some cases scholarship

The diversity of these groups created two problems when I designed the studies that led to *Mass Authorship*. First, a single project about self-publishing cannot adequately address its size and scope; second, self-publishing was developing rapidly while I was executing the research. Indeed, the term *hybrid author* is well known among commercial trade publishers now, but to my knowledge it wasn't in use when the project began in 2007.

To provide focus for this burgeoning world, my book is built around studies of four groups of writers: professional poker players, memoirists, recreational romance writers, and popular fiction writers who achieved bestseller status. This may seem like a motley crowd, and the incongruous experiences of these four groups can make some of the shifts between chapters seem mildly abrupt, but this has been a deliberate (and modest) approach that attempts to capture the diversity of self-publishing and that bears resemblance to what Ian Bogost calls "media microecology." His approach eschews strong value-laden claims about the effects of a medium on human culture in favor of documenting the "variety" and "application" of a medium and how it functions distinctively in larger media ecologies.[46] Qualitative research is particularly well suited to exploring rapidly developing and largely unknown phenomena, so I have concentrated on documenting a wide range of practices that participants deployed and that spanned different modes and mediums organized around the ideas of books and authorship.

I chose these four groups because they explain four crucial issues of digital self-publishing: poker players illustrate nonfiction niche markets, which have thrived on the web because of its capacity to help geographically diffuse populations come together over a common interest. Memoirists write personal narrative, one of the most accessible kinds of writing and very attractive to many amateur writers, and their experiences demonstrate the democratic reach of self-publishing. The recreational romance fiction writers show how readers and writers work in an open system in which ebooks are freely published and read, and bestselling popular fiction writers indicate what it's like to labor as professional and independent writers who nevertheless depend on the publishing platforms of corporate giants. I include a full account of the study's methods in the appendix, but here is a brief overview.

My work began with a four-year digital ethnography of the writing and publishing practices of professional poker players writing nonfiction niche ebooks. These players wrote and sold their works as part of coaching businesses they had created to satisfy the demand for poker strategy when online poker, and the potential to make significant money from it, began early in the first decade of the twenty-first century. The ebooks often used statistics and probability to create poker theory, and I studied their production and circulation by participating in online communities, archiving and analyzing discussion threads and blog posts, and interviewing authors face-to-face, through Skype, and through instant-messaging programs. My analysis concentrates on how these authors utilized their status and knowledge to sell ebooks without the intervention of professional publishers. Although the poker coaches were anomalous in their ability to charge high prices for their ebooks, their experience nonetheless provides a strategic way to understand some of the core issues at stake in nonfiction self-publishing: How do inexperienced writers learn to produce books? How do they achieve credibility for their work? What is the nature of their interaction with readers? How do they protect themselves from copyright infringement and preserve their texts' value when ebooks can be exchanged by readers through back channels for free?

By coincidence, I completed the study of poker players at about the same time the US government cracked down on offshore poker websites, significantly damaging (at least short-term) the US online poker economy. I then began studying two more groups of writers to compare their experiences and understand how the nature of writing conditioned the kinds of publishing practices engaged in by authors. Beginning in 2011, I interviewed self-published memoirists because of the widespread perception that the genre has increased in popularity in recent decades. Anecdotes suggest that after fiction, memoir has been one of the genres most frequently rejected by traditional publishers and one of the most frequently produced in the twentieth century through self-publishing and vanity presses. The memoirists I studied included war veterans, businesspeople, aspiring musicians, trauma victims, and social justice advocates.

I simultaneously began a study of recreational romance writers who were serializing their work on Wattpad.com, a social, open ebook website heavily populated by young writers and readers. Wattpad is a growing user-generated content site that has attracted venture capital because of its ability to keep readers' eyeballs on the screen and because it has built much of its publishing ecology with mobile technologies in mind. I interviewed romance writers for two reasons. First, studies of romance writing by ordinary writers are relatively scarce, but as a popular genre it has been the focus of studies of reading that Janice Radway's *Reading the Romance* helped initiate.[47] Second, most professional poker players are male, so studying romance writers, who were primarily female online and in my sample, ensured that the study would include a gender-balanced range of voices.

In an effort to examine practices by more self-identified professional writers, I conducted the final study in 2014 with a sample of self-published popular fiction writers whose books had appeared on Amazon bestseller lists (and sometimes on the *USA Today* and the *New York Times* bestseller lists). Benefactors of the opportunity to publish on Kindle and through other ebook retailers, these writers represent the emergent indie author movement, which is the subject of chapters 3 and 4. These authors have written a wide range of fiction, including fantasy, science fiction, thrillers, and young adult novels. Many of them earn a living from their writing and have marshaled their self-publishing platform into contracts with traditional publishers by selling print rights, foreign rights, and film rights. I use their experience to show the indie author movement's definition of itself and to examine the new kinds of intermediaries that have come to mediate the relationship of indie authors to their readers, with a particular focus on giant ebook retailers and their algorithms.

Most of the poker players and romance writers were between the ages of eighteen and thirty-four, and the memoirists, like the bestselling fiction authors, tended to be older. Only the bestselling popular fiction (or indie) authors wrote professionally; the members of the other three groups wrote books as an avocation or a hobby. Very few had formal training in creative writing. The samples were concentrated in the United States and Canada, and a few writers were from Europe and the Philippines. I collected, coded, and analyzed data using a grounded theory approach.[48] This was an emic approach to data analysis that drew many terms and concepts from the data, mainly because I wanted to understand how the participants were defining books and authorship during a time of transition and flux.

Every participant I interviewed except for one gave me permission to use his or her real name. Despite this, I do employ pseudonyms, and I use real names only in a limited number of cases. This hybrid approach is an unusual choice for a qualitative researcher, inflected with the still-developing ethics of doing Internet research; it has to do with protecting the integrity of my knowledge claims and lingering questions I have about privacy and memory online. I elaborate on this dilemma in the appendix. In addition to conducting interviews, I collected web texts like review threads and blog posts associated with the ebooks of the writers I interviewed, and I studied the authors' activity in online communities if they participated in them. The data trail on social media sites helped triangulate the data from the interviews.

There are certainly a number of limits to the claims in *Mass Authorship*. I articulate some of these in the appendix, but two of them are worth mentioning immediately. First, because the study is largely grounded in the experiences of writers in the United States, it fails to account for international developments. China has a robust self-publishing culture with dynamics that might call into question the conclusions I draw about self-publishing. In the future, it will be worth comparing sites of self-publishing to understand how it changes across cultures and how those cultures interact.

Second, I draw many of the examples I use to support my claims from writers who have amassed audiences ranging from a few hundred readers to hundreds of thousands of readers. This is probably atypical. The output of self-publishing is so copious that the more representative self-published author probably finds an audience of fewer readers than the authors I have profiled in this book. Indeed, there are certainly tens of thousands, if not many more, self-published books with no readers. The sampling methods I used tended to create a pool of interviewees who had managed to find an audience for their writing.

The poker authors were leaders in their community and had small but enthusiastic audiences for their work. I sampled romance writers from Wattpad depending on whether the authors had made contact information public, which weighted the sample in favor of authors who were aggressively cultivating audiences. The memoirists tended to reach the smallest audiences, and by definition, the popular fiction bestsellers had found many readers. Although my samples are probably not representative of self-publishing, I classify the status of the writers I profile under the heading of mass authorship because most of them produced books that would not have been published or circulated in the age of print for various reasons (even though many of the bestsellers adhered to professional print standards). The sample and the examples are not representative of all self-published authors—we don't even have the data to know what that really means—but this is typical with qualitative research.

An Outline of *Mass Authorship*

Although the four studies provided four unique perspectives on the digital shifts, the chapters concentrate on issues that appeared widely in the experiences of authors who produced books without a publisher. My major themes ultimately emerged from the analytic procedures (see the appendix), but what unites most of the themes is a focus on how the study participants collectively forged an understanding of books and authorship that harmonized with their experience as they resisted and exploited the historical legacies of book culture that bore down on them.

Chapter 1 profiles the technological and cultural conditions that led to the emergence of self-published books and some of the factors that have fostered their growth. It argues that as the vanity stigma associated with self-publishing faded, a cottage industry of support services grew to profit from, and encourage, self-publishing, and this cottage industry has in some ways mediated the void of the allegedly disintermediated experience.

Chapter 2 examines the methods writers use to refashion their authorial identities in the absence of publishers. It argues that publishers have played a constitutive role in the formation of authorial identity under the royalty system, and it examines how authors reshape these identities in self-publishing models and what that process has to say about the potential interaction among multiple publishing models.

Chapter 3 continues this work from a slightly different angle, profiling the emergence of indie authorship. It argues that independent authorship represents the growing professional sector of self-publishing and that the movement's adherence to professional textual standards represents an abandonment of the democratic ethos on which it was founded. It uses this insight to explore the factors indie authors must negotiate as they move fluidly between traditional and nontraditional models of publishing.

Chapter 4 continues the focus on independent authors and concentrates on how they experience Amazon as a publishing platform. It profiles the various kinds of labor required to achieve a bestseller as well as the experimental publishing practices that authors develop in response to the way Amazon's recommendation systems shape their books' sales potential. This chapter pays close attention to how authors shape their publishing practices in response to Amazon's algorithms and the various kinds of data they acquire when working on the system.

After the first four chapters analyze some of the technological and corporate entities that mediate the author-reader relationship, chapters 5 and 6 take a more detailed look at how authors use digital tools to interact with online communities. Chapter 5 examines intellectual property and copyright, the backbone of modern authorship. The ubiquity of publishing means that copyright issues have settled into an everyday concern for self-published authors. Few writers know the nuances of copyright law, however, and even fewer care to police their copyrights with recourse to the law. This chapter compares the experience of poker players and romance writers to trace how online writing communities develop microclimates of intellectual property to police copyright infringement and plagiarism. Respect for authorship can run so deep that the microclimates become thick and muggy, with writers taking extensive (nonlegal) measures to preserve it. These practices include readers and authors developing standards of courtesy and etiquette, authors manipulating their writing habits to prevent unauthorized circulation, community members volunteering time to police copyright violations, and system administrators introducing code designed to frustrate copyright violators. Taken together, these practices resist the unfettered circulation of ebooks and nurture systems of ownership and attribution.

Chapter 6 presents findings from my study of professional online poker players who wrote and self-published advanced poker textbooks. The chapter concentrates on the literate dynamics of book reviews and how they help create credibility for the authors of self-published nonfiction.

The reviews develop genre conventions that indicate ebook readers are coming to terms with the affordances of the ebook and the unvetted nature of information in digital environments.

The conclusion uses the framework of mass authorship to rethink complaints and laments that there are "too many" books. It discusses the economics of attention in light of a read-write understanding of the book and the consequences that self-publishing might have for how we value authorship.

The appendix describes the methodological challenges of researching distributed populations who write on various web spaces. It accounts for my approach to digital ethnography and documents the samples and analytic procedures.

Mass Authorship represents a grounded understanding of writers developing practices in the digital transition, some of which are ephemeral (indeed, designed to be ephemeral), and some of which will persist with some durability.

CHAPTER 1

The Decline of Vanity and the Rise of Self-Publishing

THIS CHAPTER SURVEYS the convergence of factors that fostered self-publishing's move from a twentieth-century fringe activity to its current and plural state as a hobby, a profession, and an expanding industry. Laura J. Miller has partly addressed this in her brief but excellent overview of self-publishing. She has documented some of the ways that we have moved from a past in which self-publishing was likely to be viewed as "a foolish act of hubris" to the current moment, in which it is more "likely to be applauded as a legitimate act of self-expression."[1] Miller has catalogued a range of factors that led to this shift, including the rise of digital technologies, the expansion of online bookselling, conditions in the publishing industry, and a new respect for amateurs in participatory culture.

Although this chapter discusses how digital technologies have enabled the growth of self-publishing, it also calls attention to two overlooked trends that have played a crucial role in its expansion. First, in the twentieth century, the vanity stigma made it deeply taboo for publishers to profit from aspiring authors, but in the first decade of the 2000s a series of events helped erode this taboo, and a number of legitimate businesses (including large publishers) coalesced to form a cottage industry to help self-published authors produce their works. This not only gave the authors access to professional editors and book designers to improve the quality of their books, it also motivated some professional publishers to stop perpetuating the stigma on self-published books, which was a common trend in the twentieth century.

Second, the emergence of digital technologies took place against a background of deeply shifting literacy practices that have fostered a hyper-abundance of book production—a point that is almost entirely absent in discussions of contemporary publishing. Deborah Brandt has called this the move from a reading-oriented literacy to a writing-oriented literacy, in which more people orient to the world as writers and develop work-related writing competencies, which then spill over into hobbyist and semiprofessional book writing. Understanding the nuances of this shift not only helps account for the increase in self-publishing, it also uncovers assumptions about reading and writing that are embedded in the vanity stigma, which, I argue, is a by-product of reading-oriented literacy. As this survey profiles the expansion of self-publishing, then, it traces some of the ways that literacy and vanity have been entwined and what that has meant, and means, for the publishing environment of amateur and aspiring book writers.

The Vanity Stigma

In the twentieth century, vanity presses were the scourge of the publishing world—the nefarious "other" to the royalty publisher. In brief, they worked like this: Vanity presses often placed ads in the back of writers' trade publications, promising to "publish" the manuscript of an aspiring writer as long as he or she subsidized the production cost. Vanity presses often marketed themselves as akin to a farm team (a minor league team affiliated with the major league) in baseball or as a precursor to the author being able to find a royalty publisher. Some vanity presses produced high-quality books at the authors' expense, whereas others produced shoddy work and shoddy marketing materials while fleecing the authors of their life savings. This created a stigma on the vanity publishers and even on the authors who used them. The dominance of the royalty system and the problems with vanity presses led to a well-known and dogmatic professional guideline sometimes referred to as Yog's Law. A dictum coined by the novelist James D. Macdonald and used by industry watchdog groups that uncover exploitative publishing companies, Yog's Law states that in a proper publishing relationship "money flows toward the writer" and that writers should never finance the publishing activities associated with their manuscripts.[2]

Self-publishing in the twentieth century was different from vanity publishing. The term defined the type of writer who did all the work of writing, designing, and distributing a book, usually after contracting a printer to print it. Some successful self-published authors enjoyed the work and became small independent publishers, a sector that saw rapid growth in the second half of the twentieth century.[3] Self-publishing has therefore never been synonymous with vanity publishing. However, some iterations of self-publishing in the twentieth century shared characteristics with the vanity press. Some self-published books were of low quality, and in many cases they signaled to industry professionals that the authors had failed to find royalty publishers to invest in the production of the works and certify their quality. In twentieth-century newspaper articles, trade literature, and editorials, self-publishing was conflated with vanity publishing enough that I think it is fair to conclude that in many cases self-publishing became tinged with the stigma that vanity presses helped produce.[4]

The vanity stigma holds power because the concern that writing and authorship are acts of vanity runs deep in the history of Western authorship. The twentieth-century iteration has a genealogy that extends to nineteenth-century commission publishing, a model that was especially popular in England; the author shouldered the financial risk for producing a book, and the publisher helped him or her market it, earning a commission on sales. Some contemporaries complained about commission publishing because they were concerned that the low quality of author-subsidized books would debase authorship and that commission publishers were overcharging for services and exploiting would-be authors who wanted to see their writing in print.[5]

Commission publishing was not as popular in the United States, where the royalty system emerged earlier than in England. Yet despite the ascent of both the royalty system and publishers as risk-taking entrepreneurs responsible for investing in the production and distribution of books, it was still quite common in the nineteenth-century United States for authors to subsidize the production of everything from local history to memoirs to fiction.[6] Ronald Zboray and Mary Saracino Zboray depict a lively culture of social authorship populated by amateur writers who flourished in antebellum America, a brief period of publishing between what they call the "elite past" and the "corporate-driven future." The authors argue that as the publishing industry morphed toward a more corporate-driven model, opportunities for amateurs began to recede, and the gap between the amateur and the professional author widened, with amateurs measured against "the new professional yardstick."[7]

The viability of professional authorship grew in fits and starts along with the protracted modernization of the book industry throughout the nineteenth and twentieth centuries, as the royalty system came to dominate commercial publishing. This was a nuanced process that resists any monolithic narrative, but the dominant trends were new systems of production and distribution, the implementation of bestseller lists, the rise of the literary agent, the growth of public libraries and professionally curated collections, and the formation of a literary canon in higher education.[8] The maturation of the book industry included few developments that would see value in the writing of the amateur, local, or self-published author. Thus an already existing antiamateur discourse grew in the late nineteenth century, whereby professional writers devalued the work of amateurs to shore up their status as authors.[9] For the most part, despite some vibrancy in localized print culture in twentieth-century America, amateur authors who wanted to realize their works in book form and could not find a royalty publisher had limited options. They could either do the difficult work to produce and design the books themselves and then contract a printer, or they could pay a vanity press to produce and print their books for them, an expensive and sometimes risky proposition.[10]

As the royalty system began to dominate commercial publishing, the author-subsidy model was virtually absent in discussions of how publishing should work, especially after vanity publishers ran a number of high-profile scams in the mid-twentieth century that cast a dark shadow over author-subsidized writing for the next seventy years.[11] The vanity stigma had multiple dimensions that generated strong feelings: scam artists tarnished the reputation of the publishing industry; the process circumvented gatekeepers; authors sometimes overestimated the quality of their works; an author who used the vanity press had to violate the taboo on a writer promoting his or her own work; some vanity presses produced books of shoddy construction; and authors who fell for scams seemed pitiful because they had failed to learn enough about publishing to avoid being fleeced.

In the late 1990s and the first decade of the 2000s, the vanity stigma was displaced onto the first digitally self-published books, with some book professionals lamenting them just as some had lamented the emergence of the "paperback revolution."[12] This had to do with both quality and the economic models made possible by digital technologies. When print-on-demand (POD) companies surfaced in the first decade of the 2000s, many functioned much like vanity presses. With POD, authors could send the companies their manuscripts and buy copies of their books with their own money. Some POD companies offered editing, design, and marketing services, for which the authors had to pay. However, POD technology could create print runs of a small number of books economically, so an author could publish a few copies of his or her own book far more cheaply than was possible with print technology. This enabled POD companies to avoid claims that they exploited desperate writers by sticking them with bills so large they had to mortgage their houses to get their book into print. Unlike vanity presses, many POD companies let the author keep the copyright, and some offered free ISBN numbers so that authors could circulate their work through online distribution databases.

Writers, then, could pay small amounts to realize their work in book form, but no one had vetted their manuscripts or invested capital in their books. At the same time, POD arrangements violated Yog's Law, and some companies used POD technology to continue dubious—and aggressive—practices that closely resembled those of the shadiest twentieth-century vanity presses. Ultimately, POD wasn't quite vanity, it wasn't quite self-publishing, and it wasn't traditional royalty publishing, but as a case it demonstrates that from their inception, new digital publishing models found themselves struggling against suspicion that derived its energy from the vanity stigma.

Reading, Writing, and the Vanity Stigma

Discussions about books often presume a certain understanding of literacy. The vanity stigma is ostensibly a rejection of an economic model of publishing, but it contains a host of assumptions about reading and writing. The most significant is that it adheres strongly to the values and expectations of reading-oriented literacy, which is now in competition with writing-oriented literacy, a change Deborah Brandt tracks in *The Rise of Writing: Redefining Mass Literacy*. She argues that although reading and writing are mutually dependent as literate activities, they have different "sponsorship" histories. Brandt claims that mass literacy began as reading-oriented and spread under the auspices of church and state because these institutions favored reading in their instruction as a way to create a shared belief system. Western institutions, and various kinds of legal and cultural protections for literacy, have been formed around the assumption that for most people, reading would be the primary form of literate development and engagement. Reading-oriented literacies create a moral imperative for reading to be taught universally, but the model places tighter ideological restrictions on the production of writers.

In contrast to reading, writing had a more limited reach in the first stage of mass literacy development, with a sponsorship history rooted in commerce, as Brandt explains:

> Reading was critical to salvation in the ideology of the Protestant church and to the promise of citizenship in the ideology of the Republic. In the initial project of mass literacy, however, writing held no great sway. Harder to teach, messy to learn, not as suitable a vehicle for religious or social control, and especially dangerous in the hands of the oppressed, mass writing emerged separately from mass reading and more slowly. . . . The association of writing with the worldly domains of art, commerce, craft, and mercantilism helps to explain why writing instruction in colonial America was largely excluded from the literacy campaigns of churches and Sunday schools as well as from the traditional grammar school, at least initially.[13]

The association of reading with salvation and writing with commerce has had a deep and lasting legacy for the way we understand literacy, and Brandt argues that in the twentieth century and into the twenty-first, writing began to overtake reading in importance as it became the engine of the information economy. Because of writing's economic value, more people have had the opportunity and motivation to orient toward writing as their primary form of literate engagement. Universities and other schools have made large investments in writing programs in the last forty years, and millions of people spend their lives engaged in high-stakes writing on a daily basis as a means of production. Indeed, many of my interviewees spoke of writing at work extensively, and some marshaled their competencies into book writing at night, on weekends, or in retirement.

Brandt's bifurcation of sponsorship history shows that the beliefs about literacy held by those in professional book culture often presume a reading-oriented literacy. Take, for example, authorship as a venerated social identity. In a reading-oriented literacy, authorship holds more power. It "gains its prestige from the power to morally uplift a civic readership," and reading-oriented literacy systems that have functioned to restrict access to writing practices also function to restrict authorship.[14] In this system, only certain people—those who have had their writing certified by publishers—are able to introduce their ideas to a reading public. The dominance of the reading-oriented model of literacy helps explain why, with limited exceptions like yearbooks and street literature, the twentieth-century book doesn't have as robust an amateur tradition as some other art forms. Haugland notes that institutions that curated book collections throughout the twentieth century have largely ignored amateur books, and in the twentieth century self-published authors had no alternatives to these institutions, unlike musicians, artists, and stage actors, who had robust networks of amateurs organizing festivals and awards.[15]

In a reading-oriented literacy, amateurs are not encouraged to become authors, and thus we see a long history of the dismissal of amateur authors, as Ann Fabian has demonstrated. She shows that as far back as the eighteenth century, aspiring and established professionals accused amateurs of threatening the value of literature with their low quality of writing. Amateurs were also accused of distorting the value of writing by flooding the market.[16] These themes recur in contemporary flare-ups over self-publishing. In 2012, bestselling mystery writer Sue Grafton made the blanket assertion that self-published authors were both "lazy" and "disrespectful" to published authors, an assertion she retreated from after self-published authors closed ranks and pointed out (as they are wont to do) that a number of them were selling hundreds of thousands of books per year and working hard to do so.[17]

Brandt's work suggests that the vanity stigma is far more powerful in systems of reading-oriented literacy. In that sense, the vanity stigma does not just warn writers about the shady dealings of scam artists; rather, it represents a mechanism to control authorship as an identity and maintain its prestige. The stigmatization of those who circumvent gatekeepers and fund their own books is an extension of systems—royalty publishing and reading-oriented literacy—that have by accident and economics complemented each other. Fueling the ideological dispositions of both is the history of book sacralization that runs deep in the history of manuscript and print culture.

Although disdain for vanity harmonizes with assumptions about literacy in a reading-oriented model of literacy, authorship is more diffuse in a writing-oriented model, and literacy "develops by way of emphasizing and embracing the social role of the writer rather than the social role of the reader."[18] Brandt's work is in many ways a study of how writing-oriented literacy challenges Western institutions of government, education, and the economy. The move to a writing-oriented literacy has been an unacknowledged motivator in the explosion of self-publishing—and, indeed, in other kinds of education movements. We can see evidence of a writing-oriented model of literacy in a variety of phenomena: Community-based publishing programs of public libraries have grown, some of which have purchased POD book machines to support production. Creative writing has become the basis for literacy development in the 826 Valencia tutoring centers. And writing takes center stage in National Novel Writing Month, a loosely affiliated network that encourages would-be writers to finish their novels each November. Almost every complaint that I have read about National Novel Writing Month is embedded with reading-oriented assumptions about mass literacy. In a reading-oriented literacy, authorship is venerated and threatened by the output of too many books, which is often what popular commentary about National Novel Writing Month claims.

I have traced the genealogy of the vanity stigma to commission publishing and to its characterization as the degenerate antithesis of the royalty model, and I have located its power in the paradigm of reading-oriented literacy. But the vanity stigma also emanates from the practical experience of book publishers and librarians. Some of them would argue that the exasperation directed at self-published authors and the stigma on their work is warranted. Publishers would note that they have limited resources for producing books and bringing them to the public. They face the prospect of using their scarce time by dealing with amateur writers who solicit them in an inappropriate way by failing to research and adhere to the standards of courtesy embedded in the protocols of professional publishing. To many professional publishers, then, amateur writers are a time-consuming distraction who stack the slush pile high and fail to recognize that they should be engaging publishers through agents.

Likewise, librarians also have a history of having to address uncomfortable situations in which a self-published author insists that his or her work is right for a collection without having a firm understanding of the quality standards of library collections. Assessing the quality of one's own writing is notoriously difficult, and some self-published authors develop extraordinarily tight relationships with their writing and act as zealous evangelists of their own work. This lack of understanding makes the work of librarians more difficult because they, as curators, must constantly make difficult decisions about which books to keep and which to throw away. Although I do believe that these professional conditions have contributed extensively to the production of stigma, I do not think they can fully account for the powerful aversion to self-publishing and vanity presses that still lingers today.

Writing-oriented literacy has not surpassed reading-oriented literacy in a comprehensive way; the two coexist and at times struggle with each other. This struggle underpins, in an unrecognized way, many debates about contemporary book and publishing culture. I will discuss the technological and publishing industry developments that diminished the vanity stigma and mainstreamed self-publishing in the next section. Here I will conclude by stating that more people have been inhabiting, or at least toying with, the identity of the writer in a writing-oriented system, and this has created a profoundly rich soil for self-publishing's growth and for a reorientation to books and authorship.

The Decline of the Stigma and the Rise of the New Intermediaries

Brandt argues that the shift to writing-oriented literacy began well before the widespread adoption of self-publishing technologies, but their availability has no doubt been a crucial part of the decline of the stigma. I am certainly not arguing that the vanity stigma has completely faded from the publishing world. That world is not homogeneous but is composed of different sectors, each with a different kind of commitment. Academic publishing still rightly holds a fierce prejudice against predatory open-access publishers with shoddy peer-review practices that engage in all the deceptions of the most notorious twentieth-century vanity presses.[19] Generally, the closer one gets to institutions built on respect for peer review and publishing (e.g., libraries, universities, and granting agencies), the more likely one is to encounter suspicion of self-publishing. Thus, when I argue in this section that the vanity stigma has receded rapidly from professional book culture, I only mean that enough of it has been erased to allow reputable businesses to profit from self-publishing. This is documented clearly below.

In the 1980s and the 1990s, desktop publishing and POD technology began to make book design and printing slightly more accessible to everyday people. Although there were some isolated success stories of authors using these technologies to find an audience, self-published authors still confronted the print distributions systems—networks of wholesalers and retailers—that made it difficult, if not nearly impossible, to find a widespread audience without a publisher. At the beginning of the twenty-first century, the continued spread of these technologies coincided with some initial success with ebooks in the publishing industry and optimism that publishing was going to change rapidly, which sparked large publishing houses and investors to spend millions of dollars preparing for the industry shift to ebooks. The bursting of the dot-com bubble and the failure of ebook sales to live up to "wildly optimistic" projections stalled the seemingly inevitable ebook revolution, and publishers scaled back their involvement.[20]

There were multiple factors involved, including the problem that the existing dedicated ebook readers were too undeveloped for a comfortable reading experience. Books exist as a constellation of technologies, many of which must advance for significant changes to occur in systems of production, distribution, and consumption. Large ebook programs like Project Gutenberg had been in place since the 1970s, ebooks were being circulated through the web, and the ebook and its affordances were playing a role in how scholars were imagining the digital transition, yet it wasn't until the second half of the first decade of the twenty-first century that readers began adopting e-readers in significant numbers. This happened when Amazon introduced Kindle and its use of e-ink, and when high-resolution screens on tablets and other mobile devices improved the reading experience. Companies selling the hardware invested heavily in marketing and advertising, and e-readers spread quickly, which boosted the popularity of ebooks.[21]

Companies that sold e-readers and tablets during this time worked to create fairly closed systems that funneled users into their content ecosystems. Apple wanted its device users to buy books from its store, and Amazon wanted its Kindle users to buy books from its store. As e-reader adoption spread, Amazon began letting writers distribute content to readers through the Kindle store. Until that point, self-published authors had had a number of fragmented ways to publish and distribute ebooks, but Amazon's system created a centralized system for self-published authors to sell and promote their works. Amazon, Apple, and others also provided authors and readers with accessible and trusted payment systems. These developments enabled self-published authors to *potentially* solve a distribution problem that had made self-publishing and finding an audience untenable in all but the most extraordinary cases in the twentieth century. Writers interested in self-publishing still faced barriers to finding a wide audience. They found competition for readers stiff, and many realized that the association of self-publishing with the vanity stigma made audiences skeptical of self-published books.

After 2007, when the opportunity to publish directly to e-readers began, self-published authors began working with models entirely unrelated to the traditional vanity press. But many of the writers I interviewed in 2011 indicated that they thought self-publishing had retained its associations with vanity. The stigma on self-publishing began to subside rapidly somewhere between 2011 and 2013, when more indicators suggested that self-publishing had morphed into an important component of the book industry and as self-publishing began to shape how some sectors of commercial publishing operated. Extensive press coverage about some successful self-published authors brought more respect, and articles often couched these instances in rhetoric about heroic writers beating the odds to amass audiences and become millionaires. In 2011, for example, Amanda Hocking marshaled sales of millions of her self-published ebooks into a $2 million contract with St. Martin's Press, an anomalous example that nevertheless demonstrated the potential for self-published authors to amass substantial sales and then enter the traditional royalty publishing system.

The various interpretations of the Hocking episode in the publishing blogosphere and on discussion boards still showed a deep skepticism toward self-publishing, even for popular genres. For advocates of self-publishing, it showed that a self-published author could earn enormous amounts of money simply through ebooks. For traditional publishers, it demonstrated that doing the enormous amount of work involved in publishing was not a sustainable activity for an author. Hocking talked about how exhausting the work of self-publishing could be, and she also noted the potential for print distribution that commercial publishers offered, telling the *New York Times*, "For me to be a billion-dollar author, I need to have people buying my books at Wal-Mart."[22] Her case demonstrated the potential symbiosis between self-publishing and traditional publishing, or at least the potential for an emergent trajectory of authorship, whereby authors build loyal followings of digital readers and from this platform gain traditional publishing contracts. Agents and publishers began to monitor self-publishing for emerging stars to sign (in fact, some were already doing this before Hocking), but the commentary also pointed out that there was no guarantee that a loyal readership built on inexpensive ebooks sold through Kindle would translate into a large print readership. Other publishers noted that they were so swamped with submissions to their houses that they had no time to search for self-published talent.

After Hocking, more bestselling authors emerged from the self-publishing ranks, and some traditionally published midlist authors went indie and found it more lucrative than working with a commercial house. Just two years after Hocking, the *New York Times* reported that self-published titles constituted roughly 25 percent of Amazon's 2012 bestsellers.[23] I address this (fragile) growth in chapter 4, but part of the reason for it was that self-published authors had nimble businesses that allowed them to adapt to what they saw as rapidly changing markets. Commercial publishers, for instance, have worried that the low price of ebooks will lead to a prolonged devaluation of books and writing, but a self-published writer worries more about amassing an audience and can offer his or her backlist for free or at a reduced price (as low as 99 cents on Amazon) to build a brand or motivate sales of a new release.

The number of authors who actually earn a livable wage by self-publishing ebooks has remained only a small percentage of those who wish to do so, but given how easy it is to self-publish a book, this percentage will always be low. However, as more self-published authors become successful, they minimize the stigma associated with their work. This partly accounts for the energy motivating the indie author movement, which I discuss in chapters 3 and 4. Largely composed of authors who treat their writing and publishing as a small business, the movement appropriated the term *indie* (independent) as a way of celebrating the control they have over their work and as a way of distancing themselves from the stigma associated with self-publishing. As more and more indie authors have earned success, and as more and more commercially published authors have turned to self-publishing some of their work, some indie authors have begun to self-identify as hybrid authors, writers who traverse multiple models of publishing.

Indie authors populate discussion boards and blogs and are organizing support networks and professional organizations as they work to eradicate the stigma. These organizations have written guidebooks on how to be an indie author, provided warnings about scam artists, and offered recommendations for freelance editorial and design help. The organizations have also established prizes for indie books, and they purchase spaces at trade shows and book fairs that their members can rent to gain exposure to new markets. One of the largest, the Alliance of Independent Authors (ALLi) has campaigned to have indie authors and their work recognized as professional and worthy of consideration for bookstores, awards, and libraries. The very fact that ALLi needs to mount such a campaign is a reminder that indie authorship is still largely a digital phenomenon and that self-publishing is still only a fraction of the publishing industry.

Although there has been growth in, excitement about, and rapid developments in self-publishing and the fading stigma, entities that operate infrastructures that have been born and grounded in systems of print publishers (e.g., brick-and-mortar stores, prizes, and many libraries) are still largely inaccessible to self-published authors. Bookstores, libraries, and prize panels operate on a model in which shelf space and judgment time are scarce. As curating institutions, these entities have operated under the assumption that the books they consider for prizes and collections have already met the professional standards of publishing, and they have had difficulty sorting through the volume of self-published titles without the help of first-step professional vetting.[24]

The New Intermediaries

Isolated author success and favorable technological developments allayed the stigma on self-publishing, but the cottage industry of support services offering editing, distribution, and retail sales for self-published authors has also played a profound role in moving self-publishing into the mainstream. These intermediaries operate under four models. First, some new intermediaries have business models that developed organically to help self-published authors produce their work. Second, some giant corporations, like Amazon and Apple, help self-published authors distribute their work, but self-publishing is not necessarily a core part of their business models. The third type consists of traditional publishers who supply services because they see lucrative potential in self-publishing. Finally, there are seedier companies who have continued the exploitative practices of the twentieth-century vanity press.

The growth of these intermediaries has had a number of crucial consequences for the publishing ecosystem that should not be underestimated. The new intermediaries provide evidence that the vanity stigma has faded enough to enable a viable (and in many cases reputable) business model built on earnings from the pockets of aspiring authors, and the intermediaries' desire to profit from self-publishing has made them disinclined to perpetuate the vanity stigma. Because some new intermediaries act as distributors and work on commission, thus earning money only when readers buy self-published books, they have an incentive to help self-published authors become better writers and book producers.

The growth of the new intermediaries was not without controversy. In 2009, the romance publisher Harlequin introduced Harlequin Horizons, a POD division that offered writers with manuscripts (some of whom had been rejected from the other Harlequin imprints) an opportunity to purchase author services to help produce and market their works. Because it had been so taboo in the twentieth century for royalty publishers to charge authors for their services, Harlequin's move would have been unthinkable at the beginning of the twenty-first century. And indeed, for some this move was still unthinkable in 2009. Authors' organizations called the new operation a vanity press and protested it vigorously.[25] Harlequin relented and changed the name of its POD operation from Harlequin Horizons to Dellarte Press in response to threats that its main imprints would no longer be eligible for industry awards.[26]

The reaction against Harlequin did not stop other long-established companies from seeking profit from self-published authors. In late 2010, *Publisher's Weekly* began "PW Select," a supplement that allowed self-published authors to buy listings, which then made them eligible for a review. Penguin's 2012 purchase of Author Solutions, a POD company with a dubious reputation for overpricing its services and using sensational marketing language to sell them, signaled that mainstream publishers would continue to seek profit from the expansion of self-publishing, at least for the time being. From the perspective of watchdog groups that worked to protect the interests of authors, Penguin's acquisition of Author Solutions didn't represent new respect for the potential of self-publishing or an organic way of fostering it; rather, it was merely a cynical lunge for the burgeoning market for self-publishing services. In the self-publishing community, Author Solutions had amassed a horrible reputation for aggressively selling what observers called overpriced and underperforming services. But Penguin's acquisition meant that at least some large commercial publishers had lost the incentive to characterize self-publishing negatively as vanity, as they had throughout the twentieth century.

In contrast to traditional publishers like Penguin that tried to enter the self-publishing industry while maintaining a commitment to print and the royalty model, other intermediaries took a start-up mentality and built their business models around digital self-publishing. They have argued (rightly or wrongly) that this approach gives them a nimbleness that commercial publishers, with their traditions and attachment to the print market, cannot match. Wattpad, for example, began as a platform that sought to be an open, YouTube-like system that enabled users to post their writing and their ebooks. The site built a number of features into its system that were designed for younger users and writers. Its users serialize much of their work, and the site is accessible because the developers designed it for mobile use. The administrators have been aggressive about promoting and curating popular content with the help of readers, and in contrast to the harsh atmosphere of many user-generated content sites, Wattpad users tend to be positive and encouraging about one another's writing, provided the contributors stay within community norms. The site has attracted venture capital because of its ability to keep eyeballs on the site for extended amounts of time. It has also served as an incubator for print publishing by working with publishers to help popular writers monetize their content, and some of its most popular writers have moved into traditional publishing as a result.

Wattpad represents one born-digital intermediary of self-publishing, and such services have been joined by other start-ups that seek to help self-published authors with distribution. Smashwords, for example, has built its business model on taking a commission for facilitating distribution. Users upload their books to Smashwords and sell them through the store, and Smashwords also distributes the books to a number of retailers and takes a commission on each sale—a model that has enabled it to distance itself from any whiff of vanity, since it doesn't cost the authors anything until they actually sell books.

The presence of start-ups like Wattpad and Smashwords have had important implications for the vanity stigma and the trajectory of self-publishing. Much of the language of the marketing attempts of these companies resembles the discourse of Web 2.0 and social media rather than that of traditional publishing. Users share content, and the language of disintermediation saturates company efforts to encourage writers to take advantage of a world without gatekeepers and reach readers directly through the democratization of publishing. This is crucial, because within this language of social networking and Web 2.0, self-publishing and sharing content are much less taboo than in the discourses employed by traditional publishing. Web technologies and social networking have made it more acceptable and technologically possible to publish all sorts of material under the auspices of empowerment and liberation. New intermediaries employing this language have used it to help erase the vanity stigma.

Traditional publishers and new intermediaries have supported self-publishing and its move to the mainstream, but Amazon has been the main sponsor of self-published books. Its influence has been overwhelming. The potential for authors to publish and earn money through Kindle self-publishing defied the conventional wisdom, in place since at least the mid-twentieth century, that it was impossible to earn a livable wage as a self-publishing author.

While Amazon has been engaged in high-profile legal disputes with traditional publishers, it has quietly been offering a platform for self-published authors that has allowed it to amass a vast catalog of self-published Kindle books in just a few short years, and it also offers the POD service CreateSpace so that self-published authors can offer works in print. Amazon sees databases of self-published texts as one more thing to sell in addition to other kinds of media content, and in that sense what enables self-published texts to thrive in the current technological environment is not the lack of gatekeepers; it is the whims, desires, and business plans of the corporate behemoths that sponsor them. It is also the struggle for market share of digital devices. Corporate giants create platforms to develop content stores that will provide low-cost reading for customers. This encourages buyers to purchase more books—and a new e-reader when their current one becomes obsolete. Contemporary self-publishing as an industry is tied to the evolving market for e-readers as much as it is tied to the empowerment of the "citizen author."

Amazon has been particularly savvy about exploiting these hundreds of thousands of writers and their content to shape the ebook publishing ecology. It gives self-published authors an incentive to sell their ebooks within a certain price range: as of this writing, the company is offering royalties of up to 70 percent for a self-published ebook priced between $2.99 and $9.99, but it cuts the royalty rate in half when writers sell their books outside that range. Some observers suggest that Amazon designed this model to accustom readers to inexpensive ebooks, building consumer sentiment that the company can marshal into power as it negotiates ebook pricing with commercial publishers.

Amazon does have regulations in place to control the kind of content writers can publish at the Kindle store, but in contrast to print publishing the barriers are low (e.g., it has not required authors to purchase ISBN numbers for their works), and it is rapidly accruing a massive database of ebooks and experimenting with subscription services for its readers. Chapter 4 will provide an understanding of the experience of authors who have self-published and achieved bestseller status on Amazon, but on the whole Amazon's influence on contemporary book culture is enormous and still poorly understood.

In addition to the new intermediaries just profiled, services and free-lancers—like editors, book designers, and agents who mentor self-published authors and/or negotiate the sale of print rights on the authors' behalf—support self-published authors. A few of these services have been crooked; some have been caught selling services to write positive reviews on online book-reviewing sites and face lawsuits from Amazon, but many have worked to build sustainable business models grounded in contemporary publishing conditions. Members of this cottage industry not only have no wish to see the vanity stigma perpetuated, they also have a vested interest in helping self-published authors improve their books. In other words, for them a sustainable business model relies on the quality of the self-published text. They have an incentive to educate would-be authors about the expectations of readers for quality of editing, design, and formatting. For example, Mark Coker, the founder of Smashwords, has analyzed data from book sales in his company to produce presentations about the shared characteristics of top-selling books. Rarely have complaints about the low production value of self-published books taken into account the possibility that mass education could measurably improve the standards, but in the last decade support systems, educational materials, and online communities have made opportunities to learn about book production and publishing much more accessible.

···

It is tempting to attribute the explosion in self-publishing to the discourses of liberation and empowerment associated with Web 2.0, and they have played a large role, but some less conspicuous yet powerful forces are also motivating the explosion of self-publishing. The fading of the vanity stigma enabled new intermediaries to rise and profit from the work of authors against a background in which the information economy has demanded that its subjects hone their writing skills to the point that they reorient and see the world as writers rather than as readers. This reorientation drives the production of value on the writing spaces of the web and in much of the writing that creates self-publishing's massive volume.

This bird's-eye view of changes to self-publishing could easily lead us down the same path of hype and excitement that fuels so much Web 2.0 discourse—revolution-laced language from which its advocates hope to profit. We could pick any number of anecdotes in publishing news in the last decade and defend the position that royalty publishing will soon wither and die. However, whereas this chapter has concentrated on change, the next chapter will show the ways in which the ideologies and publishing infrastructures of the twentieth century have persisted in the imaginations of writers as they struggle to shape their writing identities and publishing trajectories while multiple paths to authorship unfold before them and present them with challenging decisions. This grounded view shows that changes to publishing are not happening as fast as some have claimed, and it indicates the way the publishing status quo can shape the writers' relationship to their work.

CHAPTER 2

Becoming an Author without a Publisher

FOR WRITERS WHO hope to identify as authors, the ubiquity of publishing introduces a significant problem for authorial identity. What is an author without a publisher's imprimatur? When composition scholar Rebecca Moore Howard published her study on plagiarism in 1999, she argued that academics ascribed four properties to the "true author," values that conditioned the status of academic writing. The "true author" is the proprietor of his or her work and is autonomous, original, and moral. These four characteristics produced an "intellectual hierarchy of value" that placed the modern author above, for instance, writers who collaborate with partners or compile the work of others for publication.[1]

These characteristics underpin the idea of the Romantic Author, but Howard provided the caveat that her list was incomplete. Indeed, she neglected the most basic characteristic of modern authorship, perhaps because it was so obvious that it was not worth mentioning: the author has had work published. This may have been done posthumously, anonymously, or even without authorization. But to be a Romantic Author with texts attributed to one's name is to have work circulated publicly. This fifth characteristic of authorship generates another distinction, published versus unpublished, that contributes to hierarchies of value in writing. Aspiring writers querying agents and publishers know that this binary, which is endemic to the royalty system, is an acute measure of prestige, since the royalty system naturalized the assumption that authors would find a third party to publish and distribute their work.

This measure of prestige produces an acute tension when it is contextualized in the history of author-publisher relations. On the one hand, these relationships have been shot through with contention: they are strained by economic hardship, competing visions of creativity, control over the text, the prodigious quantity of unsolicited manuscripts that taxes the publishing infrastructure, the presence of scam artists, shifting technologies, intellectual property changes, and, from time to time, eccentric personalities. On the other hand, in the royalty system most writers could identify as authors only by finding and working with a publisher. Publishers became constitutive of authorial identity. How, then, is this identity jarred, reconfigured, and shaped when writers have the opportunity to amass an audience in the absence of publishers? If publishers have constituted the authorial identity, how do writers come to understand themselves as authors in environments of ubiquitous publishing?

This chapter addresses these questions by examining the theories of publishing that self-published authors have formulated and the ways those theories help the authors fashion and refashion their writing identities. How writers understand publishing is essential to how they understand their work and how they value their writing. The authors I interviewed developed their theories of publishing through popular press representations, tacit lessons learned in formal education, experience with agents and publishers, and the swirl of lore in online discourse. Their disposition toward publishing was influenced by variables like the commercial genre in which they were writing, whether they considered themselves entrepreneurially minded, the value they placed on creative control, whether they had queried agents and publishers and the responses they had received, and their imagined trajectory as authors (if they imagined a trajectory beyond a one-book project). These writers had the confusing task of orienting to publishing when multiple models were emerging alongside the persistent (and still dominant) royalty system, a process that placed them in the middle of debates filled with polarized language about the future of the book.

In this chapter, five case studies show how writers have oriented to publishing in the transitional environment, with a focus on how the legacies of royalty publishers persist in the writer's imagination and influence the decisions writers make about publishing. The studies show how important publishers have been, and still are, to authors, and how the presence of the publishing industry—and the distinction it offers— conditions the value-making processes of writers and readers who are working in environments of ubiquitous publishing. The initial four case studies depict authors who have achieved large audiences and thus are not representative of the sample. I have focused on these four to illustrate the conundrums of writers who have had to make decisions about publishers or were likely to make decisions about them in the future, in contrast to many self-published authors who have no desire to see their work spread widely. At the end of the chapter I present a case study of the latter type of writer to contrast his disposition to writing and publishing with those who wished to reach a larger audience.

Abigail Gibbs: Getting Attention and Being Published

After two years of amassing a sizable audience on Wattpad, Abigail Gibbs disappeared. Since she was fifteen years old she had built an audience for her writing by serializing more than sixty installments of her novel, *Dinner with a Vampire: Did I Mention I'm Vegetarian?* However, she stopped posting before finishing the ebook.[2] The thousands of comments on her message board, which functioned as metacommentary to *Dinner* and where Gibbs interacted with her fans, documented the reaction to her work and her eventual disappearance. Throughout the book's history, fans offered effusive praise and a constant rhythm of requests for the next upload. When Gibbs stopped, readers posted discursive moments of despair and complaints because they had followed the serialization for two years and wanted to see a resolution. As the consternation grew, some readers threatened to "unfan" Gibbs, while others claimed inside knowledge of her disappearance and reassured her fans that she had not abandoned the story. This prompted a discussion of fan entitlement: Did Gibbs owe a final installment to the fans who had helped make her ebook popular? Did communal etiquette require that she explain her absence personally? The comments made clear that her fans had been invested not simply in the story but also in the trajectory of its enormous popularity:

some fans had discovered and shared the content in its infancy, and they thought they had played a role in making Gibbs popular.

More than a year later Gibbs offered a full explanation of why the uploads had ended by announcing that the book had been finished for HarperCollins and retitled *The Dark Heroine: Dinner with a Vampire*. Her announcement betrayed a deft understanding of Wattpad's dynamics. Gibbs had to explain to her fans why she was pulling the sixty chapters from the web and why readers would have to pay to read the ending, given that some had been following the story for years for free and were anticipating its resolution. "No need for pitchforks," she implored, as she explained that only the first twenty chapters would stay on Wattpad as an original draft. "Why am I being so horrifically evil?" she asked, and explained the decision to remove most of the work as follows:

> I started posting *Dinner with a Vampire* when I was fifteen years old, and I am the first to put my hands up and say I was not the greatest writer then. The draft that has been available on Wattpad was unedited, full of random splurge on a page, and sadly, many readers are not as forgiving of a messy manuscript as us Wattpadders. Therefore I am keen for new readers to be directed to the shiny new edited version, and not be put off by fifteen-year-old me. [3]

Gibbs invoked the language of the mob through "pitchforks" as she anticipated the complaints that would come as she monetized the work and its conclusion. Her announcement acknowledged the dangerous terrain she had to traverse as she moved from a sharing economy to a sales economy while trying to retain as many fans as possible.

Although Gibbs ostensibly pulled the manuscript because of concern over the role her web juvenilia would play in her image as a published author, there were probably other considerations. The publisher most likely did not want a free version of the novel on the web while trying to sell it in bookstores and through e-readers, and there was also the potential, if the rough text remained available, that readers would pick out changes and plot discrepancies that cropped up as Gibbs and her editors cut prose and edited the serialization for traditional publishing (something readers did, anyway, in reviews of the book). Only enough of the book remained to entice Wattpad readers to buy the full version. In the months that followed, Gibbs posted updates on her message board about media events and release dates. She posted requests that readers review the book on Amazon, and she expressed gratitude when fans announced they had bought the book.

Many writers populate Wattpad and share their work, hoping to eventually find a publisher, but few do; Gibbs's success made her an outlier. Some of her fans complained loudly when she announced that the ending would be available only through purchase. Those complaints typically focus on accessibility. They show how important Wattpad's open and mobile design had been to the popularity of the story and how inaccessible brick-and-mortar distribution was to some of its readership: Why was the book accessible earlier in Britain than in the United States? Was the book going to be available in print in Pakistan? In the Philippines? What should readers do if their parents wouldn't let them use a credit card for the ebook and they didn't live near a bookstore? And how could readers access the ending if their parents wouldn't let them buy the book because the publisher stamped a giant seal on the cover announcing the book as "the sexiest romance you'll read this year"?

On the whole, fans offered overwhelming congratulations to Gibbs, and these positive comments dwarfed the complaints. Her fans vociferously praised her for "being published." Thus, despite having had her work accessed millions of times, amassing thousands of loyal followers, and achieving microcelebrity status, Gibbs had not been "published," according to her fans. Wattpad enables all the activities required to produce a self-contained ebook ecology: writing, reading, publishing, distributing, cover design, reviewing, filtering, curating, and storing. But users do not frame this activity with language drawn from professional book culture. They use language from digital culture, and as a consequence they talk about posting and sharing stories, not publishing them. This difference ultimately enabled them to draw a line of demarcation between unpublished and published that ran as an undercurrent through the congratulations Gibbs received.

Contemporary discourses about self-publishing often champion it as the ongoing democratization of publishing, and a group of professionals works to maintain the Wattpad platform, but to Gibbs and her fans, it was clear that the sixty installments *did not count* as publication: that came only through the intervention of a professional publishing house and the move into monetization. In an environment of ubiquitous publishing on Wattpad, a website praised by some media as "disruptive to publishing," the power and prestige of traditional publishing persisted deeply. For Wattpad participants, HarperCollins's acquisition of Gibbs's book was not just about the author earning a lucrative contract. It was also about the achievement of "being published." It was the very ubiquity of publication on a website (i.e., anyone can do it) that lent an element of distinction to her accomplishment, that made her a published author. So powerful was the accomplishment of "being published" that it allowed Gibbs to seamlessly insert market relations into her relationship with her fans, transitioning from a sharing relationship into a monetary relationship while maintaining her standing in the free and open community.

Gibbs's case demonstrates how many variables bear down on writers as they work in the "economics of attention." In 1997 Michael Goldhaber highlighted the importance of attention to digital economies (and attention has since been a core concept in discussions of digital content).[4] In web-based economies with abundant information that can be rapidly published, copied, and shared, attention becomes almost synonymous with value. It is a scarce resource from the perspective of audiences and a highly desirable resource from the perspective of content creators.[5] For early theorists of the web, the idea of attention provided a way to frame key questions about the digital transition: How does one monetize the attention of an audience after attracting that readership with free content? How does content attract users who surf in a never-ending stream of it? How does one restrict access and widespread sharing when one desires?

In the economics-of-attention framework, the nature of digital texts (that they can easily be copied for free) produces a binary between digital abundance and print scarcity. This opposition is somewhat helpful, but it must be highly qualified. First, Goldhaber noted that attention economies did not come into existence on the web. They have long existed and are part of the human condition; the history of the book is rife with complaints that there is too much in print and not enough time to read it all.[6] Second, once one considers the hardware and infrastructure required to spread digital texts, one cannot equate the digital with abundance, especially given the problems of access to digital devices (and print, for that matter) that exist all over the world.

Access is not an insignificant footnote to the economics of attention in digital environments: in order for the concept to have explanatory power, you often need to assume that a population has ready access to digital devices and Internet connections. Once access to a device is assumed, then the contrast between the "scarcity" of print and the "abundance" of the digital comes more into focus as an analytic lens and can matter to the economics of digital writing and publishing. It is significant to the trajectory of writing and publishing that Amazon's servers can hold more titles than their warehouses can. It is significant that Wikipedia has more space for niche topics than print encyclopedias do. And it is significant that one can read forever on the web without exhausting the resources, even if some of the most important are locked behind a paywall. The nature of digital writing technologies matters for what gets written, circulated, and read.

From a theoretical standpoint, Goldhaber took the position that in web-based information economies, amassing attention often functions as a precursor to earning money on content.[7] He was murkier about how that transformation actually happens, and digital content creators still have difficulty monetizing attention. The problem has created an enormous philosophical rift between people who, on the one hand, believe that content should be shared widely and given away for free in the hope that circulation will lead to attention and thus revenue, and people who, on the other hand, insist that content remain monetized and create architectures of distribution that lock it down through various technological and legal restrictions.

A writer like Gibbs might monetize attention by self-publishing to an e-reader or by seeking a publisher—a decision many writers face. Relative success is contingent on volatile factors like e-reader and tablet adoption, the genre of writing being published, the personality of the writer, and the policies of large online distributors. Clearly the digital economy and print economy were utterly inseparable for Gibbs; she used each to stimulate the other. Gibbs could have monetized her writing and kept it exclusively within the digital realm, self-publishing her work through a digital distributor, as many successful indie authors have done. But the following consideration shows how difficult it would have been for her to produce a professional text and draw buyers from her existing readership.

Gibbs would have been a teenager needing to raise the capital to have her book professionally edited and designed, and she would have had to learn the intricacies and regulations of the different digital publishing platforms. The success of her book would have been contingent on the possibility of a young audience, accustomed to reading her work for free on a mobile platform, migrating to an e-reader or an e-reader app and buying the book. These readers, however, could simply migrate to another free story from a different writer on Wattpad.

What is already a complex decision-making process for a writer is made even more so when we note that writing and authorship are rarely only about amassing readers, attention, or money: they are also about a status derived from the ideological residue of the royalty model, which among other dynamics places enormous emphasis on "being published." In Gibbs's case this status meant, somewhat peculiarly, that a writer who commanded a large reading public moved into publishing as the next step in her writing career.

Jessica Snowin: Authorship, Publishers, and Institutional Dynamics

The idea of "being published" represents a conundrum for first-time authors, and it is one of the most penetrating ways that the values of traditional publishing surface in the lives of writers who feel caught between established and emerging models. Those who see prestige in the accomplishment experience tensions in digital authorship as legacies of print authorship reverberate in their writing lives. This is apparent in the case of Jessica Snowin (a pseudonym), who experienced conflicting identities as a writer when she moved from a popular publishing platform to a prestigious creative writing program. In her situation we can see that the assumptions about publishers in the royalty model are inscribed in an institution that prepares professional writers.

Snowin began writing fiction after early encounters with reading, and she began serializing her work on the web at age sixteen. She posted sporadically under a pseudonym, and shortly before she entered creating writing classes in a flagship state university, an online scuffle about the originality of her ebooks boosted their readership (see chapter 5). She was accused of copying the plot of another writer, and the conflict drew attention to her story, which drove it to the top of the popularity rankings and to the front page of the website. This also initiated interest in the other stories she had posted, and at the time of our interview her fiction had been accessed tens of millions of times.

The popularity of Snowin's texts created extensive feedback loops that contributed to her development as a writer. Using the site's commenting function, the readers picked through the plot and language of her stories and noted inconsistencies and errors, but praise dominated. Although Snowin wished for more substantive feedback, she believed that the comments from her readers demonstrated her potential to satisfy an audience. She cited this experience as something that gave her confidence as she went through the nerve-wracking process of applying to the university's creative writing program.

Despite the experience with digital publishing that she had acquired on the web, Snowin refused to mention her Internet writing to her classmates and the faculty. She didn't want them to know that she had self-published because she found the program's environment to be hostile to the kind of popular writing that appealed to the web audience. In our interview she made a pointed distinction between her online writing life and her experience in her creative writing program; she was, in fact, one of the few participants in the study who wished to remain anonymous so that no one in her creative writing program would know what she had been writing online. Her Internet writing identity functioned for her as a precursor to print authorship, as she explained:

> I've very much wanted to improve my writing skill because now I've realized that I actually do want to be a published author when I graduate from college. That is what I want to do with the rest of my life. . . . I don't want to self-publish a book and have people pay for it and go "oh my god," I just wasted ten bucks on this book, look at all the spelling errors. But when I publish on the web it's more, you know, you're posting it for yourself. You're not as concerned with whether every single letter is correctly punched into the keyboard. That sounds very bad, but it is

the truth. I think I have lots and lots of room for improvement before I can ever be a published author, where a kid can wander into a bookstore and pick up my book. I think there is a huge difference between being published online where you know the main audience is teenage girls, compared to having your book in a bookstore.

To a writer enmeshed in a preprofessional creative writing program, the enormous audience Snowin amassed on the web doesn't yield the identity of a published writer. This is partly because it is free reading, and also because for Snowin the value added by publishers—editing and bookstore distribution—remains a signifier of professionalism and means greater access to a new market, even though, ironically, her online ebooks have been accessed more than the vast majority of published print books ever will be. Her sense of authorship displays a commitment to the prolonged trajectory of development that is common to formally trained professional writers, whose temporal sensibilities have been conditioned with the expectation of delayed gratification.

For this particular writer, the professional infrastructure of formal publishing creates a "huge difference" between print and digital. Digital writing is recognizable to her as a feedback system, a preliminary move to improve through engagement with readers. The success of her web writing is not an entrepreneurial moment for Snowin, an attempt to seize attention and find ways to monetize it when it is in abundance—which could happen, for example, if she self-published the sequel to her first ebook directly on an e-reader service and then sold it to her existing readership. Rather, her web writing represents a training ground, and authorship is a status that will enable her to unload the work of publishing upon acceptance of the manuscript, much as in the case of Gibbs. There is a yawning gulf for Snowin between being a web writer and a "published author," and this gulf has been made wider through her experiences in a creative writing program as well as through an interaction she had online with an editor who warned her that self-publishing might "hurt her" when she looked for an agent to find a print publisher.

Snowin's experience corroborates Gibbs's, but an important conclusion to draw from Snowin's case is that authorship, conceptualized by its relationship to publishers, is such a protected status in her creative writing program that she cannot initiate a discussion about the various trajectories of authorship afforded by new distribution systems, even though her development as a writer relied on her experience in web writing. Discussions about the benefits and drawbacks of developing as a writer while trying to satisfy the demands of thousands of readers, or the extent to which her fan base might help her attract the attention of a publisher in the future, have been foreclosed. The special status of "being published" is evident in Snowin's stance, which is similar to that of Gibbs: amassing an enormous public audience does not make one published. The serious book culture that infuses higher education remains isolated from the systems Snowin has experienced, suppressing any lessons she has learned about digital circulation and audience building.

Stephen Toulouse and the Legacy of Vanity

The ideological residue of the royalty system runs so deep that even those with prebuilt digital platforms and prefabricated reservoirs of attention feel it flow through their experience. The case of Stephen Toulouse shows how the vanity stigma profiled in chapter 1 surfaces in the lives of writers. It also shows how the desire for "being published" is induced when a writer moves from one writing medium, a blogging platform, to another, an ebook. Toulouse was an outlier among the memoirists I studied, because he has sold thousands of books. Unlike authors who publish for family and friends, and unlike those who are trying to build platforms for their work, Toulouse had a preexisting and robust digital platform when he self-published his book: he had spent more than a decade blogging about his experience working at Microsoft. But even as a limit case, his experience illustrates how powerful the legacies of publishing can be. For Toulouse, "being published" represented a "badge of accomplishment"; the thought of self-publishing represented an act of vanity, and his decision to proceed without a publisher elicited an emotional reaction that illustrates how the legacies of print publishing pierce through contemporary acts of digital writing.

After blogging for a decade, Toulouse began thinking about a book project, so he revisited his posts and organized them into a manuscript, focusing on entries that documented his fifteen-year tenure as an employee at Microsoft. After working with an editor to develop the book, Toulouse mined his connections at work to locate a publisher. He submitted his manuscript, and the house indicated that it would be willing to publish his memoir. He later blogged that at this point "my manuscript was slotted into the hell I like to call the 'Editorial Calendar.'"[8] Little contact from the publisher made Toulouse feel frustrated, as though he had entered a "holding pattern," as he kept encountering—and missing—opportunities to promote his work.

His relationship with his publisher soured after email exchanges about royalty negotiations, so Toulouse decided to self-publish the manuscript, a decision he described on his blog: "For more than four months I had played the old media publishing game, trading paltry royalties for a badge of being 'really' published. I spent a long night after that email with a bottle of scotch re-reading my manuscript."[9] When I asked him what about publishing constituted a "badge," he replied that finding a publisher "was the one thing that would prove it wasn't a vanity project." After he overcame the hesitation that the vanity stigma introduced, he self-published his book, and less than a month after making that decision Toulouse tweeted to almost twenty thousand Twitter followers that his book was for sale in print and ebook through multiple outlets.

Toulouse had self-published his writing for years, building an audience that amounted to between fifteen and twenty thousand different blog visitors per day. Yet when he revised his blog into a book, he felt a desire to locate a publisher and the perceived prestige—and potential market reach—it carries with it. (You need a publisher to get your book in the airport, Toulouse noted.) The act of polishing his prose, reorganizing it into a coherent manuscript, and working with an editor altered his emotional disposition to his writing. He understood blogs in digital terms, measuring his success through web analytics. But he understood the book in print terms, initially measuring his success through the ability to place a manuscript with a publisher. Enmeshed in the ideology of print, his decision to self-publish made him feel the sting of the vanity stigma. He wondered whether a book without a royalty publisher had already failed.

In Toulouse's case, the question of vanity was more a matter of the method of delivering his writing than of the writing itself. The issue wasn't his writing; it was how that writing would reach the public, since the vanity stigma haunted the POD technology Toulouse used to create hard copies of his book. The publisher's stamp of approval offered Toulouse a de facto measure of success, a certification that his book wasn't a vanity project. Overcoming this need meant that Toulouse had to conceptualize his writing as something other than a failure in the face of multiple discourses that appeared to him to devalue self-published books. The protracted time in the editorial calendar and the continued work on the manuscript were factors that removed the shame of vanity from his experience.

After making the decision to self-publish, Toulouse began coordinating what he described as a fairly user-friendly process. He chose a company to help him produce the book, he tapped friends to help him with graphic design, and he consulted with the owners of the websites cited in his text so that he could guard against "link rot" in the ebook. He made decisions about digital rights management, and the legal and publicity departments at Microsoft vetted his manuscript; thus gatekeepers appeared in different manifestations than in traditional publishing. With the book preparation final, Toulouse announced its publication through Twitter and his blog. His friends tweeted its arrival, and he gave readings of his work at technology gatherings.

The size of Toulouse's digital platform convinced him that he had publication choices, yet the publisher did not seem to understand his options, as he explained:

> But in discussing the things that I thought were important about the book with traditional publishing, you could see that they just didn't realize I had options. And those options were both far less work and far more lucrative than their model. I mean their model may have put me in more stores but they were going to take a lot more money and they were going to ask me to do a lot more labor. I was going to have to travel around and do a lot of different presentations at their particular events, at their particular readings.

Toulouse's sense of agency with his writing came as a result of the built-in audience he had amassed in a decade. The options he had were hard-won, the result of contributing value to the blogosphere, engaging with an audience, taking advantage of the name recognition of his company, and working within preexisting networks. Having learned from his experience in the editorial calendar, Toulouse was able to reconceptualize the criteria of success for his own writing, shaking off the vanity stigma and the need for a publisher's acceptance. This ultimately contributed to his propensity to cast publishing in the language of old media versus new media:

> My theory was that old media would be smart enough to incorporate new media and I could have a mixture. And that's one of the reasons I was researching traditional publishing. And what I realized was, I think I'm going to make a bold statement, but I think the traditional model of publication—we'll call this old media for lack of a better umbrella term for it—I think it's dead. I think its brain stem is still alive. And I think it's shambling along a bit like a zombie and probably will for another five to 10 years.

The situation shepherded him into what Paul Duguid has called the argument of supersession, a logic that assumes the new media will inevitably displace the old.[10] In this case it was the legacy of the vanity press and new opportunities that channeled Toulouse into framing his experience as print versus digital and old versus new.

Toulouse had the means to hire an editor before he approached a publisher and was therefore confident in the quality of his manuscript. He had friends who had been through the publishing process before and could advise him. He had built a successful platform through his blog. His audience was digitally savvy; his readers populated the blogosphere and Twitter, and they were the kind of people who were likely to be early adopters of e-readers. With almost twenty thousand Twitter followers, Toulouse had a robust audience to which he could market his book. But he was also just one step away from coworkers with more than ten times the number of followers he had, and they were willing to retweet and make their audiences aware of his book. This network provided the services that publishers' publicity platforms typically provide for first-book authors, who usually cannot build it themselves. Being able to draw on such a network would certainly give a writer an outlook that would make a publisher seem unnecessary.

Toulouse's experience, however, simultaneously produced ambivalence despite his bold perspective on publishing. He implemented a promotion whereby he would write a personal message and sign print books that readers ordered when the book first went on sale. He signed close to three hundred of these books, and for some time he spent his evenings signing books, packing them, and mailing them. This work exhausted him, and despite believing in the imminent demise of publishers, he noted that it would be nice to find a publisher for his next book to help distribute the work. However, he did not feel locked into the system: Toulouse's online platform created options and leverage, a sense that he could abandon a publisher if he did not find its terms satisfactory.

Hannah Leed: Publishing Activity, the Market, and the Creative Process

Hannah Leed (a pseudonym) demonstrates how the work of publishing can condition one's disposition to writing, and her case exemplifies the desire for a model of authorship in which the writer is free to work on his or her craft unencumbered by market activity. This model appeared in John Updike's much-circulated digital lament, "The End of Authorship," in which he addressed the advocates of the "digital attention" model of authorship.[11] Advocates of this model believe that finding an audience is more important than finding a publisher. They believe that the high volume of writing published on the web, and the ease with which it can be pirated, means that the writer should give digital work away for free and then earn money by selling print copies and through speaking engagements. Updike bemoaned this development because he thought it would devalue writing. He also thought it untenable that a writer could build a career based on speaking engagements; he believed that a writer's time was better spent honing his or her craft than working on promotion, a job best left to publishers. At the core of Updike's complaint was the image of the author working without concern for the market and free from the chore of self-promotion.

The author unencumbered by the market is the model of authorship closely aligned with serious books: explicit self-promotion is taboo, and the author sharpens his or her work while publishers do the "dirty" commercial work. This arrangement protects the author's art from market contaminants, and the ability to recuse oneself from market activity preserves the author as a moral being, one of the characteristics of the modern Romantic Author.[12]

There are three larger points to make about this ideal before we discuss Leed's practice. First, this model is rooted in a desire to exorcise the market from art, part of an aesthetic tradition that, as Pierre Bourdieu has argued, is largely illusory but nonetheless persistent, popular, and rooted in an "ethos of elective distance from the necessities of the natural and social world."[13] Second, studies of author economics in the twentieth century suggest that only a limited number of authors have achieved a full-time livable wage while concentrating solely on the kinds of writing they wish to do.[14] A career as an author working full-time on his or her craft has been an unattainable prospect for most writers. Writers write; they teach; they sell insurance. Third, the image also neglects the history of deft self-promotion that all kinds of print authors, including literary authors, have engaged in to boost the market value of their work. This activity can be necessitated by publishers who do little to market a book and leave the hard work of building an audience to the author. For the sake of propriety, these acts of self-promotion are typically accompanied by either an apology for the self-promotion or an explanation for why the behavior is not self-promotion.

I want to linger on the third point because it highlights a central tension in the relationship between print and digital media. The problem with a taboo on self-promotion is that self-publishing often requires it, and critics who lament self-publishing as digital narcissism find the need for self-promotion distasteful. Digital spaces create an environment in which writers publish easily but then find it difficult to attract attention. Goldhaber contends that this has led to conditions in which self-promotion has become more acceptable, and he argues that digital attention economies favor those who are comfortable cultivating it: "The ethos of the old economy which makes it often bad taste or a poor strategy to consciously seek attention seems to be giving way to an attitude that makes having a lot of attention rather admirable and seeking it not at all to be frowned upon."[15] Other characterizations of online life blame it for an intensification of narcissism.

The characterization of the web as a space in which attention seeking is socially acceptable is partly true but also highly problematic. Online communities and social networks have developed complex conventions to limit opportunities for excessive self-promotion, and they create tightly controlled conditions under which it is acceptable to seek attention. There are still many ways in which self-promotion is in bad taste online (hence the derogatory term "attention whoring," deployed in many online communities to signify obvious attempts at self-promotion). Alice Marwick and danah boyd argue that "microcelebrity" provides a way of understanding how participants seek attention in online communities.[16] Microcelebrity results from the energy of social networking, which produces "stars" who wield influence on social networks and command attention. But this microcelebrity emerges when such stars share, produce, and comment on highly valued content. It doesn't come through blatant grabs at attention.

Marwick and boyd's work shows empirically that social conventions control and discourage vacuous self-promotion, that self-promotion must be done through the standards developed by communities.[17] Because attention is scarce and content abundant, "attention whoring" registers as simply more noise rather than the high-value content that people seek in social networks. This is often categorized in online communities as a form of spam. Spam, as Finn Brunton contends, threatens online communities because it disrupts the discursive conventions established by communities that make them productive and functional (e.g., staying on topic in discussion threads). Spam is a capacious signifier capable of being deployed in different ways.[18] The reason unfettered acts of "attention whoring" are resisted, then, is that they threaten the ethos of online communities that otherwise build value through symbolic exchange.

Cultural critics are probably correct that public sharing of self-produced content has grown more acceptable, but the ethos of sharing has important implications for the circulation and recirculation of texts. Danielle DeVoss and James Porter claim that the ethos of sharing motivates youth to share content with their friends even if it involves violating copyright through peer-to-peer file sharing.[19] In a sense, then, reciprocity and sharing create conditions for the emergence of microcelebrity, but microcelebrity takes shape against cultural conventions that regulate it. This point is often absent from lamentations about digital narcissism.

Wattpad provides a crystalline example. The site encourages the sharing of original writing, the raison d'être of the space. Yet even though sharing is encouraged, actively drumming up a readership for one's own writing by "begging for reads" is taboo. "Begging for reads" not only marks a writer as a "noob" (short for *newcomer*) and annoys the more experienced participants, it also means that participants are creating noise rather than organically trying to establish themselves as valuable to the community. This establishment comes through time, experience, and valued contributions to the activity of the site: reading, commenting, and critiquing the works of others while posting your own work. Wattpad, along with other sites of self-publishing, has a dedicated forum for writers seeking readers, essentially quarantining requests for attention to keep the rest of the site free from writers "begging for reads." Self-published authors work in an environment with countless other writers, and self-promotion does have its place on the web—it has a natural affinity with self-publishing—but it is not an anarchic free-for-all.

Despite the inadequacies of the image of the author unencumbered by market concerns and the image of the self-promoting free-for-all of digital spaces, Hannah Leed's case demonstrates that Updike's concerns are real. Book publishing activates incredible amounts of work that prompts writers' continued desire to have publishers, and Leed's case shows how this situation encroaches on narrative. Leed graduated from college with a degree in English literature and maintained an active reading life, electing to read "basically whatever was at Barnes and Noble." As an undergraduate she enjoyed writing critiques of books, and after finding her way into a number of reading groups on Facebook, she began writing book reviews for Goodreads. One of her reading groups decided to have a writing contest in which the members would write the prologue to an imagined book. Leed did not win, but a number of those who entered used their prologues to write an entire manuscript. Her English-major roots betray a reading-oriented disposition to novels, a kind of moralizing in which it is difficult to imagine books whose production isn't sanctioned, and the conceptual leap she needed to write:

> I looked at being able to write an entire novel as being something that was such an honor, and you had to have this type of respect and reverence for it. Yes, I graduated with a degree in this. Yes, I took writing courses, but to do an entire story? My courses in college were focused on literature itself and not necessarily creative writing. I never took a novel writing course. Out of respect, I never thought that it was some-

thing that anybody can just do, like, "okay I have this great idea, this great story, so I'm going to do it. I've got to get 70,000 words and call it a novel, and bing bam boom it's done." That's not my approach.[20]

Despite these worries, Leed gradually finished writing a book and drew on online writing groups to learn the basics of self-publishing. She published two books in rapid succession that she classified as women's fiction/romance and began working on a third. She invested in professional editing, formatting, and cover design. Her marketing efforts placed her work on an Amazon bestseller list in early 2014, and her books amassed several hundred Amazon reviews.

Publishing required intense work, however, and it threatened to overwhelm Leed. In our interview she explained, "I do Pinterest, I do Facebook, I do Twitter, I do Google+, now Booktropolous, and Instagram. The business aspect of it becomes overwhelming, and it's very distracting from the creative process, so I've had to step back from that." I pressed her further:

TIM: That overwhelming business aspect of it, does that influence the way you are approaching writing? Is it influencing the way you are approaching the creative aspects of it?

LEED: Absolutely. I think in a sense that's why with this third book, I've had to take the approach, "I'm going to write the story that I want to write and I'll worry about the rest later." I can understand why people do want to go into traditional publishing versus self-publishing. Just alone for that factor that you don't have to necessarily be on the ball the whole time with your marketing strategy, your PR. It really does suck the creative aspect out, because before, when I was writing my first book, I would wake up and I could have a scene play out in my head. I'm dropping my son off at school, I'm walking back to my car, and it's becoming even more vivid. I get into my office, and that's when I'm going to knock that scene out. All of these things are just growing through my head, and it is so organic, just awesome.

Now I wake up to my book tracker, I wake up to, "Let me check to see what's going on Facebook. Okay, now I have to network. Now I have to check in with readers. I have to check with bloggers. . . . I have to check what are going to be my marketing strategies today." I end up doing this for about two or three hours every morning, even before I start doing my paying job. My phone is pinging all morning long, and it's book related. I'm not thinking about my characters. I'm not thinking about the plot. I'm frustrated because it's not coming to me as easily, I'm thinking about all these other things, and it becomes the business aspect of it.

There are a number of qualifications to make before I draw some tentative conclusions from Leed's case. She wrote her first book while working full-time and raising a child as a single mother. She wrote in the car, at work, while walking. Sociocultural activity has called attention to this distributed process, which is common for writers. The distributed nature of composing is clearly one reason for the prodigious number of books that get written regardless of whether a writer can dedicate all of her energy to it, regardless of whether she has a publisher. Writing is a distributed act, and for nonprofessional authors it happens amid the ebb and flow of everyday life. But for Leed, once the business of publishing worked its way into her life, writing became disrupted by technological reminders that infused every moment of her day.

Even though her books sold well, Leed saw self-publishing as subordinate to working with trade publishers in terms of prestige and reach, since for her, finding a publisher brought with it "respect" and "validation." She filtered this prestige through a problematic and gendered history that has worked to devalue some women's literary practices. She wanted to find a publisher to prove to herself that she was not just another "mommy" self-publishing. At the time of the interview, Leed had been contacted by an agent and was working on books aimed at traditional publishers, and she recognized that even with a publisher she would be marketing her work, albeit not with the same intensity.[21] Her experience confirms Updike's worry: the market can encroach so deeply on the writer's experience that it not only diverts time from one's craft, it also initiates a kind of writer's block caused by the disruptive ping of mobile technologies.

Although Leed had difficulty with the writing-publishing balance, a number of writers enjoyed (and thrived) doing both. Some writers simply had different personalities, and publishing books energized their writing. Others had spousal support, so they could work full-time on their books and carefully delineate their activities, such as by writing in the morning and publishing in the afternoon. In some instances, successful writers considered themselves heads of small publishing companies, and they hired personal assistants and family members to address the demand for labor. Others had willing fans who were eager to do things like help with marketing or web design. Reluctant to give up control of their work, these authors nevertheless saw publishers as ways of expanding their audience through print, and they needed help with complex matters such as negotiating translations and movie rights. They became hybrid authors.

The Negative Case: Memoir and the Local

The four writers described in this chapter represent cases in which the writer has an audience and needs to make a decision about publishing; however, many writers, especially the memoirists, decided from the beginning of their projects that they had no interest in finding a publisher. The memoirists I interviewed, as noted earlier, included war veterans, businesspeople, aspiring musicians, trauma victims, and social justice advocates. Memoirists wrote for catharsis or to create a record for their descendants. Some memoirists sought a large audience, and this often happened when the memoir was written to advocate for a cause. One memoirist, for example, wrote about traumatic brain injury and used her work to raise awareness of the condition. Other memoirists, however, kept their work within the family, and even though their texts were available in publicly accessible databases, they did little to acquire a readership beyond circulating the book locally.

These kinds of writers probably make up a sizable percentage of self-published authors, but we have no data that provide a good estimate of that. However, even when self-published authors decided from the outset of their projects that they had no interest in a publisher, the idea of the publisher impressed itself on their work and shaped their writing. In the case of Roland Chase (a pseudonym), the publisher represented the mediated demands of an audience that would prevent the writer from realizing the goals he had for his work.

When Chase returned from a tour of duty in Vietnam in the late 1960s, he was interested in distancing himself from the war, and he began focusing on his career. He threw himself into his work as a college basketball coach and did whatever he could to achieve intellectual and emotional distance from his military experience. For a number of decades this worked, but eventually he found it more and more difficult to suppress his memories, and finally it became apparent to him that he needed emotional closure to his experience. When he went to see the traveling Vietnam War memorial, his emotions peaked and triggered the writing that eventually became a manuscript chronicling his experience.

Chase took a number of measures to make sure that his work was a high-quality text (e.g., he hired an editor to help him develop content), but he intuited from the beginning that finding a publisher would conflict with the goals of the book, even though at that time he had no experience with publishing or self-publishing. For Chase the book was more writer-centered, defined against the reader-centered goals a publisher would have for it:

> I wanted to reveal myself emotionally. That was my goal. And to do that you have to talk about or write about things and feelings, stuff that usually I'm not accustomed to talking about or revealing. I mean simple things at times, and I also wanted to characterize some of the people who influenced me in positives and negatives through that period. And for some people who read it, they might get bored because of some of the detail I go into, characters who don't seem relevant, but to me they were very relevant, to me personally, and I wanted to acknowledge those feelings toward those people and just put it down on paper. . . . I just wanted it to be a natural telling of my story and how I changed during that period and how it [the war] affected me emotionally, and so that was my goal.

Chase's final manuscript was more than five hundred pages. He ultimately made it publicly accessible in a database, and a small newspaper ran an article about the book. The book circulated among his family and close friends, and the emotional closure he sought manifested itself in the writing process and the "thirty or so" times he read the book, reflecting on the experience he had once tried to distance himself from.

The idea of a publisher impressed itself on Chase's process as he negotiated the public-private boundaries of writing and the legacies of the writing medium in which he was working. He had almost reached the point of experiencing the book as a read-write medium, but the stalwart imaginary publisher embedded in the read-only conception of the book lingered in his imagination. Even for someone with little experience in writing, the publisher appears in the writer's imagination as an iteration of the tension between fidelity to a vision and the demands of the market. It was clear to Chase during the process that the autonomy he sought as a writer would conflict with the goals of a publisher and the desires of the reader. This autonomy doesn't necessarily mean the freedom to experiment with form or aesthetics, as in the case of high art; rather, it is simply the freedom to satisfy the emotional goals of the writer, to include details that strike in the mind of the writer but that might find no resonance with the reader.

•••

In imaginary and material ways, royalty publishers endure in the consciousness of self-publishing writers. Furthermore, authors face complex considerations in a volatile writing environment, where it can be difficult to know whether it is more advantageous to find a publisher or to self-publish.

Contemporary writers still find authorial identity closely linked to a publisher, and even when they abandon the royalty system, the ideological structures persist to condition how writing is valued and how the authors fashion their writing identities. In a somewhat counterintuitive reversal, traditional publishers can hold immense prestige in environments where a large number of writers compete for attention and the barrier to making one's writing publicly accessible is low. Publishers reinscribe a kind of exclusiveness, a badge of honor. They also represent a mediator between the writer and the demands of the market, a route to accessing new markets, a professional standard of production, and an encroachment into creativity.

The power of the royalty publisher and its eminence in the authorial imagination also means that when, as a point of identity, authors finally decide to break with publishing, they can do it with vehemence. This is one reason that some groups of self-published authors are highly antagonistic toward publishers. Indeed, the indie author identity, as we shall see next, illustrates this antagonism, revealing a movement that has worked to define itself against traditional publishers and as the professional vein of self-publishing.

CHAPTER 3

The Birth of Independent Authorship

THE PREVIOUS CHAPTER described how rooted publishers can be in the authorial imagination and how they continue to shape the identity of writers. Unlike the authors profiled there, however, some self-published authors have rejected the idea that the publisher has relevance in today's book economy, and they have done so with strong and dismissive language. In some ways this makes sense. If the publisher has existed as a crucial part of the identity of the author, then it can take considerable resources and energy to break away from that rootedness and form a new identity as an independent author. Such is the dynamic of the indie author movement. Inhabited by self-publishing authors who mostly consider themselves professionals and seek to earn a living from their writing, the indie author movement contains a number of writers who have been vocal about their break with publishers. In this chapter I will show some of the ways the movement has deployed the language of Web 2.0 to define itself and work to gel its unstable identity. Although this chapter does profile points of antagonism between indies and traditional publishing, I want to make clear at the outset that I do not mean to characterize the indie author movement as homogeneous, nor do I intend to suggest that its members are rebelling against publishers in concert. Many indie authors recognize the continued relevance of publishers and work with them in collaborative and productive relationships; however, tracing the genealogy of indie authors and some of the energy behind the movement enables us to continue to explore the formation of writing identities in an age of ubiquitous publishing.

During the second half of the twentieth century, independent publishing and small presses grew rapidly, and they often occupied various niches that were perceived to be open after the corporate conglomeration of publishing.[1] In some ways ignoring this history of independent publishing, some self-publishing authors have recently appropriated the term *independent* to describe their work, and they have networked together to create the indie author movement. Those who spend time in the blogosphere will know that this move has clearly vexed independent publishers, who argue that this indie author movement does not recognize the longer history of independent publishing. In some respects, when independent publishers express irritation, they are providing evidence that they acutely feel the negative effects of an ideology of individual authorship that they helped manufacture.

Let me explain. In the age of print, in order to sustain the image of the genius or celebrity author—an image that has motivated sales and that readers have been able to connect with—publishers have often effaced the importance of their work.[2] This has included minimizing the importance of the materiality of the book: its design, its durability, and its usability, all of which are valuable features that publishers, designers, and printers have developed and orchestrated for centuries.[3] Publishers have played a crucial role in book production, but in the twentieth century they were mostly content to remain in the shadows, and this is one reason that independent publishing does not have the same cultural weight as indie movements do in other media industries. Many people have heard of indie music; fewer people have heard of independent publishing.

The indie author movement has a number of historical continuities with twentieth-century independent publishing, especially because many independent publishers began as self-published authors. Despite these affinities, the indie authors I interviewed were more likely to associate what they do with indie film or indie music than with independent publishers. To the indie author, independent publishers represent gatekeeping in the same way that corporate publishers do, and they also represent the loss of creative control over the production of a book. These differences have allowed the indie author movement to recognize itself as different from, rather than an extension of, independent publishing. In recent years the indie author movement has been augmented by the term *hybrid author*, an author who moves back and forth between traditional publishing and self-publishing.

This chapter analyzes the rise of indie and hybrid authorship in order to define the subcultural spaces they seek to inhabit. My argument is this: Indie authorship has established its identity and broken with professional publishers by deploying the strong revolutionary language of Web 2.0 and its association with democracy and inclusion. At the same time, the indie author movement has adopted the professional standards of book production to which readers who pay for books are accustomed. When indie authorship adopted these standards, it ironically abandoned the inclusiveness it used to establish itself, since advocating standards is in many ways incommensurable with celebrating widespread access to publishing. This paradox powerfully demonstrates why the argument that we are now witnessing the fall of gatekeepers is actually an impoverished way of describing the current moment: even in conditions in which the gatekeepers' labor is absent, the standards they have programmed into readers remain. This produces powerful gatekeeping effects that influence writers who are trying to reach an audience.

The paradox is also one reason that indie authorship is a tenuous cultural space that authors must negotiate as they consider competing discourses and options for publishing. After I define some of the contours of indie authorship, I present brief case studies that show how authors experience competition between indie and hybrid systems. The rapidly emerging model of the hybrid allows us to think more carefully about how writers operate when publishing models compete, and in some ways the hybrid appears as a point of practical reconciliation between competing models of publishing that recognize they can profit from each other.

Declaring Independence, Defining Indie

In my studies, the authors who identified with the indie movement tended to do so for one of two reasons, and the two groups combined to perpetuate a discourse of indie authorship that tended to be defined against the contours of the publishing industry.

One group identified with it because they experienced traditional publishing as dysfunctional or unfair or because they were rejected by it and harbored feelings of resentment. One author, for example, experienced what she felt as cold rejection from agents and publishers for a book that she eventually self-published and that achieved bestseller status. Another considered herself indie and vowed never to return to publishing because she was receiving commission payments and sales figures on an immediate basis rather than on the more protracted basis she had experienced with traditional publishing. A third author went indie because he was an entrepreneur with a philosophy of self-reliance, and he balked at losing his copyright to a publisher. A fourth wrote a book that she thought did not nicely fit into any of the genres publishers produced, and she felt excluded from publishing. She self-published her work and had strong sales, and this success reinforced her view that publishers were out of touch with the desires of readers.

The second group of authors identified with the indie author network because they came to digital publishing with complete indifference toward traditional publishing. The routes by which such authors came to self-publishing varied. Some published books after participating in the do-it-yourself craft movement; for them indie authorship was the analogous point of identification in book culture. A number of authors were energized by the potential creativity and social interaction involved in self-publishing, and traditional publishing held no attraction for them. One author began writing fiction after working in technology start-ups. He was clearly immersed in the language of disintermediation, and he began his writing career by approaching it as just another start-up company, and the work of authorship as the company's product. Yet another author had a spouse who had begun a number of successful web companies, and they worked as a team to start a small publishing operation.

Like many terms whose definitions are caught in technological flux, *indie author* is currently being forged among different entities with different stakes involved. For instance, founded in 2012, the Alliance of Independent Authors (ALLi) is one of the largest professional groups for independent authors. ALLi offers a network for writers, publishes guidebooks and advice, and promotes the interests of indie authors in different sectors of the book industry. Adding the caveat that the terms in publishing are changing quickly, ALLi offers a definition of *indie author* on its website, differentiating it from other terms, which include *self-published author, author-publisher, trade publishing, independent press*, and *publishing service.*

ALLi positions the term as a response to the problems of self-publishing: "Many authors who publish their own work are feeling increasingly uncomfortable with the term 'self-published,' which gives the impression that they have done absolutely everything required to produce the book themselves, from cover design to editing. This is misleading. Good author publishing requires buying in carefully matched specialist services. New, more accurate, terms are becoming more commonplace, but have not yet taken precedence in search engines over the catch-all term 'self-publishing.'" For ALLi, "indie authors see themselves as the creative director of their own books, who are independent in attitude and responsible for their own publishing choices and destiny, no matter which type of publishing service they use—paid or trade."[4] This definition positions control and attitude (presumably the attitude that one be independent from publishers) as the key elements of indie authorship.

A definition grounded in the experiences of the writers I interviewed reveals more disparate interpretations. One author who wrote novels combining mystery and erotica described her approach this way: "I'm an indie author. I know there are some people who don't like that. I don't care. Language is fungible and evolving. Tough. I know that ten years ago it meant something different. There are small publishers who used to be referred to as indie and then we appropriated the term and they don't like it." Another author who self-published "literary fiction for women" described it in terms appropriated from other industries:

Think of it like indie film and the Hollywood studio system, or versus the Hollywood studio system. In the Hollywood studio system, a very few people own everything. And with the indie system, anyone who can get funding and put together a script and hire actors, etc., can produce a film. And some of the indie films are better than the big studio films. But there are indies and once they produce the film, they have to have a distribution deal. If you think of indie authors in the same way, Amazon and Nook are the distribution and promotion companies. I don't think of it as self-publishing as much as I think about it being an indie author.

This reliance on Amazon calls into question some of the assertions about the independence of indie authors (the subject of the next chapter), but it also shows the attraction of placing one's work in the context of other media histories with more visible traditions of independence. However, as I mentioned at the beginning of the chapter, the appropriation of the term *indie* was not necessarily welcomed in the publishing industry because many saw it in conflict with the history of independent publishers. This sentiment appeared among authors as well. Although Hannah Leed recognized that the term had taken on new meaning, this was the reason she did not identify with it despite experiencing its evolution: "I don't identify with Indie. I think that indie and self-publishing are interchangeable now, synonymous with one another, but originally an indie was an author working with a small house." That vestigial trace of traditional publishing made her shy away from the term.

In addition to authors and professional groups, the cottage industries that provide self-publishing services have offered some of the strongest language in support of indie authors. Mark Coker, the founder of Smashwords, wrote "The Indie Author Manifesto," which endows authors with "the right to publish" and all writers with "natural creative potential."[5] It draws on the language of democracy to free writers from the notion that they are "beholden" or "subservient" to any publisher. Overstated compared with ALLi's definition, this is a blatant example of the utopic and democratic language of Web 2.0 applied to ebooks and self-publishing.

This hyperbolic rhetoric also resembles the marketing language of the twentieth-century vanity press that claimed everyone could be an author if he or she paid for the book to be produced—overblown claims that ultimately subjected vanity presses to government scrutiny and lawsuits from customers. However, it is important to note that Smashwords is not a vanity press. It is a distributor operating on a commission model that offers its services free to authors and only takes a commission on sales. This model is precisely what enables Coker to use such strong language of liberation and adhere to a capacious definition of indie author, whereas

ALLi has a definition delineated more tightly to reflect the nuances in different models of publishing. The authors in this study who identified with the term *indie author* had different ideas of its origins and where it had been appropriated from, but they typically shared the attitude of independence and control intrinsic to the ALLi definition.

The Push for Standards

Despite language that suggests a strong break from traditional publishing, indie authorship has incorporated much of the traditional model as it strives to adhere to the textual standards developed in professional publishing. If the indie movement is about control, freedom, inclusiveness, and self-identification, it is, ironically, also about a push for standards, precisely because it is the subset of self-publishing that wants to be understood as professional. This attitude is less about literary standards for plot, character development, and other content elements than it is about the formal standards of editing, copyediting, proofreading, book design, and production.

Many people argue that the quality of self-published books has improved dramatically in the last decade, but that is difficult to determine. Because of the nature of self-publishing, it will always include books that do not adhere to professional publishing standards, an Achilles' heel that the defenders of traditional systems aim for. Moreover, as more people self-publish books, there will probably be a greater number that do not adhere to professional standards. What is evident, however, is the position taken by highly visible advocates of indie authorship, and they are unanimously uncompromising in their message: self-published books must replicate the standards of editing, design, and format of trade publishing, and for that, they argue, expect to invest capital in book production.

This message is clearly delineated in the explosion of guidebooks on how to be an indie author, which define indie authorship along with the standards to which indie books should adhere. In these texts we can see a message of democracy and inclusion as well as the imposition of more exclusively minded professional standards. ALLi has produced a series of well-researched guidebooks on the contemporary self-publishing scene. Debbie Young and Dan Holloway's *Opening Up to Indie Authors*, for example, is part of a larger campaign specifically designed to do three things: (1) provide a profile of recent changes to publishing, (2) provide a way for indie authors to work with industry sectors that have traditionally been closed to self-published authors (e.g., brick-and mortar-bookstores, prizes, and libraries), and (3) popularize ALLi's "Open Up to Indie Authors" campaign, a push that involves education, petitions, lobbying, and community building that works to "remove discrimination against self-published books."[6] Both Orna Ross's introduction and the text authored by Young and Holloway describe indie authorship as inclusive. The world of publishing is becoming "democratized," and "potentially all the world's an author—and in control of their [sic] own authorial destiny." As Young and Holloway suggest, "The defining quality of the organization is its inclusiveness and diversity of approach, and all who want to self-publish a book are welcomed."[7]

While ALLi defines itself through inclusion, however, the purpose of the guidebook is also to empower indie authors to negotiate with institutions that have defined themselves through a very particular set of exclusive professional standards, which become the yardstick for self-publishing authors:

> Used well, the sophisticated tools and services of the digital age enable authors to turn their work into professional-looking, commercially viable books. The best are indistinguishable from those published by a big traditional publishing company. . . .
>
> There are, of course, still authors who rush to push the "publish" button without making sure their book is the best it can be[:] Those who refuse to submit their golden words to proofreaders or even spell-checkers, either from artistic arrogance or from lack of appreciation of the need. Those who have no idea their book falls short of any standard of readability. There will always be those who release onto an already seething marketplace books riddled with typos, bad content, and poor cover designs that shriek "home-made," even at the thumbnail size displayed by online retailers. Not only advocates of traditional publishing cringe on the sight of such books. Self-published authors producing books to a professional standard perhaps find it even more galling.[8]

What's curious about this tension is that ALLi, like other self-publishing guides, recognizes that producing a book is a collaborative effort that requires authors to farm out work they are unprepared to do. They recognize that producing a professional book is not free. Yet here they are reproducing the very attitude their campaign is designed to combat: the deep culturally programmed aversion to nonprofessional texts, whose symptom is finding amateur books distasteful. This position fails to recognize that democratic access to publishing is antithetical to the expectation that its resulting output will meet professional expectations en masse.

I am not advocating for or against such standards; I am merely trying to define the cultural space that indie authorship seeks to inhabit. If it is a space that requires capital and draws professional boundaries similar to other kinds of professional publishing, it relinquishes its promise of inclusivity and access, because book editing standards that adhere to standard written English have remarkably powerful—and in some cases important—roles that mirror the role of standardized language in culture. They promote credibility for the author, they arrest the rate of language change and foster mutual intelligibility across time and space, they contribute to the readability of the text and the comprehension of the reader, and they contribute to the ability of writing to masquerade as timeless and universal. At the same time, standardization imposes conditions of scarcity onto language itself, what is otherwise an abundant and almost limitless resource.[9] Adhering to standards requires expertise and formal training. Creating a book that adheres to publishing standards pushes writers beyond simply needing access to a computer and a connection to the cloud. It requires more intensive capital investment.

We can see this in the general disposition to editorial services that remains remarkably consistent across indie author guidebooks. Here are several examples:

> I cannot stress enough how important it is to have your work edited. I know as an indie, it is hard to find extra cash for a book you probably think no one will read. Even if only one person picks up your work, you want it to be the best it can possibly be. Constant typos and punctuation mistakes can make the story difficult to follow and can lead to negative reviews.[10]

Beg, borrow, or steal the money you need to hire the very best that you can afford [for an editor]. Put plenty of time into getting the right one.[11]

Don't do your own book cover unless you have professional-level skills. Nothing screams "this book sucks" more than an amateurish cover. Why prejudice readers so that they never read the first sentence?[12]

If you don't engage a professional editor, you will regret it. . . . The absolute worst thing you can do is publish something that is unedited or poorly edited. All writers, no matter how talented, no matter how firm their grasp of grammar, need editors.[13]

Indie authorship seeks to adhere to the standards the book industry has already forged. Underlying this desire is a vision of the book as a public object, more read-write than previous iterations because it champions the language of inclusion (and will be inclusive, to its chagrin), but there is still only a limited tolerance of books as writable, accessible objects that do not require capital investment.

Besides being yoked to professional publishing through its methods of self-definition, indie authorship retains another profound point of continuity with professional publishing: the reader. Debates about contemporary publishing are couched in the language of innovation, disruption, revolution, and apocalypse, but the way these debates have characterized the reader does not differ greatly. Multiple models of publishing tend to agree that the reader still wants a well-written and well-edited book. Readers have daily exposure to nonstandard language on social media and in other digital spaces, and they develop reading strategies to engage this material.

With books, unlike forms of social media, however, readers are accustomed to standards of grammar and editing established in the age of print, and they tend to expect these standards when they pay for them. They displace the expectations of quality for traditionally published books onto self-published ebooks, and they impose professional standards through the intense power they can exert by influencing the recommendation systems, which largely determine whether a book will sell. In that sense, whether publishing has been democratized is a relatively insignificant question for writers who wish to earn money from their work. These writers still need to adhere to high standards. The expectations of the gatekeepers have been programmed into the reading public, and even if gatekeepers are absent, paying money for writing induces readers to deploy those expectations.

In sum, when it comes to professional publishing, even radically altered technological conditions can be tamed by the expectations and activities of readers. This is supported by my findings, which suggest that readers will lower their expectations for quality when they read for free. In peer-to-peer production economies, in which readers do not pay money for stories, they are often willing to muscle through myriad editing issues to obtain meaning, provided they value the content. Readers on Wattpad, for example, did not expect professional standards and therefore accepted relaxed standards of grammar and style. Writers could attract fans and followings, and the collectivities that emerged were influenced by, but ultimately eschewed, strict adherence to standard English. This was because of the ages of the writers and their limited command of grammar and usage, because the site was conceptualized as a space for development (where one is not a "published author"), and because readers read stories for entertainment and to create a sense of community.

Readers did, however, critique the grammar of writers when it disrupted their reading experience. Writers and readers alike shared a sitewide shame related to grammar and style mistakes. The most popular texts were often cleanly written and, though not perfect, did adhere to standard writing conventions. There were also a number of polemics published that encouraged participants to use standard written English and steer clear of "text message speak" and abbreviations when writing. Nevertheless, Wattpad participants, like readers of free poker texts, generally tended to be quite forgiving of writing that did not meet professional expectations. Free access mattered greatly to the way readers approached a text.

From Indie to Hybridity

If the discourse of indie authorship emerges from an ambivalent (or at times antagonistic) disposition toward publishers, the hybrid establishes a point at which those involved in the multiple models of publishing recognize the potential symbiosis of these models. Hybrid authorship encompasses a large group of writers who have both self-published and published through the royalty model. The reasons that authors become hybrid illustrate some of the benefits to authors that multiple models of publishing might introduce, as well as the ways that writers deal with competing interests. Some indie authors move to traditional publishing because they have used self-publishing as a launchpad. Others remain indie yet recognize that publishers still control access to the print market and have expertise in negotiating foreign rights and translations.

Authors who have had a career publishing through the royalty model have turned to self-publishing for a host of reasons. Sometimes their books have gone out of print and the rights revert back to them, at which point they self-publish. Sometimes they self-publish work that has been rejected by their publisher, to test their skill at new genres, or to reboot their careers with a different pen name. There were times when publishers or agents encouraged this hybridity. Some agents monitored self-publishing to find emerging talent and to sign authors who had already established fan bases. Some publishers engaged authors because a self-published book had sold extremely well and the publisher believed there was a print market to be exploited or a foreign market to be tapped. The examples below show how writers negotiate the indie label and its limitations when they encounter circumstances that force them to consider the boundaries of self-publishing.

Keeping Options Open

A writer of young adult and fantasy fiction, Elle Katson (a pseudonym) began querying agents early in her career to help her publish her writing. Meeting with little success, Katson came to self-publishing as it was beginning to move into the mainstream. She self-published her first book after coming to terms with the process and getting over the stigma. When she began self-publishing, she said she experienced prejudice. "When I started out there was a real stigma." she said, "Conventional wisdom was that it seemed to be a terrible choice." She self-published regardless of the criticism she received from various sources. Referring to online spaces, she said, "There were people who basically said if you're self-published we don't want you here," and she faced similar barriers offline: "I was not expecting [prejudice] even from some of my friends who basically, were like, well, I think you're making a terrible choice." Katson's husband supported her financially and emotionally, which provided her with time to write, market her work, and acquire readers. In a few years her discussions with her husband changed: she went from asking if it bothered him she wasn't earning money to asking if it bothered him that she was earning more than he was.

Katson's case is similar to that of Stephen Toulouse (see chapter 2), but with Katson we have an example of a writer who interacted with a publisher after her books were self-published rather than before her first book was self-published. She was ultimately approached by a "fairly prestigious" publisher who wanted to acquire the publishing rights to some of her books and license the film rights, but by then her disposition to publishing had changed: "It wasn't like 'oh, my gosh they like me.' It wasn't. I was over that. I think there's a feeling when you are a new author, you're trying to break into the industry, where you feel like [when you get a publishing offer] 'the cool kids want me to sit at their table.' I think I had gotten past that. I think most people get past that at some point." The platform Katson built ultimately changed her attitude to publishers, and the work reoriented her own view of writing as a creative act to writing as a creative act *and* a business: "It ruins some of the magic when it becomes your occupation. It did for me, anyway. People are really reverent with books. I think when I got down and got my hands into it and did it everyday, I was like okay, this isn't quite as magical."

This shift in her view toward writing and the influence of approaching her writing as a business led her to a "very pragmatic view" of publishing. Unlike some indies who are alienated from the royalty publishing system and would prefer to see publishers die, she talks about it without extreme language: "If the money was right or if a contract's conditions were right, I would [do it]. If it were a good choice for me from the business perspective, I would be happy to. I don't have any revolutionary commitment to a 'ruin the publishing industry' kind of thing. For me, I would be, 'Do the numbers make sense? Is the money good?'"

Katson ultimately concluded that the offer from the publisher did not make sense because of her likely identity at a large house: "I think for someone like me, who would probably be a midlist author in traditional publishing, I do a lot better with self-publishing. I make more money. I have more freedom. I don't have to feel worried about if this book doesn't perform, how is that going to affect my next book and how they want to promote it, or how they want to interact with me as an author." In contrast to Jessica Snowin or Abigail Gibbs (see chapter 2), once Katson acquired leverage through income, the lure and attraction of being published and becoming an author yielded to a different set of concerns.

Print Distribution, Publishing, and Timing

A skeptic might look at Katson's case and argue that she valued independence at the expense of the expertise, collaboration, and mentorship that publishers offer, or that she was undervaluing the potential of the print market. Because this project works from an emic perspective, my aim is not to conclude that Katson's career trajectory might be different and/or better if she signed with a publisher, but simply to frame her decisions. Such choices are complicated by the dilemmas writers face when they both self-publish and publish traditionally, particularly with regard to timing and publication. Donna Hadley (a pseudonym) published her first romance novels with a small indie press. Her first book hit the *New York Times* ebook bestseller list, and she subsequently self-published a number of books and gained a wide readership and fan following. Throughout the entire process with her first publisher and her self-publishing, she took a social marketing approach, an in-depth immersive approach of platform building with lots of interaction with her fans.

Hadley signed a four-book deal with a large corporate publisher primarily because she wanted to see her books in print. She wanted access to the market and the allure of seeing her book "at the airport." She had to sign a noncompete clause, but as a prolific storyteller she kept producing books while her traditionally published books worked their way through the editorial pipeline; this created a problem, a disjuncture between her speed of writing and the speed of traditional publishing. Fortunately for Hadley, her publisher added an addendum to her contract that enabled her to self-publish newly written books. At the time of the interview, she had completed the contract with the publisher, and she was contemplating her future direction with the discrepancy in speed and timing in mind.

Capable of writing tens of thousands of words per month, Hadley said that her avid readers constantly bought her work while wanting her "to go faster." She worried that with the prolific output enabled by self-publishing, the quality of her series would deteriorate, and she worried about the dynamics of hybridity: At what point would her output alienate future publishers because her lower-priced self-published books were competing with her traditionally published books? Which kinds of books and series are appropriate for publishers, and which kinds appropriate for self-publishing? How do you boost the sales of a previous book if you do not control the pricing? The uncertainty surrounding these kinds of questions has led to experimental publishing practices, profiled in the next chapter, but it has also shown how many variables weigh on the author's decision-making process once there are multiple viable routes to publication.

The Third Way

After working as an electrical engineer and with tech start-ups, Matthew Wilson (a pseudonym) experienced an extraordinary ascent to bestseller status after serializing a science fiction work and then publishing a novel, a thriller about the consequences of computer hacking. Wilson noted that he had sold close to two hundred thousand copies of his first two books and that he had turned down six-figure offers from publishers for his second novel. Instead he self-published it and then used an agent to sell the film rights. He did use a publisher to sell the foreign rights, however. He reported that thus far, half his revenue as an author had come from self-publishing, and the other half had come from working with commercial publishers. Acknowledging that his case was extraordinary, he drew two conclusions from it: (1) in the future the only way for popular fiction writers to find a publisher would be to build a fan base first through self-publishing, and (2) having an audience makes it possible to traverse self-publishing and traditional publishing and utilize one's success in self-publishing when negotiating with publishers.

Wilson acknowledged that having a book in print with a major publisher made him feel "very special," but in our interview he noted that business concerns were a far more significant factor in his publishing decisions than the desire to see his work in print. I'll discuss some of the ways Wilson has used his knowledge of algorithms to increase his sales in the next chapter. I had the distinct impression during our interview that his work with tech start-ups and the values and lessons learned from it conditioned his approach to publishers. Wilson came to writing as an outsider; he had few dreams of becoming a writer and decided to write a book only when he turned forty. This outsider status meant that he had fewer internal conflicts about his relationship to publishers, and his attitude was in some ways propelled by the digital ethos he had absorbed during his work with technology. Publishing was business only, and the contentious history of authors and publishers that largely comes from the world of print registered only slightly in his approach—a significant difference from the case studies in chapter 2.

•••

If the royalty system offered a stable model through which writers could begin to fashion their identities as authors, the current mixing of models has left them negotiating several possible identities. In many cases this flexibility left them balancing their interests with the interests of their readers and the potential benefits of traditional publishing. In many cases the multiple models the authors had to choose from seemed to be helping them sharpen their relationship with the business of writing and publishing. Indie status signifies control for the authors, and for some successful writers the identity may create leverage with publishers, but that control also includes the responsibility for learning the business of publishing and upholding its standards for the sake of readers. Indie authors talked fluently of their writing as a business, learned rapidly about the creative and the commercial aspects of it, and often experienced it as an integrated practice.

Despite its propensity to declare freedom from publishers, then, the indie author movement's adherence to professional standards and the demands of the labor bring it into close proximity with traditional publishing—indie is much more closely related to traditional publishing than its moniker would suggest. In the next chapter, I explicate some of the ways that indie authors depend heavily on Amazon as a new intermediary, which further complicates the notion of being an "independent" author.

CHAPTER 4

Amazon as a New Intermediary
Experimental Self-Publishing and Popular Fiction Writing

ALTHOUGH *Mass Authorship* explores the wide range of spaces in which self-published authors now work, it also recognizes that Amazon has dominated discussions about the future of publishing and self-publishing because of its size and what many see as its aggressive intervention in book culture. Self-publishing is surely not synonymous with Amazon, but Amazon's Kindle and its publishing program have provided the most robust potential audience of any new intermediary. Self-published authors who have sought to earn a livable wage hold the conventional wisdom that it was impossible to do so until they acquired access to Amazon's Kindle audience. This chapter focuses on the relationship of self-published authors to Amazon, concentrating on how Amazon (and other ebook retailers) function as publishing and retailing environments for writers. It does so from the perspective of bestselling Amazon authors: How do these writers understand the nature of their interaction with Amazon and the new intermediaries? What kind of publishing practices do the new intermediaries enable and sponsor?

Ultimately, the best way to understand new intermediary platforms is through the framework of *experimental publishing environments*. At first glance this seems an obvious choice. Digital self-publishing is in its infancy, and authors experiment with different practices to determine what will be durable, sustainable, and successful. However, what the term means to capture is the sentiment among the authors I interviewed that because they were living through a time of massive volatility, they might never be able to develop sustainable or stable practices. These authors envisioned the future of publishing as something that would require constant experimenting, tinkering, and innovating. The language of flux, change, and speed penetrated their work and shaped their relationship to the publishing platform and readers. They believed that many of the marketing and publishing strategies that had made them successful authors had expiration dates. Because they assumed flux, these authors had a hyperawareness of publishing conditions and trends.

Two attributes of Amazon and the other new intermediaries drove the spirit of experimentation. The first was the ubiquitous presence of an evolving ranking and recommendation system, or what the authors called Amazon's algorithms. These authors believed that the ranking algorithms, and whether a retailer's automated system recommended a book to readers, largely determined the success and failure of their book sales. The authors therefore worked to understand and adapt to these systems. As one author said, if the ranking algorithms were constantly modified, then so too must the publishing and marketing practices be modified: publishing practices changed because algorithms changed.

Second, the authors felt able to experiment nimbly because they had control over their text and its copyright, and this allowed them to make rapid changes to their books to propel sales. They changed metadata, cover design, and pricing in response to what they perceived as rapidly changing publishing conditions, and they did so without needing permission from a publishing firm. This control is the hallmark of indie authorship, and it allowed them to claim independent status, even as they operated with the tense recognition that their livelihoods as independent authors depended on digital corporate behemoths that set limits on their practices.

Although this chapter explores how algorithmic ranking and recommendation procedures are becoming central to the culture of books and authorship, it also examines the authors' insistence that the quality of their writing could overcome the power of such systems. Amazon's algorithms had a crucial influence on the work of the authors I interviewed, but these authors believed that the material and sociotechnical conditions of publishing could eventually recede into the background as they established an immediate and intimate relationship with readers through their books—

the kind of unmediated relationship so often fantasized about in the age of print. The authors shaped the length of their ebooks and narrative forms to make them amenable to Amazon's ranking algorithms, and they knew that finding an audience was highly contingent on machines interpreting the activity of readers. But even as they learned this, they continued to believe that good writing would float to the top because of its capacity to create a direct relationship with the reader and that this would happen because the ranking systems had a kind of objectivity to them. This belief enabled the authors to affirm the quality of their writing amid a volatile and chaotic system. This quirk adds a complex wrinkle to the way we think about book culture and the dynamics of mediation—and the continuities we can draw between print and digital reading practices—and understanding it will require a brief detour into reading and theories of mediation.

In the past decades, media scholars and book historians have called attention to how intermediaries shape literary systems. Adrian Johns has argued that the work of intermediaries in print culture was often effaced in order to establish the book as a medium that could stand on its own authority. Partly as a result, books became enormously successful at establishing a reputation for "immediacy." A concept developed by Jay Bolter and Richard Grusin, immediacy indicates a communication medium's ability to "disappear" so that a user comes to believe that he or she is having an "unmediated" media experience. Virtual reality, in which the user believes that he or she is fully immersed in an environment, represents the zenith of immediacy.[1]

In book culture, immediacy is embedded in the way we describe certain reading experiences. If readers achieve immediacy, they believe that they are inhabiting a character, experiencing a world, putting themselves in the shoes of others, or conversing directly with the author about philosophy, history, and so on.[2] Immediacy appears in sight metaphors, too: the immediate experience is one in which the reader believes the book is a clear window onto a phenomenon. Socrates may have thought that writing was stupid because it couldn't talk back when the reader asked it a question, but print culture helped produce ways of thinking about books that led us to believe we were in immediate conversation with the author.

Immediacy requires the conditions of the book's production to be obfuscated and the influence of its materiality to be minimized, and it harmonizes well with the ideology of the individual author. This philosophy of reading does not encourage readers to ask questions such as how the materiality of a book encroaches on the interpretive process, or why a distribution or delivery system favors one book over another. It is the media philosophy that led Amazon founder Jeff Bezos to say that "the key feature of a book is that it disappears."[3] This presents us with a peculiar irony: whereas scholars argue that disintermediation represents a radically new model of publishing books in the digital age in which writers and readers communicate directly (something *Mass Authorship* argues is a fantasy), readers seem to have been harboring the fantasy of disintermediation off and on for centuries, believing that they have been communicating in an unmediated relationship with the author.

We see examples of immediacy in popular sloganeering about the power of books. The commonplace notion that books can take us to faraway worlds represents the desire for, and the fantasy of, immediacy. In this fantasy the power of the book trades on its claim to allow readers to transcend time and space as they experience new worlds and expand their horizons. This fantasy has positive and negative forms. When we read canonically sanctioned books, the book as unmediated experience is said to expose us to new cultures and lead us toward tolerance as enlightened liberal subjects. Yet immediacy is also a liability. Critics have long accused female readers of romance fiction of escaping into superficial worlds at the expense of acting politically in their own world. In both the positive and negative forms, there's the deep belief that the readers of a book can achieve immediacy.

However, regardless of the intellectual training and the learning experience we may receive from reading, books on their own rarely result in the immediate geographic dislocation of the body to a new world, nor do they often allow us to immediately escape the webs of power in which we are entangled. Books can initiate powerful educational experiences, and their importance should not be minimized, but books mediate embodied experiences—beyond the site of reading they tend not to provide them. From the perspective of contemporary learning theory, which stresses the importance of embodiment to learning, reading might prepare you to exist ontologically in a new world, but it can never fully teach you to live in it. That we believe reading can dislocate us spatially or temporally from our current context testifies to the book's incredible capacity to induce the experience of immediacy.

Most of this chapter is dedicated to showing how authors adapt and work with Amazon and other new intermediaries, but it concludes by showing how authors minimize the importance of these intermediaries by the fantasy of immediacy. Holding digital change and print continuity in tension, the chapter explains how authors believe that algorithms contribute to their experience of an experimental publishing environment. It then documents a number of key practices common to successful self-publishing authors as they work on the platforms of new intermediaries: (1) adjusting practices in response to analytics, (2) executing stealth tactics, (3) harnessing fan production, and (4) experiencing exhaustion. These publishing conditions pressure the writing of authors, yet writers and their readers continue to nurture the fantasy that they can experience an immediate relationship. This faith demonstrates that at least in belief, authors and readers discount the consequences of the ways new intermediaries pressure writing and the form of the book.

The Presence of Algorithms

Amazon is a distributed configuration of personnel, warehouses, office buildings, and computing hardware and software. As a digital retailer, it is experienced by most customers as online shopping. In the case of ebooks, it is often experienced as a Kindle interface and content ecosystem. The authors I interviewed often spoke of the prominent role that Amazon's algorithms play in this system, and the work of the information scholar Tarleton Gillespie can clarify what they meant. Gillespie has noted that the meaning of the term drifts depending on who uses it. For the software engineers who create algorithms, the concept often refers to the "logical series of steps for organizing and acting on a body of data to quickly achieve a desired outcome." However, in broader public discourse, the term *algorithm* can work as a synecdoche. It functions as an "abbreviation for the sociotechnical assemblage that includes algorithm, model, target goal, data, training data, application, hardware." This abbreviation also indicates the connection of the technical assemblage with both a "broader social endeavor" and the massive number of people who design, tweak, and tune the algorithm.[4] This definition is quite consistent with the way the bestselling self-published authors I interviewed used the term, since to them Amazon's algorithms worked as a kind of black box (though one they tried to open), and they used the term to indicate both the computational and the human procedures behind the recommendation and ranking system.

The authors I interviewed rightly latched on to the importance of algorithms. In databases of millions of books, search processes are deeply implicated in the readers' ability to discover individual titles. Much like Google, Amazon seeks to collect as much data on its users as possible to provide them with "relevant" search results. The company tracks the buying and browsing habits of its users so it can recommend similar books. It also tracks the reading habits of Kindle users for the same purpose.[5] Amazon employs this data to constantly tweak its algorithms and recommendations system to provide more "relevant" results and recommendations (i.e., it constantly manipulates its procedures to increase sales), and it modifies its system to avoid the possibility of users gaming it.

The dominance of algorithms in these activities has led Gillespie to argue that we have been experiencing a shift in the way people access information and cultural goods, from an editorial model to an algorithmic model (and here Gillespie is using *algorithm* as an abbreviation for the sociotechnical assemblage discussed above). Whereas editors used to generally control access to the information that reached the public, now algorithms play an increasingly central role. For Gillespie, this shift has monumental importance, especially because so many of the algorithms, like Google search algorithms, filter the information that dominates public discourse and debate, and corporations problematically hide the intricacies of how the algorithms work as proprietary information.[6] In the realm of culture, Ted Striphas has followed media scholar Alexander Galloway in using the term "algorithmic culture" to describe our increasing dependence on "data-intensive computational processes" to sort and classify ideas and texts.[7]

Gillespie argues that the owners of search algorithms disingenuously frame them as a way of measuring the value and relevance of content and returning "objective" results to the user. This claim to objectivity underpinned Google's revolutionary contribution to the search engine industry when it began relying on a crowd-sourced model to return search results. A story rehearsed ad infinitum, Google began with the assumption that people linked to and from content that was valuable to them, and so the company assumed that the more links some content amassed, the more relevant and valuable that content was. Gillespie argues that although the companies who own the search algorithms champion their objectivity, they constantly manipulate the algorithms. Google, for example, considers hundreds of factors when returning results. The claim of objectivity for the search engine results don't pass muster when companies simultaneously need to manipulate their algorithms to increase advertising revenue, appease oppressive governments, protect brands, and guard against attempts to game them.[8]

Despite the apparent shift to algorithmic culture that relies on computationally processed and massively distributed human activity, centralized editorial processes still exist in two important ways. Search engines count links and traffic, which means that large corporations that entered the digital age with editorial prestige still hold power. They produce content that people value (and thus lots of links), and they also have the marketing resources to increase the popularity of their informational products, which initiates activity the algorithms recognize. Moreover, because algorithms are subject to interpretive shaping, the companies that own algorithms hold editorial power. Barnes and Noble's alleged reaction to a steamy romance on its bestseller list shows how the algorithmic and the editorial intertwine—an episode Hugh Howey documented in a blog post.

Howey has been a bestselling indie author and a vocal proponent of self-publishing. In 2013, drawing on Internet discussions and data shared among authors, he alleged that indie romance writers were seeing their ebooks stall at number 126 on the Barnes and Noble bestseller list, despite having sales that, compared with other authors they were sharing data with, should have ranked them much higher.[9] Howey argued that Barnes and Noble throttled the ascent of romance books with racy covers, making an editorial decision to stall the works near the bottom of the list. To my knowledge Barnes and Noble has not commented on this issue. However, if Howey's allegation is true, it shows that the bestseller list is not an objective measure of sales, it's simply a measure of sales influenced by brand protection and propriety, which is coded into the Barnes and

Noble procedures that calculate its bestsellers. Algorithms bear evidence of traditional editorial decisions about curation and taste.

New intermediaries tweak their algorithms to maximize profit, and authors put forth considerable effort to understand these tweaks because they are rarely if ever articulated to the writers. Authors read about search engine optimization, track data collaboratively, and contribute to discussion boards. The combination of editorial logic with algorithmic logic has conditioned authors to experiment and expect change and caprice in their working environment. A steamy book cover that catalyzed the sales of a romance on one platform might be rejected on another for violating terms of service. Likewise, one platform might ban material as obscene whereas another platform may simply stall its ascent in the rankings.

"I look at what works and what doesn't work," said one author, reflecting on her marketing practices, "but again, what worked last year for many people did not work six months later. A lot of it is just being flexible. Each book and experience is take what you know, be flexible, and adjust however you can or however you have to."

These necessary adaptations constantly remind indie authors how dependent they are on search engines, social media, and their algorithms. During my interviews a number of authors mentioned episodes in which algorithmic tweaks torpedoed their book sales. In late 2013 and early 2014, Facebook modified its ranking procedures to change how content from small businesses appeared in the feeds of its customers. Small businesses that had been building relationships with customers found their content reaching a far smaller population than before. Facebook reportedly made this move to force small businesses to pay for advertising instead of receiving advertising for free through organic reach. Authors who had been building platforms on Facebook, and who had used Facebook as a place to launch contests and giveaways, had a more difficult time directing attention to their pages.

An author of what she called women's lit described the consequences: "Facebook reach has changed. The algorithm has changed. It's got a smaller organic reach. . . . At least in my circle, Facebook was a huge, huge vehicle for getting our news out, and so now our wings have been clipped in that sense, and you're relying on these networks of people, not Facebook friends but bloggers and readers, to pick up your book and take off with it."

Some indies adjusted their practices to these algorithmic tweaks, relying on fans to mention ebooks on their own pages and developing ways to circumvent the filters. A romance author told me, "Getting people engaged on Facebook is huge because Facebook has now resorted to hiding posts and hiding things from pages. You really have to do all these crazy things to get people to keep liking your page."

Small algorithmic changes by the digital giants can reshape an author's strategies for reaching readers and affect the balance of which authors are best equipped to do so. One author said, when talking about the indie approach to the rankings system on Amazon, "This is the metaphor in my head. I think of Amazon as this giant beast. All of these authors are on it trying to get into his eyes or something. They're all trying to get on and it's always changing to shake them off. I do feel like Amazon is always switching the algorithms."

Analytics

The transition from the editorial to the algorithmic appears in the lives of authors as constant exposure to, and interaction with, the ranking and recommendation system on Amazon. The system encroached deeply on the writing lives of the authors I interviewed—from the way they plotted their stories to the timing of their publication dates. Amazon's system, and the algorithms that governed it, had two features that surfaced in every interview: it provided various kinds of data and analytics to the authors that allowed them to analyze their sales and publishing performance, and it determined whether authors made the bestseller lists, which I address in the next section.

The data and analytics afforded the possibilities of experimentation. When the indie authors published to giant databases, the systems returned quantitative information that allowed them to infer how the publishing platforms worked. The ability of the authors to access diverse quantitative data to intuit sales patterns, a kind of bibliometrics, enabled them to draw lessons about readers and the new intermediaries. For example, Amazon's platform provides sales statistics, and at the time of the interviews it let authors see how many ebooks they sold on an hourly basis. Indies could also see the number of reviews they had received on the system, the average review score, how those reviews had been distributed on a five-point scale, and what countries they were selling books in. They could see exactly when their competitors planned to publish books, they could see their sales ranking relative to other books and authors, and they could see where they stood on various lists. They could also see the prices and page lengths of their competitors' ebooks, which tend to be more diverse than for print books.

In addition to being able to retrieve this data from Amazon, the authors could access data from other retailers and from third-party platforms, like review sites, where their work was discussed. Some authors analyzed the data retrieved from their own web pages, and they knew the keyword searches people used to find their websites as well as their visitors' geographic locations. The indie authors shared all this data with other authors, and this collaboration allowed them to build a rough portrait of what the numbers mean: On which days and times do books sell well? How many books does it take to achieve a place on a bestseller list? How many books sold per day allow you to move up in Amazon's rankings?

The answers that indies produced to these questions were undoubtedly imprecise, but authors who sometimes had had only a year or two of publishing experience had already begun trying to answer questions, which would be challenging if not impossible to conceive of in print systems. In response to the answers, they manipulated the metadata surrounding their texts and the "paratextual" elements to see how sales responded to changes made on the fly.[10] Indies refined their blurbs and changed cover design. They manipulated metadata to recategorize their texts, and they used bibliometrics to test the efficacy of giveaways and contests that they launched through social networking sites. They tried to learn how manipulating the prices of their books affected sales. Professional publishers certainly engage in these practices as well, but how and why they do it is difficult to determine. The indies I spoke to believed they had a certain nimbleness in experimentation because of their control over the text.

Pricing in particular demonstrates a responsivity to algorithmically governed databases. Ebooks tend to offer more flexible pricing schemes than print books. Once ebooks are produced, the authors can give them away for free or for little cost to the reader. If the retailer allows it, self-published authors can charge 99 cents one day, $2.99 the next day, and $5.99 on Sundays. Conventional wisdom suggests that corporate publishers have been far less willing to experiment with ebook pricing—they fear a long-term devaluation of books and authorship. Indie authors, on the other hand, do not have magisterial backlists that extend deep into the twentieth century. They are newcomers, somewhat divorced from the ideology of previous systems, and they often prioritize finding readers over the value of writing.

Moreover, these new writers tend to write popular fiction. Unlike literary fiction, which is institutionalized in higher education and in prestigious publications, mass-market fiction has been largely unattached to institutional structure. It has long been derided as formulaic by literary critics, but the most important measure of its quality for those who write it is whether it will be read and will hold the reader's attention. This seems to make it more responsive to market fluctuations, reader taste, and publishing trends. Although some indies in this study did seek the stamp of approval of established publishers, as we have seen in previous chapters, others voiced the willingness and the flexibility to remain independent so they could exploit these trends; being unwedded to any established cultural or commercial institution that controlled their copyright afforded them the opportunity to experiment.

Matthew Wilson (profiled in chapter 3) worked as an electrical engineer before self-publishing science fiction. He serialized his first work and gave it away for free, and by his second work he had built an extensive audience. His second work became popular enough that he sold the film and print distribution rights in a number of countries. He then began charging for the first book. He attributed much of his popularity to the quality of the writing but also to the understanding of ranking systems he had acquired from his previous work in engineering. This knowledge enabled him to extend the shelf life of his books.

"I only have two books," Wilson explained, "but when they start to come down in sales and popularity you can do all kinds of stuff with them. I offered it for free for a weekend, and then it jump[ed] up in the charts and start[ed] selling. You can keep on tweaking it and playing with it.

Whereas I think a traditional publisher would just put this thing out and let it die, I've been able to keep on earning, whatever, $5,000 to $10,000 a month off each title. I just keep on tweaking and tweaking and tweaking and keeping it up in rankings." Wilson's case is not strictly about digital systems that allow him to tweak, it is also about the legal control of his text and the belief that free content can eventually be monetized. In his opinion he can attract far more attention to his text than a publishing company would for a midlist writer, even as he relies on those publishing companies to reach the print market.

In the publishing industry, ebook pricing is enormously complex, with fierce debates about the influence of digital economics on the real and perceived value of writing and fiction. My study was not designed to reveal much about pricing and the consequences of giving writing away for free. Many writers in this study believed that giving away their writing was imperative for building an audience, but they had reservations. They thought about the value of their writing, but not whether it would be depressed long-term. Rather, they worried that giving their writing away for free would categorize them as low-quality writers who did not take a professional approach to their work.

A number of authors reported that giving their writing away for free dropped their ratings. When Lancaster Cole (a pseudonym) gave his book away for free over a weekend, he saw his average review on Amazon go down by three-tenths of a point, which he connected to price: "If those people who normally don't like romance, or even fiction, review your book, it may not be as good of [a review] and your rating may come down, as opposed to charging a fee for something and then the people who only like that genre in the first place are buying it." Three-tenths of a point may not seem like a significant drop, but it becomes significant in a database that ranks hundreds of thousands, if not millions, of books.

As a writer's catalog grew, he or she manipulated the pricing scheme in more complex ways. One author yoked her pricing to the way she imagined readers progressing through her series of seven books. She made the first book free and the second and third books progressively more expensive, because she reasoned that if readers wanted to continue, it meant they valued the content and would be more likely to pay more. She made the fourth book free to encourage readers to continue to the second half of the series, and she bundled the series so that buying all the books at once was less expensive than buying them individually. These kinds of practices are common, but experimentation is circumscribed by Amazon policy: it limits the time that books can be offered for free, and its royalty system sends a clear message about the price it thinks ebooks should be. At the time of this writing Amazon was offering a 70 percent royalty rate for books priced between $2.99 and $9.99 and a 35 percent royalty rate for books priced outside that range.

The authors experimented freely with pricing and paratexts, but they did not make revisions to stories to increase sales. A number of new media practitioners have experimented with "versioning," or updating and modifying a text in response to different factors, as a form of digital cultural production. Except for its use in some of the nonfiction profiled in chapters 5 and 6, this practice was almost entirely absent from the ways authors experimented with texts. Changing a text typically happened only if it had been entirely unread, in which case the author had the freedom to "unpublish" it in order to revise or rework the story. In isolated cases, authors uploaded new versions of their texts to correct typographical errors, but this was mostly unnecessary, since they had employed professional editors.

Readers made it difficult for the authors to make any substantive changes to the content of their fiction because they had invested intense emotional resources into a story and its plotline. Fans regularly speculated about the twists and turns of a plot, so revising the plotline of a story could betray the readers' sensibilities. This problem was particularly acute for one author when she faced the prospect of having to make changes to sell a book with a particular retailer who had rejected the book because it was too racy. The author argued with the retailer and used robust sales statistics from Amazon to argue that the book was appropriate, and the would-be censoring retailer relented. When I asked the author if she would have rewritten the text to align with the content standards of the retailer, she said probably not. It wasn't just that her "dignity as an author" would have taken a hit (and in this case dignity is tightly related to control over a text and independence from influence), she also worried about having multiple plots floating around in the same book and the various ways that would disrupt a fan's reading experience: "I just don't feel like I should have to change my book and tell all the people who are buying it on that platform [that] it's a different story," she explained. "It seems unfair. Especially if it's a series, and people are invested in the details. Honestly, I couldn't imagine myself doing it."

This lack of desire to update or modify a text does not mean that ranking systems and algorithms are bereft of influence on narrative form. On the contrary, this influence surfaced immediately in my discussions with authors about serialization. Serializing texts has a long history in literary culture, and digital systems are particularly well suited to support it. Mass-market fiction's amenability to serialization is one of the reasons that this type of fiction has been so successful on e-readers. Authors can produce plot-driven writing quickly to satisfy their fans' desire for the extension or resolution of a story. Serialization allows authors to gradually build an audience throughout multiple installments, and it encourages readers to buy books instead of violating copyright and downloading them for free. (Presumably, paying readers have immediate access to a new installment, whereas readers who plan to download it have to wait for a pirated copy to appear online—a potentially significant amount of time to wait, if the work is a niche book.) Perhaps most important is not that digital systems enable friction-free serialization but that the new intermediaries and the algorithms that constitute them encourage it by requiring prolific output from self-publishing writers. Authors satisfy the demands of Amazon through serialization.

In an essay on negotiating algorithms for self-published authors, the romance writer Liliana Hart has noted that Amazon marks new releases as *new* in the Kindle store for only ninety days. Books have the most visibility during this period, and for that reason self-published authors need to "keep feeding the beast" with new writing to sell or "rankings will take a dive and you fall into oblivion."[11] This resembles the brick-and-mortar bookstore practice of keeping a book on the shelves for a short time before returning it to the publisher. An indie I interviewed shared this sentiment: "If you let it go too long, you will find your sales not just taper off, not just drop, but go off a cliff after ninety days. We all, meaning my crowd of writers, believe that this is built into the algorithms. That if you don't release, you'll fall of the cliff." With the caveat that the precise workings of the algorithms remain obscure, this sentiment has nevertheless become naturalized as conventional wisdom, and it shapes the writing and publishing habits of those working within the system.

Feeding the beast structures the output of writers: they detour from their main book series and write short stories or novellas, for example, or they repackage their books as box sets or anthologies. In these detours they introduce new characters and write backstories, and they construct their narratives in ways that let them release their writing often in order to appease the algorithms. This release schedule is paired with the intensity of ravenous fans and their ability to shape success through recommendations and reviews. One romance mystery writer noted, "I write really hard cliff-hangers at the end of my books. If I keep them [readers] waiting too long, you got a bunch of pissed-off fans. We don't want that." The demands of the new intermediaries combine with the demands of vocal fans to place intense pressure on the writers for output, including their decisions of what to write, their narrative form, and the length of their books. This, as we will see, can lead to writer exhaustion.

Stealth Tactics

Indie authors have a complex disposition toward Amazon. On the one hand, many praise Amazon for giving them a chance to circulate their ebooks and find readers when they could not get a publisher to invest in them. On the other hand, they are indie authors, and Amazon is in some ways yet another giant behemoth in the David-versus-Goliath narrative that reverberates in the identity formation process of indies. In this way indie authors have an adversarial relationship to Amazon, with few loyalties. Some have realized that since Amazon is a digital system governed by algorithms, it can be exploited and gamed for sales.

Tarleton Gillespie reviews the tactics that online writers sometimes use to encourage their writing to spread more widely. Writers will tag a social networking post, for example, with an unrelated yet popular keyword in an attempt to get the social network to promote the writing to a larger audience. "Is this gaming the system?" he asks. "Or is it a fundamental way we, to some degree, orient ourselves toward the means of distribution through which we hope to speak?"[12] Likewise, a number of indies have developed stealth tactics in response to working in an algorithm-dominated publishing environment, a way of orienting themselves to the means of distribution. This is particularly apparent in their relation to bestseller lists.

After an indie book is published, its initial success is influenced by the author's marketing push, which usually takes place through a variety of social media platforms. Initial sales matter because they register with the retailer's system, and with enough favorable reviews and sales, that system begins recommending the book to buyers (e.g., "customers who bought this item also bought . . . "). The foremost concern of indies was achieving a spot on the various kinds of bestseller lists that drive ebook sales. The most important lists at the time of the interviews—the ones that motivated sales, according to the interviewees—were the *New York Times E-Book Fiction* list, the *USA Today* bestseller list, and the top one hundred bestsellers in the Kindle eBook store. The indie authors agreed that making these lists would extend one's audience to a broader public, beyond organic social media reach and the relatively inexpensive advertising the authors could afford.

Writing about the culture of twentieth-century bookselling, Laura Miller argued that bestseller lists have been powerful marketing tools that can increase the sales and visibility of a book, but rarely do people understand how these lists are compiled. Proprietary information thwarted her attempt at a full profile of how the *New York Times* compiles its list, but Miller learned enough about the process to know that the methodology and the influence of the list itself were "actively participating in the doings of the book world rather than just passively recording it." Although the *New York Times* claims to be as systematic and representative as possible, when it was sued by an author who failed to make the list despite suspecting that his book had sold enough copies to be included, the newspaper argued that its list is an editorial product.

In addition to editorial decisions that inflect the list, publishers' marketing efforts play a crucial role in whether a title is included in the questionnaire the *Times* sends to booksellers, which is the primary data-gathering tool for the list. Books that appear on the list receive a boost from the efforts of retailers who push bestsellers, and Miller argued that this indicates that bestseller lists have a self-reinforcing quality to them. Becoming a bestseller increases sales—it often makes a text even more of a bestseller—and this invites attempts to game the list (even before the advent of the Internet). Miller reported that some authors have bought thousands of print copies of their own books in an effort to make the list. The complexities of the lists' production and the impact of their reception led Miller to conclude that they provide information about the social production of bestsellers.[13]

The *New York Times* list functions similarly to algorithms on Amazon, but without the help of digital databases yoked to the immediate activity of book buyers. It is still a ranking procedure largely determined by quantitative measures, albeit one governed by editorial decisions. For instance, the *Times* list has to account for time spans; it is not an all-time bestseller list; otherwise the Bible would never budge from the top spot. Likewise, Amazon's algorithms reflect time as well, and the timing of release dates and marketing efforts matter greatly to indie authors. Jana DeLeon, an indie author whose work has appeared on the *USA Today* and the *New York Times* lists, documents how she considered both algorithms and timing when working to make the list. She is clear about the value she believes it provides: "The absolute best thing about hitting the *USA Today* or the *New York Times* is that you get the moniker. You can put it on your website, book covers, and business cards, tattoo it across your chest, even have it chiseled into your tombstone. All it takes is a single hit on one of those lists, and that moniker is like a university degree—it's yours forever!"[14]

DeLeon writes that determining the methodology of the *USA Today* list was straightforward. She made that list by reducing the price of a previously released book to coincide with what her research suggested would be a slow week of new releases from authors who wrote in a similar genre. She then made a large advertising push on Monday, the first day that *USA Today* begins calculating sales for the week. Making the *New York Times* list, however, required a coordinated, collaborative effort with other authors. Although DeLeon's own experience taught her much about how Amazon's algorithms compiled their lists, the *Times* methodology remained a mystery. Describing it as the "granddaddy" of lists (and for DeLeon the gendered nature of her description is not accidental), she expressed strong opinions about it:

> The *NYT* best-seller list calculation is harder to solve that the Da Vinci Code, but this is what seems apparent: While industry professionals

insist that sales from Amazon do not count for *NYT* print lists, they do appear to count for the e-book list. This is great news for indie authors. The bottom line is that it appears sales alone do not dictate the *NYT* list. Somewhere in that determination, other things come into play. Maybe they consider historical sales to see if you're an author trending up or simply a flash in the pan. Maybe they look at your bio pic and if they think you're hot, they let you on the list. No one knows except the people choosing the list, and they're not talking. I always have this mental image of a bunch of old, stuffy men wearing tweed jackets and standing in a law library, deciding whether indie authors are good enough to be allowed into their club.[15]

With only a slight understanding of how the list works (e.g., that the *Times* calculates weekly lists from Sunday to Saturday), DeLeon and a group of other authors ran an experiment in April 2013. They created a box set to which eight authors each donated a mystery or a suspense novel, and they sold it through several ebook retailers for 99 cents. They convinced Amazon to let them have a preorder button (not all independent authors can get them), and they collected preorder sales, the grand total of which seemed to count as sales on the first day their collection went live. They released the collection on the first day the *Times* began calculating the list for the week, and every author used her mailing list to contact fans, giving them the opportunity to buy weeks of reading for 99 cents. They purchased ads on indie reading recommendation services and Facebook, and they blasted Twitter. As a result, they sold thirty-eight thousand copies of the box set and landed at number seven on the *New York Times* list.

DeLeon and the authors marshaled the affordances of digital publishing to acquire a *New York Times* bestseller moniker for promotional materials. Like Amazon, the *New York Times* has its own algorithmic procedure for determining the list. And learning about some of the nuances of Amazon's procedures allowed the group to boost its sales on Amazon and make some educated guesses about how the *Times* was compiling its list. This information allowed the authors to boost sales during a particular period. DeLeon describes her plan as a "stealth" move. She writes that it was a "total crapshoot," but, she argues, indie authors should be engaging in "total crapshoots" because of the sheer volumes of books they compete with.

It is possible (and perhaps likely) that the *New York Time* has adjusted its methodology to account for stealth tactics, but it's also noteworthy that indies hotly debate the propriety of these tactics—and the prudence of building a platform on unsustainable practices, a point to which I will return at the end of this chapter. These discussions forge new standards of propriety in bookselling based on algorithms and fairness and whether an author should take advantage of a quirk or a gap in the system—or rather, whether *authors* should take advantage of quirks they identify through collaboration and information sharing, since this was a critical component of DeLeon's move. In the face of giant intermediaries, indie authors sometimes seem better off collaborating than competing, sharing data and creating shadow databases.

Fan Production

Peer production played a crucial role in the work of the bestselling authors I interviewed, and they harnessed labor from readers to accomplish various publishing tasks, some of which registered as popularity on Amazon's system. This was also the case for the poker players and recreational romance writers, who are profiled in chapters 5 and 6. However, there is an important distinction: in the case of those two groups of authors, peer production was largely motivated by the author's affinity with a community. In the case of the bestselling popular fiction writers, peer production was largely motivated by the affinity of the readers with a single author, which I call fan production. These authors spoke of their fans with deep gratitude and gave them due credit for directing attention to the authors' work—a way of acknowledging the collaborative efforts of their experience with authorship. It's certainly possible to read the exchange as a cynical exploitation of fan labor, but this interpretation is complicated by the sense of meaning and belonging that fans could achieve by collaborating with the authors.

All the authors reported that fan activity motivated the sales of their books. In some cases the authors aggressively cultivated fan communities, enticing readers by giving them sneak peeks of new works and supplemental material that was not published elsewhere. Readers provided labor like website design and book cover design; they also moderated fan communities and in some cases provided editorial work. Matthew Wilson provided copies of his work to two hundred fans, and as they read it, they discovered dozens of errors that were missed by the professional editor he had hired. There are certainly limits to the wisdom of the crowd, but proofreading for minor typographical errors is one activity that fans seem well positioned to execute.

The fiction writers simultaneously benefited from fan labor and distinguished themselves from it, setting up a hierarchy. For example, Martha Byrd (a pseudonym) rewrote a plotline after her fans guessed the ending of the novel she was serializing. She wanted to maintain an element of surprise, which was lost when the fans guessed the plot, and she also worried that her fans would think she was stealing their ideas or relying on them to provide content. Despite monitoring conversations about her writing that by her own admission influenced the trajectory of her series, she moved to affirm her ownership over the text in an environment in which the line between production and consumption, between author and reader, is not always clear.

The authors spent considerable time mobilizing their fans in anticipation of a new release. Much like publishers identifying friendly readers to provide blurbs for the covers of books, the authors provided free copies of their works to fans they knew would provide friendly reviews on Amazon, since how readers review and rank books is a crucial factor in whether the company's algorithms recommend the book to other readers. At launch, the authors monitored their quality ranking carefully (on Amazon this is the number of stars it receives on a five-point scale). If a ranking began to slump, the author with a loyal fan following could send strategic emails encouraging fans to finally post reviews they had promised. The importance of this fan labor created conditions that favored authors who enjoyed communicating through social media, who could tolerate self-promotion, and who were proficient at learning the conventions and etiquette of online communities (a reminder that self-publishing might not work for writers who communicate through long-form writing because they dislike certain kinds of social interaction).

The authors extracted digital value from fan production, and they also recognized that their fans provided a route for them to access offline retail and promotional opportunities. Professional self-published authors have had a notoriously difficult time accessing the brick-and-mortar institutions of book culture—prizes, bookstores, and libraries—because these institutions have been built and operated on the assumption that publishers will vet the quality of books for them. For self-published authors who were earning a living from their writing but had not yet sold print rights, fan labor represented one of the only ways to access brick-and-mortar institutions. Called *street teams* in the romance industry, groups of fans would encourage local libraries and bookstores to stock the books. Fans would also recommend the books to readers who read primarily in print and would be unlikely to encounter the ebook without prompting. The geographical diffusion of a fan base—linked through the power of search engines and online affinity groups—leads to and contributes to a diffusion of print and its patterns of circulation.

Exhaustion

For the indie authors, data, analytics, and control gave them the opportunity to experiment, but the activity and the perceived need to constantly keep abreast of changes also induced anxiety and exhaustion. The interaction with fans led to constant requests for new writing. The writers knew they had to keep feeding the beast, and they worried that this would dilute the quality of their work. Those who took time to craft their stories lamented the missed opportunities to exploit audience interest in their work. They could not produce a second book quickly enough, and by the time they did complete it, they felt the need to begin building their platform again from scratch. And as with Hannah Leed (profiled in chapter 2), the penetration of the lives of authors by the tasks of marketing their writing through social media and mobile technologies made it difficult for some authors to write the kinds of texts that mattered to them. Most authors who addressed these intrusions successfully distinguished writing time from publishing time. A number of them wrote in the morning, until they were tired, and then worked on publicity and marketing in the afternoon and evening.

"Obsessive refreshing" surfaced as the most ubiquitous form of anxiety in response to the accessibility of sales data. A book published years before might suddenly become popular, but there was widespread feeling that the first week of sales mattered intensely to the success of a book, especially because it coincided with the biggest marketing pushes. At the time of these interviews the authors were able to access their first-week sales on an hourly basis, which induced indies to obsess over their launch. One author explained, "Usually right after I publish I'm neurotic about checking sales, and it's very nerve-wracking. But most of us will say, 'We check it like every hour. What's going on, what's going on, what's going on?' You do that maybe for the first few weeks, and then you realized that you're going crazy so you stop, you have to. If not, it's maddening." But the rapid returns enabled them to see how sales were developing, which enabled them to experiment with publishing tactics and receive feedback on their moves.

Matthew Wilson's experience shows how responsive these numbers can be. His full-length thriller novel began to sell well after he had amassed a reputation writing science fiction, and Amazon's system let him watch his sales figures update hourly. "You start to push the button and look at your sales," he stated. "Actually you can look at your sales rate per hour. I'll be selling twenty books an hour, or thirty books an hour. If you get a couple of bad reviews, it will go down to like ten or fifteen an hour. . . . I've stopped doing that now because I've got enough volume that it takes care of itself." Although only Amazon knows precisely how recommendations influence rankings and sales rates, Wilson described his reaction to his observation that a few bad reviews could significantly slow sales. He tinkered with the idea of "defending his sales," and by that he meant emailing a group of friendly readers to ask each of them to post a review of the book. Data create a feedback loop, a kind of evolving game that encourages sales.

Reintermediation

One of the most significant differences between print and digital books is how the activities of digital reading and writing register so easily in trace data on the web—as analytics, comments, blog posts, reviews, and so on. Functioning as both authors and publishers, the indies I interviewed used this data to guide their experience. They were aware of how their activity with readers was mediated and how readers were finding their work amid the sea of competing authors. Yet despite the authors' exploitation of this data to circulate their work, and the fact that the data permeated their experience, they ultimately downplayed its importance when they talked about their success. They explained the circulation of their writing by talking about the power of writing itself and the potential for it to build a relationship with readers: the mediation receded. The book—even in this environment, this physical form, and these conditions of hypermediation—had the power to induce the belief that it was unmediated. The fantasy of immediacy registered most powerfully in the belief that the recommendation algorithms could be objective.

When pressed about the power of algorithms and the influence of the new intermediaries, the authors reverted to explanations that mirrored the old web design adage that "content is king." This is the belief that no amount of flashy design or gimmicks to bring readers to a website can overcome bad content. But the authors couched their own version of "content is king" in language inflected by standards of propriety that surround bookselling. Algorithms mattered, but they ultimately believed the ability of the author to connect with readers mattered much more, and this belief allowed them to minimize their work as publishers and venerate their work as writers. One author followed an explanation of the various ways she has learned about Amazon's algorithms by talking about the desire to avoid gaming the system in favor of building audience trust. She wanted an audience that recognized the quality of her books, which she contrasted to the capacity to simply induce clicks: "I do try to be smart. I don't want to try to game the system. Maybe I'm not cutthroat enough or something, but I want to earn things fairly. I want to be savvy. I don't want to be smarmy. I don't want to do gimmicks. I want to do things that I feel good about."

Another author said, "People need to trust you, that you're going to do something interesting with their time. It's not even the 99 cents or the free or the whatever. It's just the amount of time that they have to invest in reading your book. They need to trust you, that you're going to get somewhere interesting, and that you've got something smart to say, or that you're going to entertain them, or make them cry, or whatever it is that they're reading for. You can start the ball going down the hill, using some little tricks, and this, and that, and pushing yourself at first to really get momentum, but it ultimately needs to be a good book."

These authors are forging the unsettled ethics of marketing and publicizing books when those activities rely heavily on search engines. But the trust that good writing would prevail derived from a faith that the systems would be objective, that they would register and make visible "good books" or books that succeeded in producing authentic reader engagement. This belief in algorithmic objectivity—that algorithms will help deserving books become discovered—is the return of the fantasy of disintermediation, that the book and the surrounding infrastructure can disappear or recede into the background, allowing the individual author and reader to form an unmediated connection warranted by the quality of the writing. For these authors (and the way they perceived reader experience), unmediated connections and deep relationships with readers affirmed the quality of their prose. Whereas literary fiction is grounded in the affirmation of professional critics or structures, the affirmation for this popular fiction was located in the power of the reader only—and once the process was in motion, the authors imagined the power of the algorithmic system to abate and objectively register their accomplishments insofar as it reflected the judgment of their readership. This fantasy nurtured the individual author's sense of accomplishment and sustained the power of writing amid the chaos of a changing publishing environment and the influence of machine processes on it.

...

This attempt at an initial understanding has shown what it is like to work as a professional indie author when that work depends heavily on a relationship with Amazon. By the time *Mass Authorship* is in print, many of the practices profiled in this chapter may have morphed or disappeared altogether. This fact in some ways underscores the frenetic nature of self-publishing, of what it is like to labor in a rapidly changing environment that seems to delight in its own transformation. In other words, not only do indie authors have to work amid the changing conditions, they also have to do so on a platform and from inside a discourse of digital technologies that celebrates speed and disruption.

This circumstance creates a precarious situation for authors and, from time to time, a wary attitude premised on the possibility that their publishing models can collapse if Amazon tweaks its business model (e.g., by adding all-you-can-read subscription services for Kindle readers). The speed also extends to the expectations of the fans. As writers produce more writing to feed Amazon, readers begin to expect faster updates to the serializations—writing and publishing processes that are sustainable for the platform but perhaps, not for those supplying the content.

CHAPTER 5

Microclimates of Intellectual Property

RECOUNTING INSTANCES in which their work became embroiled in copyright and plagiarism issues, two of my interviewees found themselves confronting questions of what it means to own writing in the early twenty-first century. At the time of the interviews one was twenty-two years old and the other was eighteen, and they described the experiential dynamics of intellectual property for creators as follows:

> I search for the book online to make sure nothing blatant is going on [i.e., copyright violations]. But to stop torrents I would have to sue people, and that would be a whole big hassle, and let's be honest, that isn't going to happen.

> I've had quite a few [instances of finding my work copied] where it's either been direct plagiarism or where they liked my characters so much that they'd write another story just about my characters. At the same time it's flattering. And you know if they had said, "Hey, I'm writing this," then I'd be like "Hey, just give a shout-out to me." I'm okay with that. But some people just take it and they try to make it their own. It's kind of disheartening to find things stolen, but at the same time, it's like well, they must think I was doing something right to want to take it that badly.

The first quote is from the author of a poker ebook who has an Ivy League education, and the second is from a fiction writer who was barely out of high school. The poker author spoke of how the peer-to-peer energy that helped produce his book was now appropriating it and circulating it for free through BitTorrent protocol, a distributed system that is visible to him yet well outside his control. The eighteen-year-old fiction writer spoke about attribution, uptake, and the rights associated with her characters. She contemplated on how she should react to the fact that her stories acquired such a large audience that they have spawned their own fan fiction.

These are examples of one of the most dramatic developments in recent copyright history: a law that began primarily to regulate professional bookselling has become deeply enmeshed in the everyday experience of digital writers. Before the advent of personal computing, copyright existed under the ken of professionals in the content industries; rarely did the average citizen come in contact with copyright law. When computer users gained the capacity to share copyrighted cultural products easily, it created a zone of friction between their activity and the law, enabling them to routinely run amuck of copyright.

The first chapters of this book have explored the ways that writers have been (re)fashioning their activity and identities as they orient themselves to multiple configurations of publishing and publishing platforms. The final chapters differ: they take a detailed look at writers who have published to networked participants who strongly considered themselves members of an online community, and the chapters concentrate heavily on how these communal dynamics have influenced the work of authors. No dynamic was stronger, for the authors I interviewed, than the felt tensions of copyright and plagiarism. The focus of this chapter is the intellectual property systems that have come to regulate writing in these communities in the absence of traditional publishers, who took responsibility for policing copyright infringements.

Copyright law winds through the history of modern authorship like a main circuit cable. Although it recognizes many iterations of authorship not associated with the Romantic Author, copyright has enabled writers to claim ownership of their writing, which has helped make professional authorship possible.[1] Mark Rose has argued that the development of the modern author was "inseparable from the commodification of literature":

the convergence of possessive individualism, print technology, and legal maneuvering in the seventeenth and eighteenth centuries created the author as a "proprietor," a historically contingent way of understanding writing that is now embedded in education systems, in commercial brand names, and in the way cultural productions are marketed. Copyright "makes possible the profitable manufacture and distribution of books, films, and other commodities but also, by endowing it with legal reality, helps to produce and affirm the very identity of the author."[2]

The modern author has remained quite durable even though the terms and conditions of Western copyright have not been stable across time and country. Copyright has grown into a bundle of remarkably complicated rights, and Siva Vaidhyanathan has shown that technological upheaval brings with it periods of confusion and change. Stakeholders looking to protect their investments in new media often lobby to restructure copyright to protect its output, and copyright has expanded its scope across history to include expressions like photographs, films, and cultural products published on the Internet.[3]

The growing intersection of copyright law and everyday life has occurred against a longer historical backdrop of what Vaidhyanathan calls "copyright creep." As culture industries have sought to protect their products from entering the public domain, the terms of copyright have been extended; its protections have grown more robust and invasive. Both Vaidhyanathan and Lawrence Lessig worry that this "thickening" of copyright policy has privileged owners at the expense of ordinary producers, depriving the public domain of material that would otherwise be available for users to create new cultural expressions.[4] Corporate lobbying for thick copyright ensures that ordinary creators now experience copyright law through code that powers digital rights management tools, through takedown notices that threaten lawsuits, or through actual lawsuits for violations. Lessig argues that the oppressive climate has fostered a discourse of piracy used in a blanket manner to describe diverse (and sometimes legal) uses of copyrighted material. He worries that our current situation has bred an extreme copyright fundamentalism in corporate mentality and an extreme copyright abolitionism in the minds of youth, who have very little respect for copyright and the excesses of the law.[5] Young people are not homogeneous, however, and as I will show in this chapter, they are quite capable of adopting thick notions of copyright and ownership when it comes to their own creations.

Despite the presence of copyright law in everyday life, the fact that the poker author didn't want to bother with lawsuits suggests that the massive scope of copyright makes the law inadequate to encompass all its dynamics. Even before ordinary computer use, the dynamics of copyright did not exhaust themselves under the auspices of the law. The history of publishing, William St. Clair contends, demonstrates that copyright law does not completely explain the consequences that intellectual property (IP) has had for books and authorship. IP practices have existed in opposition to established laws (and ignorance, I would add) and have developed without any basis in law at all. St. Clair thinks that a fuller account of IP regimes would examine factors beyond the law. Many facets of these regimes are capable of conditioning the work of authors, publishers, and distributors. The history of IP is as much about how regimes and their circulating ideologies, metaphors, and levels of understanding influence the practices of stakeholders as it is about the law, which is just one element (albeit at times a dominant one) that produces these ideologies. These regimes shape business and trade practices as well as the output of literary production, such as price, accessibility, and distribution patterns.[6]

If St. Clair's point holds for the age of print, when publishers engaged in heterogeneous practices, it holds even more so for ordinary writers publishing in digital environments. When authors self-publish with neither the means nor the desire to involve the law in copyright disputes, IP concerns become woven into the fabric of their literacy experiences, appearing at all stages of the writing and publishing process. In the absence of the law, the writers and readers in this study communally forged "microclimates" of intellectual property that regulated publishing and attribution.[7] Such microclimates appear in online environments that are "caught between two regimes [of authorship]" that are "bound to assumptions about the ownership and originality of texts that derive from older, Enlightenment-era notions of the self, while using technologies that lend themselves to the distributed, the collective, the process-oriented, the anonymous, and the remix."[8]

In the two communities I examine, the respect for authorship and IP rights run so deep that the microclimates could become thick and muggy, with the participants taking extensive measures to preserve authorship and thwart copyright violations. These measures include readers and authors developing standards of courtesy and etiquette, authors manipulating their writing habits to prevent unauthorized circulation, readers policing copyright violations, and website administrators introducing code into websites to frustrate copyright violators. These strategies and tactics operate against the background and under the threat of copyright law but never formally involve it. The practices help authors temporarily control their work in contexts where readers could also be distributors, a process I refer to as *manufacturing scarcity*. Their practices sought to disrupt unfettered circulation, either because it could decrease an ebook's value or because it could sever attribution and thus the original authorship. However, while the communities work to preserve the integrity of copyright, the authors' writing experiences and their bids to find readers can produce ambivalence about the very microclimates that sustain their authorship.

Microclimates and the Individual Author

The dynamics of these microclimates call into question some assertions about the influence of technology on the multiple trajectories of digital authorship. In 2001 Mark Poster argued that the author function would not be able to "endure the change" to digital technologies.[9] Although he believed that the author function had become socially irrelevant, anyway—because the rise of mass media meant that control of creative production shifted away from the individual author and to the producers of the culture industry—Poster nevertheless argued that the author function had continued to exist as status, propped up in particular by academic humanism.[10]

While taking measures to avoid technological determinism, Poster voiced the concerns of early hypertext theorists that digital texts decentered the author; one reason for this was that the "instability" of digital texts reconfigured the relationship of the author to writing media. This instability is related to the potential to circulate digital texts for free and the potential for agents to easily transform a text during circulation. For Poster, the affordances of digital texts would yield a "new regime of authorship" that would not be premised on the stability and authority of texts.[11]

Poster's analysis is representative of academic commentary about the web in the late 1990s and the first decade of the 2000s, which operated on a series of print-digital binaries, including of offline-online, stable-unstable, permanent-ephemeral, real-virtual, and credible-uncredible. These binaries inflected early hypertext theory.[12] Despite the desire of early theorists of digital authorship to avoid technological determinism, they were still confident that networked writing would influence writing in certain ways—in particular, that it would dissolve a strong notion of individual authorship. This prediction has not always clearly accounted for how writers might resist, modify, or manipulate the affordances of digital writing technologies. For Poster, and indeed for many academics who have theorized about authorship, the modern author is something that has outlived its tenability, inevitably enjoying a measure of prestige until it slowly dissolves over time.

Yet because it was initially theorized as historically contingent and socially constructed, the author function has always had the inherent capacity to dissolve, and the affordances of writing and publishing technologies are only a few of the cultural elements that sustain it. Technology is certainly implicated in the trajectory of authorship, but so are multiple institutions, like libraries, schools, and the law. Kathleen Fitzpatrick notes, "Our assumptions about authorship . . . . derive less from the technologies and processes that produce the author's texts than from the legislative and economic systems that govern those technologies and processes.[13] Moreover, web affordances and associated practices have evolved somewhat in the last decade to bring the database to the fore. Hypertext theory tended to proceed from the assumption that readers would often traverse the vastness of the web through hyperlinks—for them the hyperlink was the defining feature of the web. Although users undoubtedly do that, an enormous amount of Web writing has been corralled into and published on centralized database systems, which introduces the possibility that computer code can stabilize the author function and bring it in line to reflect strong notions of IP and copyright.[14]

Even as we consider the argument that the model of the Romantic Author simply doesn't reflect the way writing happens, my analysis of two different microclimates will show some of the precise activity that supports its durability.[15] Writers can develop social media practices that preserve a strong notion of the author and that resist the technological affordances that can threaten it. For books, at least, the writers in this study valued a strong notion of the author and the ownership and system of attribution that it implies—far more than the circulation or manipulation of digital texts.

This is true even when writers publish their work online and distribute it for free in open systems, since in these cases the economics of copyright yield to the moral economy of authorship and plagiarism. This strong iteration of ownership is publicly asserted and supported, and it provides writers with a limited ability to protect themselves from copyright infringement. But even writers who support strong notions of textual ownership embedded in copyright law may simultaneously share copyrighted material through back channels. Thus, public respect for the author coexists with the private activity that resists the legal regime that helped put that respect in place. This tenuous coexistence resists, but does not completely dissolve, the ways in which the modern author continues to dominate the microclimates.

Microclimates also encompass a ubiquitous misunderstanding about which elements of a text—ideas and expression—can be protected. This results in a widespread conflation of copyright and plagiarism that shapes the microclimates and other situations. Martine Courant Rife's study of 334 digital writers, students, and teachers found similar confusion. She suggests that a misunderstanding of copyright is often an essential part of writing online. Almost half the respondents in her study had difficulty understanding the difference between plagiarism and the fair use doctrine, and they believed that attribution was a key factor when the courts determined fair use (it is not). Thus, much of this chapter focuses on copyright, but I have lumped it together with other issues, like plagiarism, under the umbrella term *intellectual property*. IP scholars make precise distinctions among issues like copyright violation, fair use, and plagiarism, but many writers in the study, like the writers in Rife's survey, were confused about the differences and conflated the terminology. Rife attributes this conflation to the vehemence with which academics treat plagiarism; this vehemence is intensified because systems of attribution help establish cultural capital and function as measures of success for academic authors. Antiplagiarism efforts, she speculates, "might easily be characterized as having the force of law in disciplinary life. In fact, the survey data shows the requirement of attribution is conflated to a legal standard and meshes together with whatever restrictions copyright law might impose upon the creator."[16] As I will show, antiplagiarism sentiment online can be just as austere as the sentiment among academics.

This chapter compares and contrasts the dynamics of the two distinct microclimates, the Wattpad romance writers and the poker players, to reveal the contrast between fiction and nonfiction. Both groups of writers published using online spaces in which the participants strongly represented themselves as communities. The communal ethos helped generate the microclimates of IP that inflected the writing and publishing practices of the authors. In contrast to the memoirists, who had to manufacture ad hoc audiences for their texts, the romance writers and poker players had online communities that both preexisted and survived the liveliest portion of the life span of an author's book. The imagined communities largely coalesced around centralized websites, which had administrators willing to intervene in copyright disputes. And although members of the community certainly engaged in unauthorized sharing and copyright infringement, other members of the community eagerly reported such activity when they discovered it.

As the chapter proceeds, I document the methods that romance writers used to limit unauthorized distribution of their writing and establish a microclimate of antiplagiarism that supported authorship. From the perspective of these writers, copyright violation and plagiarism robbed them of credit, attribution, and originality. Because their texts circulated for free, and because people posted their writing primarily for the sake of status and social standing in their online communities, plagiarism represented a direct threat to authorship and the existence of the communities. However, the individual responses of the writers to this climate show how their experiences with writing and publishing generated ambivalence toward and tension with the oppressive climate, since plagiarism also indicated the existence of a significant audience.

After documenting the practices of the romance writers, I make some major points of comparison between fiction and nonfiction before I start to discuss the poker players. In the latter section I suggest that rather than an antiplagiarism regime, a microclimate of "idea protection" was created that became more secretive over time. Poker players were primarily concerned with copyright and the wholesale theft of their ebooks and the information they contained. In the process of manufacturing scarcity, they worked to keep their books from circulating in back channels and from being posted for free on the web, which eroded the monetary value of the text. In their perspective, they walked a thin line between distribution and secrecy: they believed that the widespread circulation of their ideas deflated their value and that if enough players followed their advice, the profitability of the games would decrease.

The two groups demonstrate the emergence of microclimates in two radically different contexts, a reminder that understanding digital publishing means understanding precisely how responsive networked publishing practices can be to the nature of information contained in circulated texts.

Authorship and Status among Romance Writers

During my time observing Wattpad, a few writers managed to monetize their writing after building an audience on the site. As the site grew, traditionally published authors began frequenting the site and releasing some work for free to drum up publicity for upcoming works they had for sale. But as a user-generated content site, Wattpad primarily drew writers who were there for the pleasure of reading and writing, to obtain feedback on their work, or to finally find a readership after years of consigning their stories to hard drives and desk drawers. These writers quickly learned that they were surrounded by data. The site tracked how many people had accessed a given chapter and aggregated that into a number for how many times a book had been read. Readers voted for their favorite ebooks, and enough votes moved a story up in the recommendation rankings. There were also annual awards for stories. The home page of each story tallied the number of readings, the votes, and the comments the story had received. New writers sought readers not just for qualitative feedback but also for the increasing numbers that came along with them.

The qualitative comments and the quantitative feedback formed the backbone of the status systems that developed across the site. Stars emerged as their stories cracked the "What's Hot" lists, as they were chosen by the administrators to have a "featured story," or as they won contests and received the "Watty" awards. Although very few of the writers I interviewed expressed a desire for Internet fame, they still enjoyed the rising numbers that accompanied audience building on Wattpad. It was, perhaps, less about pure vanity or celebrity than it was an indicator that their writing had sparked interest—that someone was enjoying their stories and entering the worlds they had created.

The notions of IP that the writers brought with them mixed with the status system to seed an intense ethos of antiplagiarism. The participants subsumed copyright under this ethos. Plagiarism indicated a complex group of practices that range from borrowing plotlines to purloining a whole story, copying it, and posting it on another website. Wattpadders developed a widely distributed and extremely intense antagonism with which to combat these practices, fostering a microclimate that often defaulted to a kind of permission culture in which many authors asserted some kind of moral rights over their work. This attitude was distributed among many of the participants because as writers, they were concerned about having their work stolen. Readers and fans also participated, not simply out of respect for the writers but also because letting authors know that their work had been copied and/or stolen was a kind of community engagement that bred goodwill and was its own kind of status.

That fiction writers would ground their microclimate in plagiarism is not surprising. Fiction has been one of the most tightly protected forms of expression in copyright law, and the Romantic Author is often implicitly a literary writer. The concept of the individual author has been developed, rooted, and nurtured in discussions of literary fiction. And where the modern fiction author goes, so too goes the plagiarist: Rebecca Moore Howard has shown that the nefarious "other" to the modern author is the plagiarist, an outcast who has violated the ideals of originality and autonomy, the characteristics on which the modern author was built.[17]

Plagiarists were regarded with similar scorn on Wattpad. If status consisted of emerging from millions upon millions of stories to achieve numbers and recognition, then the antiplagiarism climate was about protecting recognition, making sure the readers and feedback were channeled to the original author. Plagiarism threatened authorship not simply because it was the inverse of originality but because copyright violations, and the reposting practices subsumed under it, diverted attention away from an author's page, robbing the author of readers, votes, and comments.

The threat of plagiarism meant that the authors had to engage in IP work as a routine element of digital authorship, and it prompted them to consider questions about the nature of writing, sharing, and originality. How closely could one plotline imitate another before an author was forced to deal with accusations of plagiarism? Did a fan of a story need an author's permission to write "lemons"? (These are romantic scenes rewritten by fans to include sexually explicit material; they are called "lemons" because the new scenes are supposed to make a reader's face pucker.) And if a fan wanted to share an "orphaned" story—a story originally posted on what is now a mostly abandoned website—could he or she repost it without getting into trouble? Some of these questions are easily answered by copyright law or by the website's terms of service, whereas some are not. But because of the sheer volume of participation and communal turnover, website users mostly negotiate these issues among themselves.

Communal Antiplagiarism Practices

Wattpad's microclimate of antiplagiarism relies heavily on educational texts, computer code, and roaming bands of amateur copyright sleuths to function. The site's terms of service include detailed instructions for reporting copyright violations, and the administrators had a reputation among the writers I interviewed for being responsive to copyright concerns and creating an environment in which the writers believed that someone in a position of power cared whether their work was stolen. Beyond the formal terms of service, there were user-created metatexts as guides for the site, similar to a "frequently asked questions" (FAQ) page but in narrative form. Etienne Wenger's *Communities of Practice* is an influential analysis of the various routines, ways of being, tools, and discourses that people must learn to participate in communities. In online spaces, instructional texts like FAQs, or more unofficial documents like the metatexts, have played an important role in socializing the "noobs" in the values and expectations for behavior that exist in a given community (although in isolation learning such texts are an insufficient way of becoming a full participant in a community). In Wenger's terms, these texts exist as a process of "reification," or the "process of giving form to our experiences by producing objects that congeal this experience into 'thingness.'"[18]

Like many of the FAQ pages, the Wattpad metatexts were born in moments of frustration, when established members of the community recognized the recurrence of questions and began articulating the tacit norms by which the community operated. In Wattpad parlance these metatexts were "rants" or "vents" that, because Wattpad is a fiction site, often functioned simultaneously as communal guidelines and forms of vernacular literary criticism. They sometimes bemoaned the quality of grammar on the site. They identified clichés (no more vampires!), and they encouraged writing trends. They also worked as instructional texts that sought to define and stop acts of plagiarism and copyright infringement, in the process reifying and reproducing communally valued notions of authorship.

The "Wattpad Writers Rant" began as a guide to the site but morphed into an antiplagiarism text because it was being plagiarized as it was being serialized.[19] The user Nadie Rae began the text in frustration over the abundance of clichés in Wattpad stories. The "Rant" railed against inane detail in stories, poor spelling, and stories that began with alarm clocks. As the rant developed through serialization, a reader let the author know that her text was being replicated and posted by another user who was only changing minor details before reposting. Nadie Rae responded with a chapter that condemned plagiarism; it simultaneously shamed the plagiarizer and left an antiplagiarism text that persisted after the initial conflict was settled. She wrote, "I would just like to let the person know that if you are stealing a rant—not even an actual story, just a rant—of my ridiculous thoughts that I spew out over fifteen minutes on the computer, then you are kind of pathetic." She continued by discussing what she thought the motivation was for the theft. The plagiarizers, she asserted, were seeking "votes": "The point is to entertain them and make them laugh, not get them to vote for your plagiarism[,] you imbecile." This rant reinforced the norms of plagiarism on the site, indexed value by ranking texts (rants are "spews" worth less than original stories), and sought to initiate "unpublishing" by shaming the plagiarizer into taking down the offending text.

Nadie Rae's attempt to shame the plagiarizer was a softer yet similar replication of tactics from early Usenet communities that shamed spammers who plastered—and disrupted—the communities with commercial messages. In his wickedly incisive study of the history of spam, Finn Brunton documents this strategy and argues that it functions as a "charivari." A kind of mob vigilantism common in premodern Europe, a charivari was a shaming technique turned on anything a community found "unnatural." The charivari is distinct from vigilantism because it does not resort to physical violence. Rather, it is a kind of public performance that uses mockery, humiliation, and harassment. In its digital manifestation, the charivari "is a distinct network-mediated social structure, a mode of collective surveillance and punishment for the violation of norms and mores." It is efficacious because it makes a public racket that announces to the offender that "everyone knows—while spreading the word to those who don't know yet." Brunton shows how the charivari has been deployed to combat spam on Usenet in the early 1990s and persists to this day in many manifestations of online culture.[20]

There are two important dynamics of the charivari that surface in Wattpad's antiplagiarism movements and help stabilize the microclimate. First, there can be a dimension of pleasure that motivates participation in the charivari. Second, the charivari is most effective when deployed against a community member who shares the value system of the mob. The charivari is limited if an offender brazenly rejects the values that produce the sense of shame the charivari seeks to instill. In the case of Usenet spam, the charivari lost its efficacy as the user base of the Internet expanded into a more diverse group.[21] For fiction writers, the point at which the charivari fails is the point at which they are compelled to seek a more formal intervention—that is, contacting the administrators.

The first inclination of Wattpad writers is to address plagiarism cases through peer pressure, and I've seen this pressure applied so intensely that it can resemble online bullying. Writers believe that plagiarism and copyright infringement threaten the existence of their community, and this threat is not just an imagined one. Besides contacting the administrators of a website and publicly shaming plagiarists, Wattpad writers have stopped unauthorized sharing by threatening to withhold installments of their texts, actually withholding them, or threatening to abandon the site if the copying did not stop. These tactics can lead to disappointment for fans who have been following a story for weeks or even years, waiting to see a resolution.

These threats have intensified the atmosphere of the antiplagiarism microclimate and mobilized the site's version of the charivari. If a popular author threatened to withhold an installment, the fan base visited the copyright violator's page and posted threats or sent the person direct messages, putting as much pressure as possible on him or her to stop the reposting. When an author decided to involve the site administrators, fans were encouraged to email them as well. These crowd dynamics have worked to resolve the threat to the community.

Code and Authorship

Readers often report instances of copyright infringement. This is one of the most common ways that authors discover that their texts have been reposted. But Nadie Rae's case shows how code itself permeates online microclimates. As she noted when writing about the episode, Wattpad's recommendation system had detected similarities between the text she was writing and the plagiarized version the offender was posting. Because of the similarities, Wattpad's system recommended that Nadie Rae read it. Although the precise workings of the Wattpad system are not open to observation, I would assume that the Wattpad system tracks user taste through an analysis of reading patterns and metadata and then makes recommendations to readers in ways similar to Amazon's methods. In this case it detected similar material and perhaps similar people reading both texts.

For Nadie Rae this was a serendipitous recommendation, but it also reveals how problematic it is to conclude that the instability of digital texts threaten the author function, especially now that so much web writing has been corralled into centralized databases. This is a precise example of a text being "reauthored" and reposted almost instantaneously, a form of recirculation that happens shortly after a text is published by its original author. But in this case the recommendation system that Wattpad employs was complicit in preserving the author function, in exposing the modified text to the original author while simultaneously exposing the plagiarist, and in thwarting the transformation of texts that poses a threat to the author function in hypertext theory.

Computer code works to thwart copyright violations not simply through serendipity but in other ways as well. Like many other user-generated content sites, Wattpad has designed technological fixes to make it easier to root out copyright infringement. In the site's early days, it became the target of complaints in the popular press that it was providing a platform for piracy and hiding behind "safe harbor" laws. At the time, some users were posting copyrighted material instead of their own work. Wattpad worked to keep the material off its site and encouraged writers to post their own content. The site wanted to be the YouTube of ebooks, and for that it needed user-generated writing. The complaints about copyright infringement came from the publishing industry as well as from early adopters who had had their stories reposted on other Wattpad accounts. One of Wattpad's technological moves was to create code so that when a writer posted a chapter, the text was rendered on the page as an image, which made it difficult to copy the story from the website and post it elsewhere. Technically, however, it wasn't impossible to copy and paste. A reader who was savvy enough could simply right-click on the page, view the source of the web page, and then copy and paste the story directly from the HTML format.

Despite the ways around this copyright-infringement solution, it surfaced in the interviews as something that the writers believed made a large difference in the dynamics of the site. One writer spoke of it creating a sense of security that, when added to the other checks on the site, allowed her to post her work: "It's secure because you can put your work there and it's fixed so that people can't plagiarize your work because you can't copy and paste . . . so they can read your work and they can comment on your work, but there's no way for them to actually access your work, no way for them to copy and paste it or anything like that." This sentiment appeared in more than one interview, and it shows why it can be so problematic to theorize patterns of textual circulation and distribution from the "intrinsic" affordances of digital texts (i.e., that they can be copied easily and replicated for free). With this simple solution, the Wattpad administrators were able to make the digital texts *appear* as if their affordances had changed.

It was merely the appearance of this, coupled with the fact that many people just don't know much about the inner workings of web technologies, that has made this a somewhat successful solution—at least until the knowledge of how to circumvent it becomes widely known among the community's users (there is already a YouTube video on how to do it). Textual distribution becomes *somewhat* locked in a system that functions on the precarious assumption that most people will use the technology as its immediate and transparent design features suggest it should be used. And even though the system does not thwart people who are determined to copy a story and repost it elsewhere, it does work to influence the climate, providing both a feeling of security and a feeling of confidence that the administrators are actually working to address plagiarism.

The technological measures taken by the Wattpad administrators, then, could be as much about good faith as about providing a leak-free system, since they created an atmosphere of security that changed the emotional tenor of the site. Even as the writers I interviewed perceived the website they frequented as a free economy, they still wanted a sense of security that the gift they posted on the Internet would not circulate without attribution, as stolen writing, or as a text for sale through Amazon's Kindle. (Some people actually attempt to download masses of web content and republish it through Kindle in the hope of earning ebook sales on a short-term basis before they are discovered.) The writers' gifts came tethered to expectations about authorship, and reposting and unfettered circulation were seen as *threats* to a free economy of sharing. They diminished the emotional value of the feedback on which the economy operated. Although copyright law has supported the potential for professional authorship, its ideology—possession of a piece of writing by an individual author—structures the free economy of writing as well.

Antiplagiarism Coalitions

Fans have routinely notified authors on an ad hoc basis when they have discovered instances of copyright infringement, but organized groups have also launched plagiarism watchdog websites. The website of the Fictionpress Watchers bills itself as an antiplagiarism coalition whose purpose, according to its slogan, is to "smack plagiarizers in the face."[22] This site was originally developed solely to monitor the website Fictionpress.com, but many of the participants patrol Wattpad as well as fan fiction sites and Amazon publishing. From the blog posts, it is clear that the members of the coalition concern themselves mostly with copyright infringement, which they label plagiarism. The site functions not simply as a way to expose plagiarizers but also as a launching point for collective action. The posts indicate that the site administrators are likely to act swiftly to terminate the account of a copyright infringer when they have received multiple complaints about the account.

Members spend considerable time sleuthing with Google, searching for story titles, character names, and plot summaries in an effort to determine whether their stories have been reposted elsewhere. They traverse Facebook, GoogleBooks, various fiction websites, and Amazon to determine the extent of the infringement and to find contact information for the infringer. The coalition's work shows that the alleged plagiarism it finds is not strictly wholesale copyright infringement in which texts are simply reposted. Some texts are modified in different ways: plot lines are changed, and there are "search and replace texts" in which a user has searched for the characters' names and replaced them with new names. In some cases a text has been recirculated in so many ways that the effort to find the original author has been frustrated, an example of the "authorless text" in hypertext theory: "I did a Google search for the story 'The Final Game,' and its summary appears so many times and under so many different titles that I'm not honestly sure where it originated. It's a similar situation with the one-shot 'Game Over,' though it appears to be some kind of manga [a type of Japanese comic book or graphic novel] by someone named Fuka Mizutani. Again, I'm honestly not sure. It's definitely stolen, though."[23]

Although the posts follow a standard format, there is a smattering of commentary on the discoveries (e.g., "I nearly vomited when I came across this") that betrays the emotional register of the coalition. Fictionpress Watchers is run from the blog site Livejournal, which allows "mood updates," and members of the coalition list their moods as "enraged" or "irate" at the discovery of plagiarism. These responses mirror the reactions of teachers to plagiarism, which Amy Robillard attributes to the teachers' emotional investment in their students' success and their stake in differentiating authentic from inauthentic writing.[24]

The source of the FictionPress Watchers' emotional investment is both individual and communal: much like what I discovered in the interviews, there's a feeling of violation when one's own work has been stolen and an underlying sense that such reposting threatens authorship and the fabric of the communities involved. The absence of legal intervention pushed the antiplagiarism discourse into both moral and embodied terms against a backdrop of discourse about originality. Upon finding one of her own stories copied, one participant reported having a "rage shudder" and encouraged group action with a comment that manifested the pleasure of participating in the charivari: "I've emailed the site moderators in regards to the first violation I found, but a bit of urging would be appreciated if anyone has an account on that site and/or enjoys righteous indignation."[25]

There was no shortage of anger in the writers I interviewed when they spoke about their work being copied. The moral outrage emanated from writers who had failed to receive credit for their work, and they believed that these instances of plagiarism had violated the authentic relationship they had with their writing. The romance writers expressed sheer astonishment that someone would steal their work and repost it in an attempt to claim credit and votes. This astonishment suggested a singularly narrow conception of the relationship between the publishing environment and authenticity. For the writers I interviewed, the site held value only for its ability to publish authentic writing, and authorless or falsely claimed texts had no value.

Beyond Outrage: Ambivalence and the Economics of Attention

Studies of online communities have long investigated the term *community* to determine whether online collectivities can, in fact, really be called communities.[26] Often noted in these explorations is that whether online or offline, *community* has always been deployed in a positive way; it has had no obvious negation. Finn Brunton asserts that for online communities, spam is the obverse, the negation, of community. Spam is a threat to the fabric of imagined communities, a line of demarcation, a spot of chafing where the gift economy of the Internet and its peer-produced value rubs against the commercial attempts to extract value from individuals' interactions. Spam is not simply a nuisance but something that often instigates conversations that define the kinds of discourse by a which a community constitutes itself.

Given the reactions against plagiarism on Wattpad, and given the perception that plagiarism threatens the site's community, it would be tempting to classify plagiarism as a kind of spam. But although I have mostly pointed to examples of alleged plagiarism that are actually copyright infringement, *plagiarism* encompasses a variety of practices that traverse issues of imitation, originality, and influence. These practices of copying were often murkier than outright theft. As the incidents moved from wholesale copying to more nuanced and complex processes, so too did ambivalence, doubt, and contradiction grow about textual ownership. This was most obvious when plagiarism indicated to the writers that their work was being noticed.

The writers I spoke to craved feedback because it meant that readers were engaging their texts, but, ironically, acts of plagiarism meant the same thing: despite the moral outrage that plagiarism provoked, it also signaled that people were paying attention. Jessica Snowin (profiled in chapter 2) saw her work gain popularity during a conflict over its originality. She wrote a book inspired by a story she had read and enjoyed. She made use of a plot that is hundreds of years old in which a heroine is sent to live in a strange place among many related members of the opposite sex. Sibling rivalry ensues, and there are romantic results. Snowin was not the only writer to have ever been inspired by this plot, and as the popularity of the story line spread, Snowin began to face accusations of plagiarism, despite having included a disclaimer that the story was an imitation of a book that had inspired her. Apparently a number of readers had not seen Snowin attribute the plotline to another writer.

Snowin's responses were tactful yet progressively more sarcastic. In her initial disclaimer she drew a line between stealing an idea and being inspired by it, stressing that she had credited the original author. Snowin became increasingly exasperated by claims that she stole from other ebooks; her imitation spawned more imitations, and the plotline became more recognizable on the website as months and years passed. Despite her irritation, Snowin understood that it was the popularity of the plotline and the questions of plagiarism that had initially brought her text from obscure to popular.

She attributed the clicks her story got to the first accusation of plagiarism: "I think a lot of people clicked on the story to see: Did this girl really copy, you know, one of our favorite authors on Wattpad? And the funny thing was I had actually posted my story about a year before she ever started writing hers. That was a little frustrating because I'd been working on it for a while and then all of a sudden people are like 'oh my god you are copying her.' So that was a little frustrating, but in the end it did pay off because it brought people to check out my story."

The user comments that accuse Snowin of plagiarism suggest that this episode helped cultivate a very specific kind of intertextual reading. Although it's a truism to say that all reading is intertextual, a number of comments on Wattpad indicated that the users were reading specifically to compare two texts; that is, their acts of reading were motivated simply by the desire to see whether there were any transgressions—a peculiar kind of "plagiarism lust" evident in the comments that once again demonstrates the pleasure that motivates charivari.

Recommendation systems like Wattpad's have more success tracking *what* a user has read than *why* he or she has read it: the systems register reading, and they do not distinguish hate reading from reading for enjoyment. The by-product of this plagiarism flap was that Snowin's story jumped onto lists that track the most popular stories, thus directing more readers to her text, which eventually aided the recirculation of the plotline as imitators spawned more imitators. This became something of a break for Snowin, since some of the readers who enjoyed her story began reading other stories she had written. Ultimately the accusations increased her readership and fan base significantly, launching the number of readings her work had received from a few thousand to tens of millions in just a few short months.

Much like Snowin, Jennifer Bilson (a pseudonym) found herself ambivalent about copyright violation when she discovered a book posted on Wattpad that she had recently self-published through Kindle. The incident introduced her to a new set of readers. Bilson had published her young adult fiction independently and with publishers. As she began selling her most recent book as an ebook, an administrator from Wattpad contacted her to let her know that her story had been posted on the website under a different title. It had become popular, but a reader recognized it as Bilson's work and alerted Wattpad. Bilson describes her reaction: "I was devastated. She [the reposter] hadn't put the whole book up yet, but she was definitely saying it was hers and saying that she had written it. So I was a little bit stressed at first. It's one of those sick feelings. But she wasn't selling it, so that was kind of nice. But then at the same time, it had become one of the most popular books on Wattpad. So that was really reassuring for me to know that I had the teen voice down. I just took a breather when they first told me. . . . I was like I'm going to use this for marketing. It got two hundred thousand reads in one week."

In order to exploit the book's immediate popularity, Bilson did not pursue legal action because she "wanted to come in as the gracious person instead of the meanie and it seemed to work better with the teens." Instead of suing teenagers, Bilson recorded a video of herself, as an introduction to the community, that identified her as the author of the filched story. Combined with the popularity of the story, this gave her a splashy entrée to the community of readers, and she began a page on which she posted stories, links to the books she had for sale, and links to creative writing tutorials that she ran from her website. The event created circumstances that Bilson could exploit to gain access to a stream of attention she channeled toward her work. A victim of copyright infringement, Bilson looked at it as an opportunity to be taken advantage of, salvaging from the situation a new potential audience to establish a relationship with. This move required gaining some distance from her initial reaction, since Bilson, like the other writers, described the moment she found her work had been stolen as surreal and devastating.

Plagiarism breeds ambivalence because it shows that an author's writing is doing something other than languishing in a cyber vacuum. One writer noted that she hadn't found her stories reposted elsewhere, but she admitted that it would have been an indicator of success: "I always say I don't know if I'm good enough for people to actually start copying me." Likewise, the eighteen-year-old fiction writer quoted at the beginning of this chapter, Sade Ragnin (a pseudonym), had an attitude toward plagiarism and her own work that resembled moral rights. Her characters had been used by fans to write derivative works, and rather than assuming a kind of fair use, she argued that permission was important, coupled with attribution. She expected fan writers to ask before they adopted her characters and to credit her for creating them. Yet even as she asserted such moral rights, she realized that their violation indicated reader approbation.

There is a kind of resignation here, a struggle with "coming out" in the public and the ensuing loss of control it represents. Creative writers have long talked about losing control of their texts, being unable to follow them around and guide the interpretations of them. But many creative writers have had publishers managing the copyrights of the texts, and whatever acts of (re)production readers engaged in with the books have been largely invisible. But in this moment of convergence between writing and publishing, issues of control over interpretation and reuse have become attached to questions of copyright, often hashed out in interactions between writers and readers; these issues have blended with questions of (re)composition and permission as, for instance, an eighteen-year-old confronts a general rule of writing: the more popular it becomes, the more it becomes the property of the public, regardless of how oppressive a copyright regime or microclimate might be.

From Fiction to Nonfiction

The poker players displayed a similar concern with IP and, like the romance writers, conflated plagiarism, attribution, and copyright. Like the romance writers, most of the poker players did not consider invoking the law to be a viable option. Among insiders, back-channel sharing of ebooks was common, but there was a publicly stated respect for copyright, and copyright protection was a communal endeavor as readers alerted authors about flagrant copyright violations. However, there were also several differences between the poker writers and the romance writers. The core one was this: in the poker community, copyright violations and plagiarism weren't perceived to threaten the status of the author and the community of writers. Rather, they were threatening because the content of the texts—the knowledge applied to the games—could become widespread. This broad circulation of insider knowledge would, many players alleged, lower the profitability of poker in general. Unlike the information in most books, which acquires value (or at least holds its value) as it spreads widely, the information in poker ebooks is "rivalrous."[27] It is not like Thomas Jefferson's metaphor of a candle that can pass its flame without exhausting itself. The impetus of IP protection, to the poker writers, was less about protecting the authors and more about protecting the games through a microclimate of "idea protection" that sought to limit the spread of information.[28]

Many of the key differences between the romance writers and the poker authors stemmed from the differences between fiction and nonfiction—or, in the words of the writers, storytelling and information—especially in terms of assessing originality. The Wattpad writers clearly drew on robust communal resources that ranged from character types and myths to plotlines, settings, and themes. The value in an original text derived from how an author spun these elements in new directions. At the same time, the communal resources were a source of conflict, friction, and embarrassment. Writers who drew from them too closely were accused of plagiarism. The romance writers acknowledged being influenced by other authors they admired, but they located this influence in an individual writer, and they rarely spoke of resources as communally shared. Originality emanated from the self. There are several potential explanations for this: The romance writers have internalized a vision of creative writers from romantic theories of originality. Or they have internalized critiques of genre fiction that call it formulaic, and acknowledging communal resources would smack of formula. This originality emanated from the self, but from the perspective of readers, it did not matter who the self was. This was a fiction community that invited anonymity and identity bending. The attribution of an author was enormously important, but as long as that attribution was in place, and as long as the story had value for the readers, the flesh-and-blood characteristics of the author mattered very little.

The poker players, in contrast, needed to be accomplished in the game to write a book. Their texts had value only inasmuch as they were anchored to the ethos of the player. Unlike many of the cases of alleged plagiarism in fiction, copyright violators in poker did not necessarily claim the information they appropriated to be their own, since in many cases that would have significantly diminished its value. For example, a player would buy a book in English, translate it to another language without permission, and then sell it, but this had to be done with an attribution in place. The value of the text was anchored deep within the ethos of the flesh-and-blood writer and poker player.

These differences between fiction and nonfiction authorship seem traditional, but they mattered to how the writers conceptualized their relation to communal resources. The poker players recognized more willingly that they were drawing on communal resources to produce their texts, even as they asserted ownership over them. Authors and readers shared an expectation that in books, and in discussions, some information would be repeated, shared, and held in common. This was a point of fact for the poker players, not a point of embarrassment. Having a shared body of knowledge helped them identify "original" information that had not yet leaked into widespread circulation and was therefore highly valued. But it also created the possibility for value to emerge strictly from shared resources: books were sold that took information that wasn't necessarily new and rearticulated it and/or synthesized it in lucid ways that made the information easy to apply during games. Reviewers would often note this in their book reviews, but they would not level charges of plagiarism.

The poker players recognized communal resources as their "debt to the community." They acknowledged that they had drawn from a collection of collaboratively produced strategy texts to help them learn. In practice, they had a well-developed sense of the digital commons, even if they did not use that term. When they monetized their books, they were operating on the borders of the commons and the market, an experience that many of the romance writers had not yet had.[29]

The poker writers' sense of the commons is the focus of the rest of this chapter. As the perception grew that the games were becoming more difficult, there was a greater push to protect high-quality information. This led the poker players to manipulate their writing practices in an effort to eliminate the commons and enact a kind of idea protection. In contrast to the earlier description of the contours of an emerging antiplagiarism regime in the romance writers, the next section concentrates on a time in which the poker players considered their economic environment to be changing and examines how they changed their IP practices with it.

Poker Authors, the Market, and Peer Production

In an article about why the Napster music-copyrighting phenomenon should matter to writing teachers, Dànielle DeVoss and James Porter argued that peer-to-peer file sharing has fostered a new ethic of digital delivery that has contributed to the copyright crisis. They documented public conflicts and court cases related to Napster. Untangling different strands of the copyright crisis, DeVoss and Porter drew "battle lines" between those in favor of open access and distribution, on the one hand, and those in favor of copyright control, proprietorship, and the constraint of information on the other. Those in favor of open access push for information to be a shared resource, whereas those in favor of control take a more proprietary stance, regarding information as something to be owned and regulated.[30]

In light of the surge of user-generated web content examined in this book, the battle lines drawn by DeVoss and Porter make it difficult to account for the dynamics of copyright and IP on what Yochai Benkler has called the "constructive interface" between market and nonmarket social production on the Internet—that is, web spaces where the labor of commercial firms and entrepreneurs and the labor of voluntary peer production interact to create informational goods.[31] This interface often confounds clear distinctions between commercial and noncommercial textual production. If, according to DeVoss and Porter, focusing on the delivery of texts is an important component of understanding digital writing, and if in some ways peer-to-peer networks contribute to an ethics of sharing, then sharing can become layered into literate activity meant to create textual proprietorship. The ethics of sharing can become an integral part of the efforts to commodify information.

The poker players wrote on this constructive interface between market production and nonmarket production, and during my ethnography of them, many of the players perceived online poker strategy to move away from collaborative peer production to a proprietary economy of instruction. There was talk of the "good old days" when strategy was freely shared, but then coaching sites showed how to successfully monetize the information, and the games seemingly became more difficult. As writing and instruction began to achieve commodity status, the instructors worked with readers and students to arrest the flow of advanced poker theory and texts to the public. That is, they manufactured scarcity. In general, much of the strategy that the experts produced through electronic media has been monetized through subscription-based websites, a coaching industry, and ebook sales. However, this shift to proprietorship was not linear or monolithic. Peer production continued as the players generated poker strategy collaboratively on free and public discussion boards through robust information gift economies. Commercial and noncommercial textual production have not been discrete processes; they competed, informed, complemented, and struggled in an irreducibly constitutive relationship. For example, the self-publishing authors monetized their texts by articulating a strategy that had not yet been disseminated through the commons, but at the same time they relied on commons-based poker communities to produce book reviews that sanctioned their work and verified its quality.

Writing, Instruction, and the Move to Idea Protection

There were two reasons that the poker players worried about the games becoming more difficult. First, many players worried that coaching websites were too successful in their efforts to educate the bad players. Second, there was the persistent worry that the legal gray area occupied by online poker made it increasingly difficult for recreational players to play online, and recreational players were the people who made the games lucrative. There has been no publicly available research to verify that the games actually became harder, but the sentiment was almost ubiquitous in my interviews and in online discourse; so too were accounts of how digital writing changed in response to difficult games. Competition put mounting pressure on writing practices, and the disclosure of strategy shifted from anonymous sharing to a more protectionist model. One instructor explained, "There's kind of a backlash against posting anything groundbreaking on the forums because you don't want to give it up free, especially with coaching sites everywhere. I've been realizing the games are getting tougher. People are much more reluctant to release their secrets, so to speak, and so at least not without a price."

The enormous number of educational resources made available online and through bookstores means that many players have acquired an understanding of the game by using methods that were not accessible when poker strategy was spread through the limited resources that David Hayano documented in *Poker Faces*, a 1982 ethnography of professional card players. In response to difficult conditions, players and instructors began posting less on public forums and instead posted articles on private forums that were accessible only to paying subscribers. They also changed their blogging practices.[32]

The decisions of the authors to change their writing practices were often explained in relation to a growing professionalism and a responsibility to students. Tomasz Wlodarczyk (a pseudonym) began posting to the forums of a training site when they were "relatively blank." As a public school teacher, Wlodarczyk gained satisfaction from helping people learn: "I was at a level where I felt that I could really help people out in the forums, so I just took a very involved approach to that and I would write twenty or thirty posts a day, and people seemed to appreciate that. I really enjoyed helping people, and I think a lot of teachers have that. That is kind of what I did."

Wlodarczyk eventually contributed enough lucid writing on forums that a "grassroots effort" emerged to have him hired as an instructor. He began making instructional videos that concentrated on teaching poker fundamentals using mathematics, and he maintained a well-read blog that documented his own thoughts on strategy. Working and coaching supplemented his poker income and provided him with the means to become a full-time player, which Wlodarczyk described as a "leap of faith."

But as his income came to rely solely on poker, the professional identity Wlodarczyk had created led him to change his blogging practices: "I cut down a little bit on the strategy that I post in there because I don't want people to know exactly what is going through my head. So I am still thinking about the things that I can write on my blog right now, and I think my blog is going to become more general reflections on broader things, maybe a little bit more abstract. I definitely think my involvement with my blog has cut down in the last couple of months."

Competitive pressures linked to a sustainable professional identity led Wlodarczyk to reflect on the types of strategy he might write about on his blog, and his writing moved from concrete and specific to more general and abstract in order to protect his "win rate."

As his coaching business grew, Wlodarczyk began writing private articles for the students he was coaching about issues that recurred in many of his lessons. He did not post these articles online because, as he explained, "They are kind of like my own intellectual property, and I don't want to educate everybody. I want to educate students, and I am definitely going to give more resources to my individual students because they are pay-ing for more." The responsibility to his students and its relationship to protecting information reverberated in the way Wlodarczyk talked about his writing. Although this responsibility pushed information away from commons-based strategy forums into private writing spaces, Wlodarczyk continued to contribute to forum discussions, helping beginners and intermediate players with strategy questions.

Likewise, as the professional coaching business of twenty-eight-year-old Jeff Saviten (a pseudonym) grew, so did his awareness that his strategy writing had monetary value, and this changed his approach to blogging. Saviten linked the withholding of information from public forums to the responsibility he felt toward his students:

> At the beginning I put way more poker content in my blogs. But it had a kind of change for me because I was charging people on an hourly basis for the information I was gleaning from playing. I didn't really feel like it was fair to them or good business for myself to start giving away a whole bunch of information on my blog in terms of strategy, especially after I became a professional poker player and after I began getting into coaching. So I would say my blog now is more about life.

The responsibility to students caused Saviten to withhold information from blog posts. This was a significant move because in the past, indi-vidually written poker blog posts have sparked peer-produced forum de-bate. Withholding information from a blog reduces the material available to create commons-based texts, which is what happened when Saviten shifted much of his poker writing to private forums accessible only to his students.

Reproducing Secrecy

Formalizing and monetizing relationships between teachers and students produced a sentiment that militated against anonymous sharing. This sen-timent can be reproduced as students become instructors and they need to make their own decisions about what information to bring into the public domain. Scott Huntler (a pseudonym), for example, earned a reputation as a prolific writer in online strategy forums. As his reputation spread, a website approached him and asked him to make instructional videos for its library. Huntler first spoke with his own mentor before agreeing to make them because, as he told me, "My coach was very reluctant to allow me to put certain materials out into the public domain because he taught them to me and they jeopardize his trade secrets, essentially." Despite claiming such information as a trade secret, Huntler gave no indication that he had a contract with his coach to prevent such trade secrets from moving into the public domain. Such secrets, then, might have less to do with contractual obligation than with affinity and social norms that emerge in the relationship between coach and student as they negotiate terms of information flow, speaking of it in discourses of trade secrets and IP.

The move toward protecting information to sustain proprietorship over knowledge fundamentally altered the way many players approached a variety of online writing media and applications as they thought through what information they wanted to prevent from leaking into the public domain. The transition of these coaches' participation from public to private writing spaces has much to do with ad hoc measures of idea protection often laced in discourses of IP. This move toward proprietorship exists in connection with the writers' own web participation, since these shifting writing practices suggest a quasi-withdrawal from open online strategy communities.

However, as I have suggested, it is not an absolute shift. Despite having a thriving coaching business that he writes weekly articles for, Huntler continues to post prolifically on public forums, offering basic and intermediate information to players who are soliciting advice. Huntler claimed that he does this because he still feels an obligation "to give back to the community" that helped him learn poker. These contributions have cemented his electronic reputation as a solid coach and mentor, and they keep his name circulating. In addition, up-and-coming players still heavily populate public discussion forums because, as one player told me, writing about his thought processes online meant that his erroneous assumptions about poker might be corrected as other players responded to his strategy advice. An ethic of sharing combined with a desire for social standing compelled the coaches to contribute to strategy forums as the interface of commercial and noncommercial complicates how and why people protect written texts.

The articles that the coaches wrote came to mediate their relationships with their students, and the texts also activated discussions among the students whose learning was based on instruction with a particular coach. Wlodarczyk, Saviten, and Huntler created private forums for their coaching programs, which provided spaces for their students to interact in. All these students were serious enough about improving to invest large amounts of money in professional coaching. Their interaction distributed the work of teaching through the network, and it helped the students form symbiotic bonds with players of a similar caliber. Saviten found that his own students began to share strategy and respond to one another's questions when he was not available to comment. Some of Wlodarczyk's students interacted online to discuss concepts they learned during his training sessions. The move to a proprietary model of coaching and instruction increased the importance of these private writing spaces because they enabled the students to engage in social learning through reciprocity contextualized in established monetary relations with the coach—a type of information sharing that hinged on personal relationships and not on anonymous peer-to-peer relationships, in which sharing is often motivated through an affinity with community.

These learning networks have stalled the flow of new poker strategy to the commons and contained it temporarily. This phenomenon illustrates the conditions under which players manipulate the public and private flow of information to preserve the value of their knowledge or coaching program yet still engage in learning through social media, especially as relationships among people with different competencies become more formalized and monetized.

The Ebook: Copyright Meets Idea Protection

Although many poker instructors have changed their writing practices to protect new developments in poker theory, coaches who have developed theory in ebooks and want to guard it face a distinct set of challenges. In a survey of poker literature for his ethnography of professional poker players, David Hayano found that many poker texts were basic. This changed in 1987, when David Sklansky wrote what is widely considered to be a seminal text, *The Theory of Poker*.[33] In the first decade of the 2000s, a poker boom increased the number of poker strategy books available, but many skilled players exhausted the information in hard-copy texts and looked for advanced books with strategies specific to the online game dynamics that were beginning to emerge from the coaching programs. A good deal of coaching happens as individual instruction through Voice over Internet Protocol (VoIP) and screen-sharing technologies, and such sessions and information are not conducive to mass dissemination. But coaches who have written ebooks have faced the prospect of their coaching knowledge being traded freely through a single text through copyright infringement and unauthorized distribution, and the writing and publishing strategies of ebook authors are intensely inflected with attempts to prevent their texts and the information contained therein from circulating widely and becoming part of the commons. This could presumably happen quite rapidly, given how fast electronic texts can circulate through peer-to-peer networks.

Copyright infringement, piracy, and IP issues loomed large in the way many of the ebook authors in my study talked about their composing experiences. However, the measures they took to protect their ideas as well as to prevent unauthorized distribution have not been homogeneous. Much like the romance writers, the poker authors responded differently to the microclimate around them; in this case, their responses had less to do with their conception of the creative act and more to do with an author's own conception of information and his knowledge of technology.

Frederick Gregorus (a pseudonym), for example, ran an information technology business in Copenhagen, Denmark, before learning how to play poker. As his own poker skill grew, he began coaching small-stakes players. Gregorus wanted a textbook to accompany his program, so he wrote an ebook that he sold in a package with two hours of coaching and six instructional videos. Gregorus decided against protecting the ebook with digital rights management software because he had little faith that such a measure would protect the book from unauthorized distribution. Eschewing the practice authors have of answering questions about their book only in private forums, Gregorus initially kept his discussion public, acknowledging that attempts to keep information private were often futile. He relied on the intellectual services that he provided with the sale of the book to preserve the value of it. These services included coaching, instant-messaging sessions to explain concepts, and attending to a long comments section where his students discussed the book. Like other ebook writers, Gregorus has offered updates of the book that are conditioned by his readers' feedback on the content and style. This has sharpened both his ability to articulate concepts and his ability to write in a second language.

In many cases, readers' feedback contributed not only to revisions but also to copyright and idea protection, since the relationship between teacher and student, ebook writer and reader, conditioned the dissemination patterns of ebooks to make them scarce. The authors reported that many students approached them before publishing book reviews. These reviews are a primary mechanism for helping ebooks achieve credibility, and the students wanted to know if they could discuss specific strategy terms in their evaluations. The material would probably fall under the terms of fair use, but the measure shows how the conceptions of idea protection condition the writing practices of ebook readers as well, pushing them to a kind of permission culture that they adhere to after developing a personal relationship with an author.

As we saw with the recreational romance writers, the poker writers' readers contributed to copyright protection by policing unauthorized distribution. Readers who have paid for information are not inclined to encourage widespread free dissemination, so copyright and idea protection become distributed through readership. Rob Eckstut priced his ebook at $750, which was half the price of his three-day coaching program. He initially sold more than a hundred copies and offered the buyers access to private forums where he answered questions. Well aware that the price of the book meant that many people would try to acquire his text for free, he tried policing it by searching BitTorrents and by following discussions of it on different forums. Eckstut initiated a screening process whereby he interviewed potential buyers. He denied several applicants because he thought they were going to resell it at lower price after buying it. To complete the screening, the applicants had to speak English, and Eckstut did everything he could to keep the book in English, even denying offers of translation into Dutch and Russian so that he could retain control of the material. After a while he began making subtle changes to punctuation marks on certain pages so he would know who owned the original copy if a pirated copy appeared on the Internet.

Eckstut could afford to withhold sales because the dissemination of his book was of secondary importance to him. He primarily identified and earned a living as a poker player, not as an author, and this afforded him the opportunity to keep greater control of the information. His buyers helped him police unauthorized reproduction: after paying $750 for the ebook, they wanted to protect the book just as much as Eckstut did. He received frequent emails from his customers after someone had approached them asking to buy a discounted copy. After identifying the seekers of illicit copies, Eckstut created a blacklist. A number of his international customers who spoke French and Russian monitored discussion forums, and they alerted Eckstut to conspiracies hatched on poker forums to obtain the book, translate it, and redistribute it. Buyers formed a type of networked electronic guild to help protect the information for which they had paid.[34]

Of course, anyone can publish a poker ebook, but to commodify one's text it takes a relatively untarnished reputation, a proper author's name with an ethos derived from online communities. Many of the ebook writers I interviewed intuitively understood the potential cost of threats to their credibility, and this process became saturated with IP concerns as well. David Brody (a pseudonym) faced the threat of peer alienation during the production of an ebook that emerged from his coaching program. He solicited a chapter from a coauthor, but during the final stages of editing, a former coach of the coauthor contacted Brody to express concern that his ideas were being stolen, published, and profited from in the book. Brody offered to send the coach a copy of the book before it was published to ensure that none of his ideas were being stolen.

While I was conducting this interview, I thought that this was just another case in which a writer's unfamiliarity with copyright laws had led to conflating copyright violation with plagiarism. But when I mentioned to Brody that ideas cannot be copyrighted, he said, "It wasn't an issue of legality. What I didn't want to have happen was for this very reputable coach to come out in a public sphere and say, 'This book is a rip-off, don't buy it.' It was a question of credibility. If I have someone attacking the credibility of my coauthor, that's not a good thing for me." The possibility of Brody's selling the text was contingent on him being able to benefit from the name recognition he had established on online poker forums. Yet status is so fragile online that he imagined that the originator of an idea could wield enough power to disrupt his reputation as an author. In fact, here it did not matter that ideas cannot be copyrighted, because in an attempt to commodify digital writing, peer pressure enacts a kind of idea protection that the law does not.

The Threat of the Torrent

Even the authors who had the most open stances toward informational flow believed that peer-to-peer file sharing via BitTorrent protocols would significantly reduce the value of their texts if they were distributed widely for free. Although some of these ebooks have been traded through anonymous peer-to-peer networks, some of the poker players suggested that this file sharing has been limited. First, many of the discussion forums on which these ebooks are peer-reviewed are hosted on content-producing websites whose administrators are concerned with piracy. The moderators on these forums often suppress discussions of BitTorrent protocols in order to prevent anonymous file sharing. Second, poker ebooks are so specialized and geared toward a niche market that the number of people interested in reading them is small, and so too are the potential number of anonymous peers who would want to share the files.

Third, the presence of online scammers is large in the culture of Internet poker, and ironically, these scammers may help prevent the dissemination of ebooks. The web discussions I followed suggested that some players were nervous about downloading poker ebooks because there were rumors that the files could contain spyware. In the past, software applications relevant to poker players have appeared on anonymous peer-to-peer networks, and these applications have contained key-logger programs—or so went the online lore. Once installed, these programs could allegedly provide a hacker with the log-in information to the players' online poker account. Thus a fear of viruses embedded in ebook files may have slowed their circulation, and although peer-to-peer file sharing of these texts did exist, such sharing appeared to me to make its way through networks of friends, not exclusively—or even primarily—through anonymous channels.

Copyright and Intellectual Property without Control

Many of these writers, while trying to control their texts, also took relatively commonsense approaches to conceptualizing IP flow as something that functioned beyond their control. Brody sent emails to online forums that were hosting discussions about how to pirate copies of his ebook and asked the forums to shut the discussions down. He knew that the emails would help only marginally: "Of course, once something goes onto the Internet you lose most control. But it is important to choke off the marketing capabilities of those who are trying to buy the text and resell it at a lower price." Another ebook writer said, of trying to sell digital texts: "Tons of people are going to read it without paying for it, which is why you have to offer revisions and make yourself available for questions. Those who get a pirated copy will not have access to private forums or the updates to the text." We can see here the knowledge work that comes along with authorship as instructors offer incentives to those who purchase the book.

But these incentives also extend the work of authorship past the point of publication, into an ongoing process that lasts through the commercial life of the ebook. This is an important point, because these texts gradually leak into the public domain: the buyers of an ebook master the information in it and, months or years later, find no value left in the book and thus feel little need to withhold it from public forums; up-and-coming students become coaches, and they rearticulate the knowledge in less expensive manifestations.

Even the author of the ebook may provide this information in different forms. This was the case with one author, who sold copies of his ebooks for several hundred dollars and then included some of the information in a less expensive instructional DVD series. When I asked whether his readers complained, he said, "I think people implicitly understood the risk that this is an investment and it hinges on them knowing the information and others not knowing it . . . it occurs to people that if it leaks out it won't be as valuable, but even with that in mind they approached me and bought it anyway." The value and commodity status of such a text relies on uncertain and ephemeral measures to prevent the information inside from becoming a public good; idea protection strategies are leaky, and when an author lost interest in protecting the text, most of it appeared months later posted for free on the web.

The economy of instruction that surrounds online poker is a somewhat negative case of online writing. Because poker players work with rivalrous information, their writing practices are a rather dramatic way of showing how IP microclimates can become integrated into the fabric of literate activity as writers work to manipulate textual production and informational flow. Yet despite sharing most of their writing for free, the romance writers' experiences suggested a similar concern with IP, generating similar tactics to stabilize attribution and distribution and thus authorship. Although authorship in this context was probably more unstable than in certain print contexts, and readers could read entire books without knowing whether its professed author had created an identity-bending online persona, the ad hoc networks protected authorship and its attribution. They allowed people to establish reputations, fan bases, and audiences who waited eagerly for the next installments of the text. Microclimates stabilized authorship in the absence of entities that policed copyright.

The presence of microclimates complicates Lessig's worry that copyright extremism has led youth to be contemptuous of the law, at least from the vantage of their own production. The issues of originality, plagiarism, authenticity, and textual ownership are utterly bound to issues of copyright, and users share an ambiguous respect for the entire system. The respect for attribution stalls recirculation, but it is also complicated by matter-of-fact sharing that violates the letter of copyright law. Copyright violations in back channels are rife even in microclimates that otherwise stifle the most public acts of unauthorized sharing. Users gain status in authoring texts and in reporting plagiarism, but they can also build goodwill among friends by sharing texts. Close relationships almost require one to forward a copy of a much sought-after and expensive ebook for free to a friend if one has a copy. Other groups of friends pool their money to buy a single copy and then share it within the group.

Kathleen Fitzpatrick argues that scholarly publishing could achieve a new kind of vibrancy with the help of networked technologies. She advocates a new model of scholarly publishing that reflects theoretical developments in authorship and makes use of the technological affordances of digital publishing. This model includes the possibility of moving away from the idea of the closed text, moving toward new forms of collaboration, participating in a gift economy, and rethinking the credit that academics take for original research.[35]

Poker players built their initial economy of instruction on these practices, but as they perceived the economy changing, they altered their authoring practices accordingly. After five years of obsessively observing their online activity, I noted a playful irony that demonstrated some of the fickleness of microclimates: as Fitzpatrick was arguing that humanists should adopt the more open and collaborative practices that I had seen permeating the poker economy in its nascent state, the poker authors were taking steps to become more like humanists by trying to reboot practices of individual ownership and secrecy—at least to the extent that they could while working in environments in which collaboration is rife. In other words, although the humanities are often seen as the last bastion of individual authorship, the poker players—and the romance writers, too—recruited this model because it harmonized so well with the knowledge regimes and status systems they attempted to put in place.

CHAPTER 6

Book Reviews and Credibility in a Nonfiction Niche Market

ON APRIL 15, 2011, the US Department of Justice unsealed an indictment for money laundering and fraud against the most prominent online poker companies in the world. The sites had operated in a legal gray area in the United States for almost a decade, but on that day the Justice Department blocked the sites. Almost immediately a recreational activity and multibillion dollar industry became completely inaccessible to US players. Insiders of the American poker community called this Black Friday.

As of this writing, fully regulated online poker has begun in a number of states, and online poker's death in the United States, followed by its partial rebirth, provides another example of how fickle the state's position toward gambling has been for hundreds of years: sometimes the state suppresses gambling and sometimes it sponsors it.[1] But the shutdown also provided a stark reminder of how literacy practices can be highly contingent on the economies that motivate them.[2] For more than a decade, professional and semiprofessional players had been building an economy of poker instruction to satisfy the demand that grew with online poker. The instructors doled out advice through video instruction, blog posts, and ebooks. They populated online forums and built coaching businesses. Just before the shutdown, a winning and articulate midstakes player could make several hundred dollars per hour coaching aspiring players.

The shutdown did not completely destroy the economy of instruction, however. The global spread of poker in the twenty-first century meant that demand still came from Europe and the Pacific Rim, and people continued to play live poker in casinos. Some video instruction sites have survived, and some coaches continued creating instructional materials simply through inertia. A former math teacher turned poker player wrote, "So I'm in the final stages of putting my book together. While it sucks that poker is mostly dead in the U.S., this has been a long-term goal of mine and I feel like I'm getting really close to the end. All the major content is there, and right now I am getting it peer-reviewed and edited."[3]

Since the United States had been the most robust market for online poker, the general feeling registered on online forums was that it was time for professionals to move to a new country, begin playing in casinos, or get a different job, because the only online operators left were small and fragile sites. The value of instructional materials online began to fall as well, decreasing partly because of falling demand but also because as copyright vigilance diminished, more and more materials began to circulate for free through digital channels. Ebooks that had once been tightly protected, as described in chapter 5, began appearing in abundance on the web as one-click downloads from file-sharing sites.

Nonfiction Niche Writing

As the poker economy shows, the web enables geographically diffuse populations with similar interests to locate and interact with one another; this is one of the Internet's most powerful affordances. The economics of print distribution made it difficult for publishers to produce books about niche subjects without some sort of subsidy; it was difficult for readers to coalesce into an ad hoc public and provide a visible audience large enough to make obscure texts economically viable for publishers to produce.[4] But the ability of readers to use search engines and digital networks to find one another has led to an apparent increase in so-called long-tail cultural products, and nonfiction niche markets are a hot spot for understanding the particular dynamics of self-publishing.[5] Yet while self-publishing systems enable the production and circulation of niche nonfiction, they also operate without the publishing systems that vetted the quality of information in twentieth-century nonfiction. Since publishers played a crucial gatekeeping function in nonfiction quality control, how do the self-published authors of nonfiction produce books and establish credibility? And how do readers assess the value of the information?

This chapter attempts to answer that question in a preliminary way by returning to my study of professional poker players who authored ebooks as part of their coaching programs. It sets their experience in motion against a background of peer-to-peer production that generated book reviews and discussions, which helped stabilize the publishing environment. In the absence of publishers and printed objects, these reviews have functioned as an intermediary to establish what counts as a reputable book. They have been a powerful form of gatekeeping, not just because the reviews assessed books but also because they helped publicize them. This chapter shows that the potential of nonfiction self-publishing may nowhere be more instantiated than in the ubiquitous book review, which is itself only a focal text that leads to prolonged discussions.

Focusing on the book review can clarify what it means for readers to become networked participants with the capacity to publish with little editorial oversight. The power of readers is why self-published book reviews have become a hotly contested issue in contemporary book culture and the subject of lawsuits. Amazon's book-reviewing system, for example, has been controversial because of the potential for quasi-anonymous identity bending that has enabled writers (or their family members) to post glowing reviews of their own work, which Amazon has tried to stop. These user-generated systems have sparked outrage, such as when the *New York Times* reported on a service that sold positive reviews to self-published authors.[6] This was just one service among a number of shady outfits that work to game corporate giants with search engines in a digital cat-and-mouse game. Nor has the controversy been limited to self-publishing; incidents have emerged in which scholars extracted revenge on rivals by posting nasty reviews of their books.[7]

In the world of poker ebooks, the reviews had power because they were bound to conceptions of online community and other systems of peer review and reputation. The reviews worked as spaces for interaction and functioned as nodes of attention that channeled awareness to an author's work and shaped its status through critical assessment. All the authors in my study had their books reviewed and criticized in discussion threads that sometimes stayed active for months. Reviewers were not immune from criticism, either, and discussion constantly focused on the quality of each evaluation. These texts were scrutinized according to the status of the reviewer, his post count in various online forums, and the quality of his writing. Rhetorical advocates of the book were often discredited if they were friends of the author and did not provide a disclaimer of their prior relationship. This was a messy process that often relied on previous knowledge of community conventions. Peer review could at times be manifested through small textual fragments: even a "lol" from a well-respected member of a poker community could be charged with enormous semiotic meaning that shaped the trajectory of the way a book was received.

The Poker Ebook Context

Poker authorship was a rich and strategic area of nonfiction writing to study, despite the fact that it was largely ephemeral. As I have noted, in 2007 I began an ethnographic study that tracked ebook authors who were producing and mostly selling self-published textbooks (in two cases the books were given away for free). The authors reported writing ebooks to make their coaching programs more efficient, since they had been repeating similar points in multiple sessions. In some cases, the coaches wrote books because their instruction was in high demand, because they were bored with poker, or because writing fed their egos. Since expert coaching was expensive, the ebooks were expensive, too, with a median price of $100, although some of the books were sold, temporarily, for more than $1,000. The poker theory in the books was an amalgam drawn from principles of algebra, probability, psychology, and statistics. Most of the authors in this study had at least the equivalent of a bachelor's degree, and some had graduate degrees. The ebooks were part of a mediascape of multimodal and interactive learning resources on the web. Because they competed with other materials, the rhetoric used in marketing these books emphasized their various affordances as a learning medium. In promotional materials, the authors highlighted that ebooks were updatable, flexible, holistic, and interactive. The speed with which they came to the market was championed as a virtue, and the authors contrasted them to print books, claiming that the ebooks were responsive to the current state of poker and the rapidly changing nature of the games.

Two dynamics show the extent to which digital writing practices can coalesce around, and respond to, the nature of information in books. The first concerns the unique nature of poker writing. As I documented in the previous chapter, my study took place during a peculiar time in the economy of instruction that inflected the ways ebooks were produced and distributed. In the years I studied the writing activity of poker players, there was a palpable sense that the instruction was improving poker play on the whole and that the games were becoming less lucrative; however, the demand for poker knowledge was still intense. The move to commodify the information, combined with the generally rivalrous nature of the information, made the writing practices a somewhat negative case compared with other web writing. The authors were not necessarily trying to find as many readers as possible, because the perceived value of poker knowledge declined as it spread. The authors faced the task of acquiring publicity and recognition while also trying to limit the pace at which the most valuable information circulated. They sold their books privately yet relied on public and collaborative peer production to provide them with publicity, attention, and credibility. This meant that the poker authors had to preserve ownership (temporarily) over their texts yet simultaneously rely on the peer-to-peer energy that in many ways resists the ownership regimes of copyright.

The second dynamic stems from the skepticism that surrounded the texts and whether they were worth the large sums of money authors were charging for them; the history of gambling instructional materials is rife with scamlike "systems" sold to naive readers who hope to get rich by beating the casino. The debates over the ebooks' value were often heated, especially because experts and newcomers, believers and skeptics, occupied the same public writing spaces and had different ideas about the value of materials. Some participants on the forums accused the authors of selling snake oil. They were convinced that the books were overpriced and that the authors were cashing in on the pipe dreams of those who wanted to strike gold playing poker. They often warned new players about expensive ebooks and encouraged them to exhaust inexpensive material first. Others warned that the texts would quickly lose value and be available for free once the information filtered out and appeared in less expensive manifestations. Mason Malmuth, the owner and publisher of Two Plus Two Publishing, and the only professional publisher I ever witnessed to comment on the price of the ebooks, voiced his concern about their price on the forums on a number of occasions; he essentially argued that if the books were as good as the price tags indicated, then the authors would ultimately make more money using a mass distribution print publishing model.

Coaches, authors, and readers defended the books by arguing that the detractors misunderstood the target audience. The defenders argued that expensive ebooks enabled players who were already highly competent to increase their win rate. The authors I interviewed said that the books often represented their coaching systems, and the book prices were consistent with the prices they charged for coaching (which were also hotly debated). I asked a winning high-stakes player, who had not authored a book, whether a particular text whose cost surpassed $1,000 was a good value. He said, "I have no idea. But a lot of this information is closely guarded, and it isn't out there, so they essentially can charge whatever they want." With few precedents to guide the authors, there was room for experimentation. One author stated, in an interview about his approach to pricing, "You can always charge $30 for a book. In some ways I decided to put a crazy-high price on it just to see what would happen."

Book Reviews in Larger Systems of Credibility

Book reviews were the main ways that the authors' books were discussed, but the reviews existed in a media ecology with a robust infrastructure of name recognition, credibility, and reputation. Players built reputations based on poker performance and the ability to articulate and teach poker theory. Concerned with questions of accountability, online poker sites have published the histories and results of every hand dealt. This has enabled websites to aggregate results, and these websites tracked the results of the best players (although following all of a player's hands was often difficult, and the systems were unreliable). Likewise, many serious players had database programs that tracked their own hand histories as they played. This allowed them to study the plays of their opponents and to publish graphs of their winnings, the stakes they played, and their win rates to demonstrate their skills. Digital communications and mainstream media exposure fueled word-of-mouth reputation building, and most of the authors were prodigious public writers, which let prospective buyers and students (as well as peers) understand their thought processes. These reputation economies tended to be kept in check by self-appointed watchdogs who used statistics to uncover and prosecute cheating scandals, which could destroy the guilty players' reputations and make them communal outcasts.

These reputation systems were a form of community in the lives of writers, whose public writing and the reasons for it were bound to how they conceptualized their place in such a community. The term *online community* is particularly problematic, given its nebulous definition and the way in which Internet researchers have employed it without precise definition.[8] For players, an online community has been an imaginary entity that helps create discursive systems that provide peer review, publicity, and trust. This is a key difference between this niche market and Amazon: the poker players had a broad loyalty to their online communities; Amazon has a more ambiguous relationship with its authors and customers because of its market-based relationship with them. In an environment of expensive specialized texts, an ebook not sanctioned by participants in a community could run the risk of being labeled a scam. If the capital investment of publishers has provided a measure of reputability to book authors, then online communities provide a way for authors to recover that ethos after they self-publish.

In a posting about the value of ebooks, print publisher Malmuth summarized how the value of ebooks was partly achieved through the forum contributions that were a major part of the community: "The best way to tell if this stuff is worth the money is through peer review. And specifically what I mean by this are his strategy posts on our forums and the reaction to them by our posters, particularly those who are considered the better players."[9] Although public response to an author's discussion posts shaped the author's reputation, another form of review came through underground peer-to-peer file sharing of ebooks. Not easily traceable, and often an act that infringed on copyright, peer-to-peer file sharing surfaced in my interview data as a de facto method of review, the digital equivalent of word-of-mouth recommendations.

Bill Vosti experienced issues of ethos when he lost a screen name in an online community that would have otherwise helped him confirm the quality of his work through name recognition. Book reviews helped save his ebook from obscurity. When he wrote the text, he didn't look for a publisher because he wanted to hurry the process of publication, keep total control of the content, and provide updates to the book that included hyperlinks to videos. When he tried to publicize his work through press releases, Vosti encountered resistance despite having a record as a successful professional player. His book was priced fairly low, and he tried to market it with a number of different poker websites, but their resistance shows the lingering distrust that buyers had of ebooks when he released his ebook in 2007 and 2008: "I definitely ran into some troubles in this area because I found most people don't take ebooks seriously. There is this whole 'Oh, ebooks are scams, or ebooks are not worthwhile books.' I didn't get responded to by most people."

Vosti noticed a spike in sales when the book was reviewed in the "Books and Publications" forum of Two Plus Two Publishing's website. Coincidentally, Vosti, who had posted on that site close to ten thousand times in several years, had been banned from the site just months before releasing his ebook for irritating the forum's moderators. Vosti returned to the forum and began posting to it using a new screen name and, with the blessing of the moderators, answered questions about his book in the discussion thread. But he did not entirely recover the ethos attached to his old screen name and his more established online persona: "I got permanently banned on that name. For being a little punk, I guess. This was before I had the vision to do an ebook, because I think having that name and that many posts . . . people knew who I was. I had been posting for over four years."

In the years before writing the ebook, Vosti contributed to strategy discussions and posted free videos in the beginner's section. Many community members knew that he was a successful player at fairly high stakes. Vosti's banning, however, detached him from that online identity, and without the ethos of name recognition attached to what Vosti said was an "online community to verify the quality" of the work, he found himself facing skepticism that ebooks were "scammy." He faced this barrier until a growing number of user-generated book reviews praised his book's content.

Identity and Authenticity

The importance of reviews came into sharp relief in episodes in which a review's authenticity was in doubt. Many of the book reviews I studied were on the Two Plus Two forums, which were owned and sponsored by the largest and most reputable publisher of print poker books. When I observed the site, it was receiving two hundred thousands posts per day on forums that ranged from poker strategy to politics, science, math, and philosophy. Because Two Plus Two publishes and sells poker books in print, the company objected to ebooks being explicitly marketed through its site. But it did allow book reviews and discussion of any kind of poker book in their "Books and Publications" forum as long as the author was not shilling his or her own work. These dynamics essentially meant that the poker authors had to negotiate the policies of the website and discuss their books without appearing to be selling them or promoting them. The authors answered questions about their works in the book-review section and provided advice on the strategy forums to demonstrate their teaching competency.

In an ideal (though rarely realized) form, the book review is an organic response to a book from a disinterested but credible reviewer; however, some reviewing practices in this context walked a fine line between communal propriety and forum policy, and these etiquette violations showed how resistant online communities could be toward threats to authenticity. Some of these threats were minor. For example, it was possible for an author to work through back channels with friends and have them move the discussion of his book to the front page of the forum when it became buried under other discussion threads. A friend or an acquaintance would accomplish this move by posting a question or comment about the book. This visibility gave the author another chance to comment on the review thread, and it could rejuvenate the discussion and keep the thread on the front page of the forum.

This was a common if somewhat problematic tactic, from the perspective of the community, but the reaction to it did not compare to the rage that phony reviews could ignite. In one book-review thread, moderators matched the same Internet Protocol address to two different user accounts. One account was that of an author of an ebook, and the other account was for a user who had posted a positive review of the author's book. The moderators accused the author of posting a positive review of his own work, which the author denied in a post on another poker forum. The reactions at the Two Plus Two forum were split: One group defended the author, vouched for his character, and noted that the author had worked in information technology and would therefore know that the moderators would discover it if he posted a review of his own book. The other group picked out inconsistencies in the author's story.

We can look back more than a hundred years and find it amusing that Walt Whitman published anonymous reviews of his own work. Yet this modern discussion of deceptive self-promotion has been cantankerous. It shows how long-held expectations for author behavior have become recontextualized in online spaces, where contempt is already high for the practice of astroturfing (masking the sponsors of a message to make it look like it has grassroots support), which violates the Web 2.0 ideals of transparency and authenticity.[10] Regardless of whether the author did in fact post the review, it was immediately clear that the very idea of it ignited moral outrage, reflecting the taboo against autocommentary in print authorship.[11]

In the poker community, there has been a history of scandals related to people playing games under alternate screen names to hide their identities. If a player participates in a poker game against other players whom he has a long history of playing against, he has an enormous advantage over the other participants if his identity is hidden. This is called *multiaccounting*, and it violates the terms of service of most poker sites. This language of multiaccounting appeared in the Two Plus Two discussion thread, further charging the emotions that swirled in it.

The discourse on the poker forums suggested that all these elements converged to fuel the discussion that unfolded across days, a dramatic flair-up of activity that stabilized credibility in technological spaces that enabled identity bending. This was certainly a high-stakes discussion: the Two Plus Two forums are so popular that their discussion threads often show up on the first page of Google search results. A popular discussion critical of a coach or an author on Two Plus Two can inflict serious damage on a player's reputation and his ebook sales.

Features of the Book Reviews

Authenticity is crucial to the book-reviewing system, but we can look beyond the metadiscussion to the evolution of the reviews themselves to see how the book-review genre evolved to address credibility gaps and how the readers conceptualized their relationships to the ebooks and the authors. I tend to use *genre* as it is commonly used in the publishing industry: as a commercially recognizable classification system for books. In this chapter, however, I employ the term as it is used in writing and rhetoric studies.[12] Although the formal elements of the text matter in this definition, so does the rhetorical action that a given genre mediates. Carolyn Miller first posited this in her foundational definition of *genre* as a kind of recurrent social situation that represents "typified rhetorical action." For Miller, and for writing and rhetoric studies at large, genre is "centered not on the substance or form of the discourse but on the action it is used to accomplish."[13] These actions typify into recurring features, and an analysis shows that generic conventions have emerged in response to writers interacting with the changing materiality of the text and the technological conditions of writing in digital environments.

The most prominent feature of the poker ebook review had long existed in the age of print: reviewers situated an ebook in relation to previously published material, building an imagined annals by which to evaluate a book's contribution. They also addressed the same question that was used to justify the value of many print books: To what extent did the book advance new concepts, or to what extent did it present old concepts in a new or lucid manner? The answer had an important influence on the quality of ebooks. Reviewers made no distinction between print book and ebooks; the latter were evaluated as much against one another as they were against the print poker books of the 1970s and the 1980s.

This move created a rapidly accruing communal memory, and authors who sold ebooks after a number of them had already been published faced increased expectations from readers. These included higher expectations for original content, increased length, and more professional standards of grammar, style, editing, and layout. Later ebook authors had the advantage of learning from the experience of those who had published earlier. Despite not being publishers, the participants became more proficient at publishing, motivated in part by the demands of the readers. Thus the collective experience of online communities with self-published books influenced how authors produced ebooks and experienced authorship. In general, as the textual history of self-published poker ebooks grew, the books that were produced adhered more closely to the traditional publishing standards of print publications.

Reviewers went beyond intertextual evaluation to situate the ebooks not only against competing books but also against competing modes of learning online. Reviewers compared the time and money one needed to extract value from a text with that of subscription video resources, interactive personal coaching, free articles, forum posts, blog posts, and printed material. This rhetorical move thus appraised the value of a book by its novelty of contribution as well as its relation to various forms of media.

The move to evaluate a book in terms of existing multimedia appeared in the discussion thread of Ed Miller, Matt Flynn, and Sunny Mehta's ebook on small-stakes poker. One reviewer criticized the laudatory tone of previous reviews before offering his own assessment: "I've finally finished the book and I found it to be pretty good, but I do think some of the hyperbole in this thread is a little overboard. The information in this book isn't anything new or groundbreaking, and if you are subscribing to any of the video training sites then most of this information should be familiar to you. What the book does well is driving those points home with a ton of well thought out examples."[14]

The first part of this review checks the temporary elation that can appear in early reviews when a reviewer is close to the author or a reader wants to share a fabulous reading experience. In the second part, the estimation of the value of the book is derived not from new knowledge but rather from carefully planned examples that reinforce preexisting concepts. The video instruction to which the book is compared often tends to be more extemporaneously produced, with more loosely defined patterns of organization than ebooks have. This reviewer has identified those differences, registering the book's value insofar as it organizes and illustrates existing knowledge in more extensive ways than could be found elsewhere in different media.

When other reviewers measured the book's value against competing media, they recommended that potential readers carefully consider their own learning styles before they bought the book, or that they buy the book in conjunction with other modalities of learning. The assessment of the book became inseparable from the imagined learning styles of the potential buyers:

> The book is good for people who are self-learners, or are already doing well at say 2/4 or above. . . . The book was good for my situation, since I could read it faster than going through his 13-lesson coaching program. It is also much cheaper. Coaching would be better for someone needing a complete overhaul and confidence boost in their game.[15]

> Beyond just putting in time, which is required of everyone to grasp the material, you should also consider how you learn. This book is very math heavy and reminds me of my engineering days.[16]

> If you buy the book, you have to learn from it and be good at thinking on your own. . . . You have to be a receptive individual who is capable of self-critique and highlighting ones strengths and weaknesses. . . . You should combine the book purchase with hiring a top-level coach.[17]

These recommendations consider the relationship between book learning and the learners' emotional state, ability for reflection, and time needed to extract information from the materials. The reviews show some consistency in attitude toward the function of the book compared to other media; the book enables, for example, self-paced learning in solitude in ways that coaching does not. But this function and its usefulness are always contingent upon the personal history and learning style of the reader. To extract value the readers must have certain characteristics as learners: formal education, an emotional disposition for individual learning, and preferences for certain modes of communication styles. These contingencies frustrate the possibility of imagining the book's trajectory in multimodal systems of online learning: it competes with and complements other media only in relation to personal learning preferences and styles. Even within a single review these contradictions emerge. The third reviewer, for example, urges readers to buy the text only if they are able to think and work on their own, yet at the same time he tells them to seek help from a coach if they buy the book.

Like the ebooks whose value they influenced, the book reviews were also self-published, and they suffered from the same crisis of credibility as the ebooks did. In a click-to-publish environment, the credibility of any single review is limited. The status of these reviews as self-published texts led potential readers and recreational onlookers to scrutinize them. The publication of a book review thus functioned less as an end point in the evaluation of a book and more as an opening point of discussion. Two genre conventions emerged from this constellation. The first convention was a disclaimer disclosing why the reviewer was not an objective evaluator. The disclaimer facilitated productive discussion and steered the written interaction away from ad hominem attacks on the reviewer, lest he be accused of posting inflated reviews to artificially increase the value of the book. The following disclaimer was made in an emotionally charged review thread: "I am a personal friend of all three authors; however, I'm also fair, and a goddamn genius to boot."[18]

Taken in context, the playful comment of this reviewer was a rhetorical attempt to defuse the tone of the heated review thread in which it was posted. Because third parties would usually expose personal relationships between an author and a reviewer, he documented his relationship with the authors before providing a positive review of their book. This disclaimer surfaced as a response to the freedom of self-publishing, and its rhetorical effect sought to prevent the discussion thread from devolving into simplistic critiques of the reviewer's ethos. It focused discussion on the merits of the book, not on the allegiances or credibility of the reviewer. A disclaimer was attached to a review if the reviewer knew the author, was a student of the author, or had received a free copy of the book in exchange for reviewing it. Although these relationships have often existed between reviewers and authors in print culture, without the ethos of a print venue endowing a review with credibility, the relationships become a necessary point of articulation to sustain productive discussion in an emotionally charged writing environment.

When reviewers treated the review as a form of interaction that created space for discussion among readers and potential readers, another rhetorical move emerged: the reviewer anticipated the author as an active audience member of the review. Although the reviews were only a small part of establishing a reputation, the ebook authors understood that the reviews directed attention to their work; they read the reviews, monitored discussions of them, and intervened when asked. The authors engaged in these discussion threads with rhetorical dexterity to avoid the appearance of shilling their own book. This constellation of activity crystallized into a generic feature that anticipated interaction with the author's future literate activity. Here we see that the alleged potential of the ebook's affordances—easy revision and redistribution—appear as a recurring feature in ebook reviews: "So on an overall scale of 1 to 10 . . . I would give this book an 8.8. Keep in mind that Tri gave me this book before it was completely finished, and my review may encourage him to add a section or two, at which point I would probably edit this review."[19] This reviewer attempted to exert agency on the book's reception and production. Writing to the author as well as to readers, he noted that both the book and his review are contingent upon future literate activity that he was attempting to shape.

This recurring relationship among reviewer, author, and revisable text created a synergy that surfaced in reviews as "wish lists" of potential improvements, which ranged from global additions to local corrections and included requests for additional chapters, better editing, and improved layout. These lists exposed weaknesses in the quality of the books and suggested that the author make revisions before distribution or in subsequent versions. Feedback helped the reviewers negotiate status differentials between themselves and the authors, providing space for the language of critique to be cloaked in the language of revision. In other words, suggestions for revision often softened the critiques of the books, providing qualifiers that diffident reviewers used to hedge the harshness of their reviews. The reviewers seemed to use this convention as a social lubricant in a niche where many people knew each other and shared a sense of community.

The author as audience member showed that the reviewers often expected—and evaluated—interactions with the authors that moved beyond the point of sale. The reviewers expected authorship to include private exchanges:

> I think a private forum would add tremendous value to the book, and since most people are going to have questions after reading it, many of which will be the same questions, the best way to answer them

would be posting responses in one location available to everyone who bought the book.[20]

I would like to add that after buying the book I have IMd Rob a few times and hes [sic] answered some of my questions, which was probably worth nearly as much as the book itself.[21]

The interactions that occurred through these reviews contributed to the value of the book. This extended engagement resulted partly from how easy it was for the author to interact with his audience online, but also from textual distribution patterns. Given the ease with which copies of their books could circulate, the writers provided incentive to potential purchasers by answering questions through private forums and office hours on instant messaging software. This incentive was also the impetus for revisions and additions to the text, which provided value beyond the sale. The reviewers reflected on an author's availability and willingness to help, which emerged as a consistent evaluative feature in the book reviews.

Digital Responsivity and Time

When book reviewers anticipated author revisions, they were contributing to a larger trend to address the material characteristics and digital affordances of electronic books in book reviews. The reviewers thought through this fluidity and the changing form of the book, as we can see in Andrew Brokos's review of Tri Nguyen's book about the poker game pot-limit Omaha (PLO). The review, and this passage in particular, addressed how the quick publication of an ebook can make it responsive to current game conditions:

> The text provides plenty of examples and in-depth analysis of advanced concepts like blockers, backdoor draws, and floating. It just makes me realize what a tall mountain there is to climb. Thankfully, Nguyen also emphasizes how many players in today's PLO games don't have an inkling about any of this stuff, which is reassuring. It does beg the question of the book's longevity, though. There's a mix of tactics that seem fundamental to playing the game well in any context and those designed to exploit mistakes and tendencies common in contemporary

PLO games. It will be interesting to see how long the latter remain viable. Since *Transitioning* is an e-book, Nguyen could theoretically update it, though to my knowledge he hasn't promised anything like this.[22]

In this portion of the review, an assessment of poker content mingles with an assessment of the technological potential of the ebook, which produces ambivalence in the reader: praise for the book's immediate responsiveness to the dynamics of contemporary poker trends, on the one hand, and questions about the permanence of the material, on the other hand. The book form as a medium of communication does not come under question; rather, the concern derives from the temporal relationship between the expertise of the book and its relevance for future players. The expectations of—and anxieties over—temporal stability have less to do with the technology itself and more to do with how the book's legacy induces the reviewer to conceptualize the relationship between time and stability. The legacy of the book as a slow medium provokes uncertainty about the value of a text whose relevance might fade quickly.

Carla Hesse has addressed the relationship between books and time in ways that anticipate Brokos's ambivalence. Citing the history of the book in eighteenth-century France, she argues that the book's mode of temporality enabled it to become a revered medium of communication. Perceived to be an "unhurried form of mediation," the book was censored less because it less often responded to unfolding events the way incendiary—and quickly produced—political pamphlets did.[23] For Hesse, the potential change in the book's mode of temporality when moving from print to digital form becomes a pivotal difference. Her modes of temporality are an elegant way of expressing the umbrella concept of Shirky's well-known formulation of new information technologies: "faster is different."[24] Torn between the unhurried legacy of the book coloring his expectations for durability and the affordance of the ebook's quick responsiveness, Brokos confronted these temporalities with both ambivalence about the object's stability and interest in the opportunity to observe the unfolding of the history of a specific book. The outcome was a curiosity for the reviewer, an "interesting" point of observation and an opportunity to bear witness to the consequences of technological change.

The relationship among book, time, and value extends beyond the durability of content to ruminations on rapid dissemination and the consequences for the buyer. In the following example, the reviewer worries that a substantial investment will diminish through rapid dissemination:

> Before I talk about some of the details of the book, I want to talk about its "packaging." First of all, you aren't getting a hard copy, so you are essentially paying for an "e-book." I think most people know this. Before purchasing, you are to agree to not distribute his book to anybody, period. I kind of want to talk briefly about that concept. Surely, in a perfect world, all buyers are honest and won't break their agreement. But we don't live in a perfect world. People lie and do a lot of shady things. It's very easy for the book to get distributed, especially being in the digital age, and there is almost no way to track who distributed [it]. As a consumer, you SHOULD be a little worried that something you paid $750 [for] today might be worth $0 tomorrow because anyone can obtain it from a one-click download.[25]

Addressing the liabilities of the ebook's affordances is a preliminary move to discussing the ebook's content. The perceived value hinges on a readership willing to protect it because poker strategy decreases in value as more people have it. Eschewing the notion that a book's value derives from widespread distribution, the reviewer weighs potential value as a risky investment contingent on the likelihood that the readers will respect the copyright. Its worth depends on limited circulation. The evidence I have collected suggests that the authors' books sustained commercial viability for six to eighteen months before they lost their monetary value, either because sales slowed or because of widespread sharing of free copies on the Internet, in their original form or in unauthorized translations.

Authors Pushing Back

The conversion of readers into networked participants with the capacity to publish was apparent in all the online book reviews I consulted, and these reviews often provided the authors with a steady stream of feedback. There were, however, two limits to this feedback loop from the perspective of the book writers: the incredible volume of it, and the potential of it to be wrong. As some of the reviews suggested, the readers often wanted the authors to revise their ebooks and adapt them to the current playing conditions. And in many cases the poker authors integrated feedback into an ongoing series of revisions provided to the buyers, a quasi-serialization of the textbook. Reviews helped them do that, but the characteristics of digital texts at times clashed with the writing disposition of the authors: the sheer volume of feedback became a limitation and a pressure point; enormous amounts could produce intellectual fatigue in the writer toward his text.

In general, the authors used the feedback from their readers to make a number of rounds of revisions to their texts. As the reviews showed, readers challenged the poker theory, generated questions about clarity, rooted out inaccuracies in math calculations, and spotted errors in grammar, style, and punctuation. This feedback helped the writers improve their work—a learning curve that readers tolerated, given the authors' poker expertise and the potential value of their knowledge. In certain cases this feedback process helped international authors learn to write in a second or third language, because the readers' comments taught them some of the idiosyncrasies and conventions of written English.

This interaction was an important part of how authorship became sustained over the life of an ebook. However, because the online communities that read and purchased these books also produced free strategy texts through peer production (like blog posts and lengthy discussion threads) that competed with the ebooks, the authors often invoked their expertise to delineate knowledge boundaries between themselves and their readers, and between themselves and the collective intelligence of the cultures of participation in which they published. Invoking hierarchy based on expertise became a way to preserve ownership of a text.

Ryan Fee, for example, began writing his ebook as a freshman in college. He was one of the first poker players to self-publish an ebook, and one of only two to distribute his ebook for free, which he did under the auspices of "giving back to the community" that had helped him learn poker. Because he published the book early in its development, Fee received enormous volumes of feedback through forum discussions and emails. An inexperienced writer when he started, he soon became acquainted with the reception of his text through the criticism and comments and made plans for revision: "I've gotten some perspective on the audience. . . . I know what to change so that they can understand it. I didn't understand everything when I wrote it. And my understanding now is a lot better so when I go back to do a revision to it, it's going to make a lot more sense and it's going to look at things in a different light."

In the midst of the reader responses that influenced the trajectory of revisions, however, Fee maintained the desire (or necessity) to claim authority over the poker content and text:

> People posted in the thread "I don't understand this. I want to see more of this," all these concepts. They would tell me and I would go put it in the book—the one that we have now, it would be version two. So version two is updated with things that were posted in the thread. . . . and now I have not been keeping up on the emails. In the beginning I replied to a lot of them. But I have not been keeping up with them. To be honest I don't really need them because people don't even know what they need. They can ask these questions but sometimes they will ask me a question and they will get an answer they weren't expecting because what they were asking is irrelevant.

Although Fee admitted that feedback has shaped the text, he invoked, as other authors did in their interviews, an individual authority discrete from, and in contradistinction to, the collective intelligence of the cultures of participation. Here mass participation and collaboration conflict with authors' assertiveness and perceptions of their own knowledge, an ironic persistence, perhaps, precisely because networked web structures are often alleged to produce a decentered authority.

Fee's experience complicates Gunther Kress's claims about authorship in the age of new media. On the one hand, the ease with which Fee self-published his ebook affirms Kress's contention that "authorship is no longer rare." On the other hand, the poker expert's experience goes against the grain of Kress's claim that as the "selection process" of the author wrought by mass communications and publishers fades, so too will there be "a consequent lessening in the author's or the text's authority."[26] Poker players wanted Fee's text precisely because it held authority. His poker performance contributed to the book's reputation, and online book reviews sanctioned the quality of the text. Poker strategy can inform decisions worth hundreds of dollars, and the authority of the text, whether digital or hard copy, is intensely important. In an activity in which less than 10 percent of players are long-term winners, the authority of the writer and his success at the game matter a great deal.

As noted, when the authors marketed their ebooks, they often promised revisions, and they championed the flexibility of the ebook as a virtue. However, the feedback that propelled these revisions—its volume, ubiquity, and speed—often threatened to exhaust the resources of the author and his desire to continually revise the text. The affordances of the medium and the patience of the authors were often at odds. Fee read through thousands of forum responses, private messages, and emails, all the correspondence that shaped the trajectory of his book; it was a daunting task, and the constant engagement with the text's readers brought fatigue and frustration. Revisions often stalled, in some cases because an author's developing skill eventually outstripped his ability or desire to update the ebook. This happened with Fee: as his poker knowledge and skill rapidly improved, his ebook became for him an affective instantiation of youth and immaturity; he began to view it as representing a period of naiveté in his development as a player. This was part of the reason that he stopped updating his text a year after it was published. Updating a text, having it become a serialized process, and exploiting the affordances of the medium presupposes a desire to engage the ideas of the text, which stops if an author's affective disposition toward the text becomes negative.

■■■

As a genre, the book review establishes a writer's authority in the absence of formal institutional or commercial publishing structures; it acts as a mediator, with characteristics of the publishing environment appearing as conventions in the review. Book reviews provide metacommentary on the value of the information contained in texts. This is an important point, since in some cases the potential buyer can only preview certain pages of an ebook before buying it; to browse an entire copy of a digital text is often to own a copy.

Because the poker texts were often expensive, book reviews became the sites of remarkably contentious discourse as writers and readers tried to assess whether a book was worth the investment. The reviews represented not only an assessment of the book but also a space for opening sustained discussion that acted as a surrogate for the presumed authority that marks print publications. At times unruly, the discussion channeled attention to a book and lent partial credibility; it joined back-channel recommendations and file sharing as ad hoc measures that readers took to assess the text's value.

The relationship of these debates to imaginary conceptions of community, to social writing practices, and to authorial ethos reinforce the idea that *self-publishing* is a misnomer. These books would be unlikely to have robust commercial lives if they were not published in established online communities. In this sense, *self-publishing* as a term that signifies publishing in online environments reinscribes the problematic individualism of the Romantic Author.

The processes that establish the credibility of digital texts exist as debates that are simultaneously situated and localized but also subjected to a multitude of pressures from the widely dispersed history of books and authorship. The characteristics of digital books and the interactions that surrounded them surfaced as genre conventions, and they provide evidence of how the destandardization of traditional publishing procedures occurring through digital environments enables the nature of information found in texts to exert intense pressure on writing practices. Although it's possible that these conventions will not surface in other contexts—and indeed, they might collapse with the poker economy—documenting them has provided evidence of the measures that participants will take to exploit the properties of new writing technologies in the service of achieving value for their work.

Hyperabundance and the Future of Books

MANY OF THE practices documented in this book represent precarious and transitional activity, writers learning to exploit tools that have significantly different affordances from tools in the age of print. Few of these practices are particularly stable, and in a sense this book has profiled pop-up economies that coalesce around particular sites or activities. There is no way to determine how sustainable or durable these practices might be, but it would be a mistake to think that the trajectory of self-publishing is tied to particular websites, companies, practices, or writing spaces. Amazon's policies have an enormous impact on self-published authors hoping to earn a living, and the identity of Wattpadders is contingent on the continued maintenance of that application, but neither Wattpad nor Amazon has had much to do with the deeper shifts that motivate the impetus to self-publish books—output that, along with other forms of web communication, has created extensive networks of digital culture.

Mass Authorship has outlined emerging literacy practices as they are forged in the midst of book cultures in the making in order to explicate an understanding of the activity emerging from the spread of widely accessible book-publishing technologies. Because of the relatively monolithic understanding of value that emanates from serious book culture, in which books hold value for their durability, rigor of research, contribution to knowledge, advancement of aesthetic form, and/or ability to influence the public discourse and debate, we have been unable to grasp the significance of the activity of self-publishing—some of it amateur and some of it professional. Here I have built a framework to elide the values of serious book culture in order to understand the urge of everyday people to write, network around, review, and discuss the books they produce. However, as each chapter has made clear, the centuries of history, expectations, and ideologies of the book surface in chaotic ways in the everyday practices this book has theorized. This ideological freight works simultaneously to arrest change and foster it. Any discussion of changes in book culture has to take into account the vast history of the codex, which has provided a litany of precedent practices—and recurring fears—that makes change difficult to understand. (It does not help that people who write about and study books also tend to be great fans of them.) The freight extends beyond the producers of book culture to the participants, bearing down on them through practices like reviewing and reading.

Mass authorship as an analytic framework allows us to rethink the questions of hyperabundance that have long dogged book culture. In her historical survey of complaints about book abundance, Ann Blair shows that scholars from antiquity have felt overwhelmed by the number of books and volume of knowledge. The printing press and the networked computer may have exacerbated the feeling, but Blair's examples, which predate the printing press, demonstrate that technological change does not necessarily cause the concerns. A number of these complaints sound contemporary. In 1680 Gottfried Wilhelm Leibniz lamented "the horrible mass of books which keep on growing . . . ; the indefinite multitude of authors will shortly expose them all to the danger of general oblivion." Another editor complained of the "flood and overflow of books," and yet another expressed the concern that "we have reason to fear that the multitude of books which grows every day in a prodigious fashion will make the following centuries fall into a state as barbarous as that of the centuries that followed the fall of the Roman Empire."[1]

Faced with hyperabundance and framed by gatekeeping, contemporary commentary creates the same lament: we will be flooded with books, and writing will be devalued. This complaint faces opposition from champions of new technologies who celebrate liberation from publishers and the fall of gatekeepers.

Mass Authorship has moved beyond these positions, concentrating less on the number of books and more on the practices that surround them. These practices complicate the extent to which digital publishing represents an exercise in freedom, and they show the gatekeepers (intermediaries) that appear in the vacuum that is left when professional publishers are no longer part of the value chain. These intermediaries include computer code, websites' terms of service, ideological residue from print, reader expectations, legal departments, family members, book reviews, microclimates, and technological access. As *Mass Authorship* has shown, these gatekeepers regulate abundance and quality by stalling or facilitating the circulation of books.

However those of us committed to serious books still worry about abundance not only because we want audiences for our own books and the books we like but also because accumulating stacks of unread books are grim reminders to bibliophiles of mortality and ignorance. Today we see a measurable increase in the quantity of books that are publicly accessible, but letting book lovers (a category in which I include myself) dictate the terms of the debate leads to potential distortions in how we understand the impact of abundance. Bibliophiles blithely describe abundance with metaphors of natural disasters—floods and tsunamis are favorites—without considering whether it is appropriate to compare the two situations: one situation consists of untold human misery, suffering, and cholera outbreaks, and the other situation consists of people having too many books to read.

I have a deep suspicion that the response of a popular fiction writer I interviewed is probably more representative of the way everyday readers treat the condition of hyperabundance. Toward the end of the interview, in which my interviewee had said that she reads many self-published books, I asked her how she negotiated the hyperabundance of them and their uneven quality. Preparing myself for a dramatic answer from someone who has been in the trenches of hyperabundance, I instead was surprised to hear her respond with a flatness that indicated she was somewhat puzzled by the question: "If I don't like a book, I stop reading it."

Gabriel Zaid's *So Many Books* is one of the few bibliophilic texts that does not lament the existence of too many books. With a pithy appreciation of reading and a measured admiration of the potential of digital technologies to create greater diversity in books, Zaid argues that the ability to scale down the book as a medium—that is, for writers to reach small audiences through inexpensively produced texts—is one of the book's greatest strengths. Zaid notes that when authors become anxious because their books do not sell well, it thwarts their ability to recognize the potential of small-scale publishing. Rather than recalibrate one's expectations toward the hardened fact that most books will only ever reach small audiences, the serious author, Zaid writes, frets about the dysfunction of the system: "Of course there will always be some author who, instead of appreciating the benefits of this system, will say, 'How is it possible that no more than fifty (or one hundred) copies of my *Deconstructive Hermeneutics* have been sold! There must be a conspiracy against me. Publishers and booksellers are in it for the money—they only promote books that are easy to sell. How will humanity, numbed by television and consumerism, hermeneutically deconstruct itself?'"[2]

In the same way that poststructuralism failed to dislodge the Romantic Author, so too have insights about intertextuality failed to dislodge many of the entrenched assumptions in the existing expectations for books—especially authors' expectations that their books should be widespread and influential, that their books should be something other than a quickly evaporating focal point in a never-ending stream of multimediated discourse. Understanding hyperabundance requires fundamentally reconfiguring how one conceives of the place of the book in discourse and developing a more nuanced understanding of how it shapes, and is shaped by, the networked media ecologies that surround it.

Zaid locates the fear of too many books, and the disappointment when a book does not sell well, in the author's dream of the world's undivided attention: "We complain about the confusion of languages, the multiplicity of conversations, because we dream of the world's undivided attention, beyond the grasp of our finiteness. But culture is a conversation without a center. The true universal culture isn't the utopian Global Village, gathered around a microphone; it is the Babel-like multitude of villages, each the center of the world."[3] Zaid's effort to situate the book as a medium in the decentered conversation of culture militates against the author's desire for his or her voice to be a medium that unifies and centralizes.

There are echoes of Mikhail Bakhtin's theory of discourse in the novel in Zaid's language. For Bakhtin, centripetal forces that unified language do exist, but centralization was never achievable; it was always an "essence posited" that stood in contrast to heteroglossia, the multiple and overlapping discourses that diversified and stratified language.[4] Zaid is applying a heteroglossic notion of language to the complete sum of books, whose abundance lays bare as fantasy the possibility of any individual author's voice centralizing attention.

Mass Authorship shows that if one situates the book deep in systems of literate activity in a way that accounts for multiple modes of communication and concentrates on embodied practice rather than on the object, complaints about too many books appear to make as much sense as complaints that there is too much language. The individual book may be a focal point of a diffuse conversation, but it is a focal point of limited privilege. This does not mean that so-called great books do not exist. It does mean that in an activity framework, the language, tools, material environments, and technological systems we use to venerate, canonize, appreciate, and preserve individual books are *part of*, and inseparable from, the individual book in its media ecology. This is something like a material, environmental, and embodied expansion of the poststructuralist account of intertextuality.

From this perspective, the systems used to venerate great books, effaced though they may be, also demonstrate the minute influence that any one text can have on the system as a whole. Popular books are often dismissed because of their ephemerality; such books do not lend themselves to re-reading or preservation. The consideration of hyperabundance and media ecologies, however, demands that we begin to rethink ephemeral engagement with books, precisely because in an environment of hyperabundance, ephemeral engagement with books is the dominant and normative mode of reading with any text, even a culture's most canonical.

The disappointed book author's failure to command the world's undivided attention is less about "the world" in Zaid's sense and more about the norm of the nation-state embedded in notions of the public and publicity that have constituted our conceptions of books. Book circulation has been transnational, but the processes and institutions that helped venerate individual books—like literary canon formation and educational institutions—were often involved in the formation of national languages, the nation-state, and national subjectivity.[5] These processes and institutions that codified certain "serious" books as canonical simultaneously created a standard for the publicness of the ideal book against which other authors and books would be judged. Thus the notion of publicity often embedded in our expectations for books is also laden with expectations of national influence, which underpins the disappointment when books do not spread widely. The size of the expected public is the source of disappointment Zaid finds in dispirited authors. To the extent that the book is tightly wrapped in vestiges of what constitutes a national public, then one of the most jarring changes to the book is not simply the transition to the economics of digital technologies but rather the deep renegotiations of public and private that are a defining feature of digital media.

If Deborah Brandt is correct, then what is motivating this drastic renegotiation of the book to a read-write medium and the renegotiations of the public embedded in it is closely linked to factors beyond technological change—to information capitalism, which set in motion a deep change in literacy. Brandt's claim about writing as the second stage of mass literacy indicates that never before have so many people been equipped with the competencies, tools, and technologies to engage in extended writing projects, but it also resituates discussions about gatekeepers in ways that go beyond the attempts I have made in this book. Brandt suggests that systems and discourses surrounding church and state have acted as pseudo-gatekeepers to writing writ large. But in her vision, these guardians have lost their influence over writing and have yielded to the demands of the information economy, which requires intense writing production. The surplus of this economy has manifested in this study in multifaceted ways: as writers either poaching time from work to write their books or appropriating digital competencies learned at work and bringing them to bear in their publishing practices. But beyond these immediate manifestations, this second stage of literacy does not portend that the number of books published will abate without some sort of drastic intervention. We can debate the value of hyperabundance, but we certainly cannot stop it.

The increasing value of writing to the economy and the spread of advanced writing competencies provide a curious background against which the wages of professional book authors appear to be falling. In 2014 the Authors Licensing and Collecting Society (ALCS) published a survey that showed a drastic decrease in the number of authors earning a living exclusively from writing. The survey also found a decrease in the wages of all writers, compared to a similar survey's results in 2005.[6] In response to this report, Nicola Solomon, the chief executive of the Society of Authors, railed against publishers, noting that for authors, traditional publishing was no longer "fair or sustainable"; writers saw earnings shrink while profits in the publishing industry increased. Solomon commented that traditional publishing still held prestige but that authors should consider whether they are better off self-publishing—a recommendation that would have been highly unlikely from an authors' guild when I began this project in 2007.[7]

I am neither an economist nor an expert in contemporary book-industry statistics. Yet these statistics fit into the narrative that networked computing and the web drive down the value of professional writing, a decline that seems to have had its most immediate impact on journalists. The decline in author salaries might be the result of amateur book production or digital technologies, and this decline might accelerate with the introduction of all-you-can-read book subscriptions to e-reader services. However, in terms of the relationship between authors and publishers, these statistics also fit into a century-old decline narrative that seems endemic to professional authorship and has always posited the past as a better time for book professionals. The ALCS survey looks grim, but it remains to be seen whether authors will increase their earnings when the multiple models of publishing now emerging stabilize. Even then *Mass Authorship* has shown that the outcome for each writer will be contingent on genres, reading cultures, technologies, legal regimes, and algorithms.

Although the ALCS report voiced concern that the decline in author salaries could have "serious implications for the breadth and quality of success of our creative industries in the UK," other considerations call this sweeping claim into question.[8] The overall quality and the breadth of human creative output is a difficult thing to measure, because regardless of the prima facie homogeneity or diversity of content, any measurement of this must also account for the ways that audiences exert their own creative energies on content through acts of interpretation and reimagination. Despite the intense difficulty of measuring the status of human creativity, cultural commentators have not been shy about making sweeping statements about the health of culture industries by drawing on personal experience and anecdote, statistics and surveys, dogma and belief. It is undoubtedly true that professional writers have produced magnificent works of culture, but that professional output has continually been linked to sponsorship that has attempted to insulate book production and authorship from the market: fellowships and grants, teaching posts, the largesse of wealthy benefactors, and spousal support. If cultures work to build infrastructures and institutions that provide a measure of insulation from the market, then the health (and politics) of those institutions must also be taken into account to determine the range of book production.

The perceived falling fortunes of professional writers aren't necessarily linked in a simple causal relationship to the health and breadth of a culture's creativity. Likewise, the health of a media technology, even one that we love, is not linked to the health of a culture in any simple causal way. Books that imply such a relationship (such as Nicholas Carr's *The Shallows*) misunderstand both the difficulty of establishing causal relationships and the synergy between media and modes of communication that makes it nearly impossible to isolate the effects of either one alone. Even with a number of twentieth-century studies about the economics of authorship, our understanding of who, how, and under what conditions writers became professional authors in the age of print is incomplete, and that makes it difficult to measure decline as we move toward hybrid print-digital models.

Although contemporary reports create serious concerns about the viability of creative professions in a time of horrendous and catastrophic income inequality, there are, I suspect, more influential factors in the growth and breadth of human creativity and the extent to which that creativity becomes inscribed in books; these factors include the size of human population and its growth, investment in education, distribution of wealth, nutrition, censorship and oppression, linguistic diversity, and access to writing, reading, and publishing technologies. This is not to be flippant about the difficulties of professional authors and the culture they produce. It is to recognize somewhat how widespread a competency writing has become, even if writers with what serious book culture recognizes as copious talent and training and dedication still remain scarce.

If we push the read-write understanding of the book to its extreme, perhaps the most radical question we can ask is whether, for particular commercial genres, the idea of writing a book will be as economically viable as the idea of reading a book, now that there are legions of writers willing to circulate their work for free or place it in databases that already have more ebooks than a reader could exhaust in ten lifetimes. This isn't simply about giant aggressive retailers working to destabilize the economics of content creation (although they probably are doing this to sell more devices), and it isn't just about consumers wanting inexpensive content or free content (although they do); it is also about the urge to create and the fact that writers will not stop writing no matter how often cultural elites plead with them.

The curmudgeonly book reviewer Will Manley once reflected on his career and noted that 99.9 percent of self-published print books were "drivel" but that 0.1 percent of self-published books were worthy of "serious consideration" and potential "gems."[9] If Manley was even partially correct, and if we think about books from a read-only perspective that applies professional standards of value, then self-published authors in the next decade will produce more inexpensively priced "gems" than a single reader could exhaust in a lifetime, if they haven't already. Again, it is crucial to note that hyperabundance looks different in various contemporary book cultures and for various reading practices, and the state of the book is never determined solely by the state of the market for it. Fiction and memoir do not have the same barriers to production as intensely researched works of nonfiction do, for example.

Amazon illustrates the conundrum of abundance and its potential benefits and drawbacks. Amazon has a reputation for dubious—if not outright exploitative—labor practices and deals aggressively with suppliers. It requires particular hardware and software to access, and its willingness to subsist on anemic profits for the sake of expansion has earned it the accusation that it is driving independent bookstores out of business as it rapidly approaches monopoly status. At the same time, for those with access to it, this centralization has produced a far more diverse selection of materials than any brick-and-mortar bookstore. This diversity is tenuous, however—regulated through human activity, interaction, and algorithms and all in the service of profit and aggressive expansion.

Laura Miller found that booksellers often misunderstood the history of their own occupation as they imagined a golden age of flourishing book culture that has forever receded.[10] The history of authors, books, and publishing shows many iterations of this nostalgia, particularly in the twentieth century. Such nostalgia is problematically directed to a golden age dominated by men, but the nostalgia nonetheless often betrays a commitment among book professionals to truth, craft, and art. Although the ideology is flawed in many ways, it has contained a series of ideals that problematized the book's relationship to the commercial market through mechanisms like cross-subsidies.

By being an intermediary that operates through algorithms that always maximize profit under the auspices of consumer empowerment and relevance, Amazon can have profound influence on book culture with no particular commitment to anything except profit, the alleged scientific objectivity of algorithms that maximizes its earnings, and the interests of the nebulous consumer whom it knows intimately because of aggressive and invasive data collection. For indie authors, Amazon has been a boon, but many of those I interviewed cast as wary an eye on Amazon as they did on professional publishers.

If nothing else, complaints about abundance remind us how damaging the brachylogy of the book has been to understanding plural forms of books and authorship by homogenizing a group of practices that should be not homogenized. This is especially true because even though digital book cultures are never very far away from one another on the Internet, they can become quite siloed to the degree that the only point of commonality is the communications media to which they are oriented.

A better approach would be sensitive to drastically different media ecologies. Contemporary book ecologies require that books and authors be understood with plural standards of value, without one standard being inappropriately or blindly imposed on an alien situation. When this does happen, the result is all too often crass elitism from book professionals toward popular practice and blind dismissal from ordinary readers toward serious books. A classic example appears in portrayals of booksellers and libraries in twentieth-century trade literature: a book professional complains about the quality of a self-published book after a sour experience with a self-published author who was aggressively marketing his or her work and insisting that the bookstore or library offer a copy for sale or loan. In many cases, the professional who is criticizing the self-published author acts with the same misrecognition as the self-published author whose book does not meet the professional standards of the institutions he or she wants to access: both fail to recognize the mutual coexistence of the standards of value that the term *book* obscures, and both fail to treat the book by the appropriate standard, which is itself slippery and contextual, existing in relationship to writer and reader experience.

The writers who have been profiled in *Mass Authorship* live on the cusp of the book's transition from read-only to read-write, and they experienced this when the very technologies that allowed them to publish also rendered outmoded their notions of the book. One writer noted her exasperation with the very technology she used to publish when it was applied to finding readers, because the read-only expectations she had for the book clashed with they ways she deployed self-publishing technologies: "In part, I can't go say, 'You're kidding me. Everybody and their mother is writing a book,' because I was, and I have been, everybody and their mother." Ultimately, *Mass Authorship* has grappled with shifting systems of mediation, and it has attempted to rethink some of the dynamics that exist—and that will either intensify or disappear—as the abundance of books increases, in a time when it only *seems* like everyone's an author.

APPENDIX

Notes on Methods

QUALITATIVE RESEARCH works well for studying emerging practices and nebulously defined populations. It can be exploratory, and it can document a wide range of practices rather than concentrate on what is representative. The knowledge claims in this book come from studies of four different groups of writers, with the research methods adjusted slightly to account for the context of each study, and I received Institutional Review Board (IRB) approval for each study and informed consent from every participant I interviewed. On the whole, I blended Barney Glaser and Anselm Strauss's grounded theory approach to qualitative research with Christine Hine's approach to Internet ethnography. Grounded theory enabled me to compare the experiences of the authors in different groups to generate a midrange theoretical understanding of their writing experience, whereas Internet ethnography offered guidance on how to proceed studying online populations.[1] Internet ethnography focuses attention on mediated social interaction; concentrates on flow and connectivity with an ongoing negotiation of ethnographic boundaries; works through spatial and temporal disjunctions with research participants; and refuses to make a clear-cut distinction between online and offline contexts.[2] In this appendix I document the methods I used to produce my knowledge claims, and then I address some particular research challenges that arose during the process.

Because I blended grounded theory with Internet ethnography, my knowledge claims materialized from three different kinds of investigation. First, there was a defined corpus of data that I subjected to grounded theory coding and analytic procedures. This corpus was slightly different for each group of writers, but it included eighty-one original interviews, follow-up interviews, and the web texts I collected that were related to the authors' books. I coded the data from each group of writers separately to account for their diverse experiences, and then I analyzed the groups as a whole using categories that commonly appeared across the entire data set.

The second source of the knowledge claims came from the tacit ethnographic knowledge I acquired about writing and publishing dynamics, which came from participating and lurking in two online writing communities that read and discussed ebooks and digital publishing. These communities were the Two Plus Two poker community, centralized on the discussion forums of Two Plus Two Publishing's website, and the online community at Wattpad.com. I spent a large amount of time reading blog posts, book reviews, and forum discussions in a volume that far exceeded my ability to use this information in a formal way. This enabled me to contextualize the data I did code in the larger dynamics of the online writing communities from which the ebooks I studied emerged. It could be argued that this experience was not ethnographic because it was primarily mediated engagement with the online communities, but I think that seeing writing and events unfold in almost real time in online communities leads to tacit understanding that is analogous to, but certainly not the same as, embodied interaction with a community, the hallmark of ethnography.

The third source of my knowledge claims has been the nebulously defined stream of online discourse related to contemporary writing and publishing. I have spent substantial time wading through the copious amount of contemporary commentary on digital publishing that often appears on the web. I read industry and popular news sources. I read popular blogs, viral content, and Twitter streams. I lurked on discussion boards populated by writing and publishing professionals for about seven years. Although this "grazing" was no doubt an unsystematic part of the study, it is nevertheless worth mentioning because it provided me with a litany of different voices and perspectives to consider as the claims in this book came into focus, and epistemologically speaking, it was not discourse that I could bracket or completely ignore when I analyzed the more restricted data set.

Studying Nonfiction Niche Writing

In 2007 my own experience of learning to play poker led me to believe that it was a strategic setting for studying participants negotiating problems of interest to contemporary writing researchers: they were establishing credibility in online spaces, producing multimodal texts, and collaborating through peer-to-peer production to produce informational goods. After observing the activity on various discussion forums for some time, I witnessed the gradual emergence of more than a dozen ebooks that were self-published by the players and that became the anchor for an incredible amount of discussion in the community. Some players who built individual coaching programs began codifying their programs in ebooks. Other players wrote books simply because they had time on their hands when they weren't playing poker, and some just wanted to give back to the community that helped them learn poker, so they wrote books and posted them for free. I began concentrating on ebooks because they were a way of binding the project that had, to that point, suffered from sprawl as it followed participants' mediated engagement throughout multiple contexts and media.

I created an archive of digital data that documented interactions between ebook authors and reader-writers. I used this archive to begin open coding to develop provisional categories to explain how ebooks and authorship were being created.[3] Four provisional categories accounted for many of the literacy practices that surrounded the ebooks: (1) textual production, (2) publicity generation, (3) distribution and intellectual property, and (4) peer review and communal sanction. I used these four categories as an analytic basis for the theoretical sampling that drove the second round of data collection, a series of hour-long interviews conducted over the course of three months with semistructured interview techniques. I interviewed thirty-five participants involved in ebook production, distribution, and review, including authors, editors, web designers, readers, and book reviewers. I conducted face-to-face interviews with nine of the participants, and I interviewed twenty-six using Voice over Internet Protocol.

I selected the interview participants on the basis of theoretical sampling, which Strauss describes as a process of data collection that is controlled by an emerging theory.[4] In practice, however, because the emerging theory concentrated on authorship (and thus authority), the sample closely resembled one derived from purposive sampling, and most of the participants were community insiders. The age, sex, and ethnicity of the participants largely reflected the conventional wisdom of poker players in the Two Plus Two community at the time, who imagined their demographics as young, white, American males. Thirty-two of the participants were between the ages of twenty and twenty-nine. The sample was exclusively male. Thirty-one of the participants identified as white, and four identified as Asian American.

My interviewing techniques remained constant with all four groups. I worked from different protocols for each group, but the interviews were semistructured and unfolded like a conversation. Each interview was directed by the prior knowledge I had amassed about a participant by the web data available about him or her, and I did not pose each question to the participants with the precise language of the protocols. Rather, the questions indicated the information that I sought about each participant, and as that information came up during the interview I checked it off the list I had created. This enabled me to create a more fluid interview and to ask follow-up questions specific to each participant.

I began coding the interview data for the poker players using the four initial categories outlined above as a guide. I relied on some codes I had already established, whereas others emerged from the interview data that had not stemmed from the web data. I discovered that the experiences the authors revealed in the interviews aligned closely with the experiences described in the web data I had already archived. Thus, my four initial categories remained durable through the second round of data collection, and I used those categories to finalize the more elaborate coding scheme I used throughout the rest of the study, at which point I went through and recoded the interviews.

After I had analyzed the data, I conducted follow-up interviews with some participants to clarify points in the original interviews; many of these follow-up interviews were text based, completed through email and instant-messaging systems. I also continued to archive new digital data about ebooks and authorship from various websites, and I coded the data using the established scheme. I continued this process until 2011.

From Poker Ebooks to Memoir Writing

Because the publishing practices of the poker players were highly contextual, I expanded the study to include different kinds of writers—groups that would offer points of comparison with the data from the study of online poker communities. At the time, self-publishing was growing rapidly, in part because e-readers and tablets were growing in popularity, and books could be published for them for minimal cost. I chose to study memoir writers because that genre had increased in popularity in the 1990s and the first decade of the 2000s, leading to what some were calling a memoir boom. Personal experience forms the basis for the text, so it is often referred to as an accessible genre. Anecdotal evidence from the publishing industry suggests that during the twentieth century, memoirs were one of the most frequently rejected genres from publishers and thus a common genre for vanity presses. Many memoirs were reported to have come from the pens of retirees who had worked in lettered professions, such as clergy and teachers.

I found the memoirists by searching the public database of Lulu.com, a print-on-demand site that offers a number of different services to self-published authors. Because at the time the driving concept of my project was focused on an emerging theory of authorship, theoretical sampling techniques did little to narrow the potential sample; I was interested in interviewing people who claimed authorship of texts about their experiences. To establish the sample, I used Lulu's sorting filters to find autobiographies. I sorted them by publication date, with the most recently published memoirs appearing first, a choice I made specifically because the publication process of the authors would be recent. At the time, Lulu had some professionally published memoirs in its database, so I went through its listings using the metadata to find self-published memoirs.

After I found names of memoirists, I used search engines to try to locate the authors, which I was able to do because many had personal websites about their books. I contacted authors only if their contact information was public and accessible on the web. Truly random sampling in qualitative research is difficult to achieve; I had no control over which books would appear from the database, and the process was thus somewhat more random than some other sampling methods available to qualitative researchers. To follow I discuss some of the consequences of my sampling methods on the knowledge claims I make in this book.

Before I interviewed the memoirists through Skype, I studied the web texts associated with their work, including reviews, personal websites, and promotional materials. I also read as many of the memoirs as I could before I interviewed the writers, although in some cases I interviewed them before reading their books. Based on information gleaned from the web texts, I developed a semistructured interview protocol about the memoirists' writing and publishing practices. Some of these questions were specific to memoir writing, but to the extent that I could, I asked similar questions of the memoirists as of the poker players so I could compare their experiences. I open-coded the interview data and developed four categories to explain the experiences of the memoirists: (1) writing process and emotions, (2) legacies of books and authorship, (3) the process of learning to publish, and (4) micropublics. Each category included a number of codes.

I interviewed a total of eighteen memoirists. Their ages ranged from twenty-five to eighty. Eleven were men and seven were women, and their educations ranged from some high school to advanced graduate degrees. This sample was concentrated in the United States, with one participant from England. Fourteen memoirists identified as white, and four identified as African American.

Recreational Romance Writers

In the summer and fall of 2011, I conducted a study of writers who published on Wattpad, an open, free, user-generated content website that allows writers and readers to share ebooks. Wattpad is dominated by fiction. At the time the site was heavily trafficked and has since only grown larger. To narrow the potential participant pool, I concentrated on romance writing. It was the most popular genre of writing on Wattpad at the time, and popular romance reading also has an extensive body of academic literature developed around it, which helped acquaint me with some of the history and dynamics of the genre. The choice was also an attempt to include a gender-balanced range of voices in the study: romance fiction has historically been written by women, and up to that point my sample was male-dominated because of the poker study.

Sampling proved difficult. Many of the participants on Wattpad were anonymous by choice and had no public contact information available on the web. In addition, my IRB approval limited the potential participant pool to writers at least eighteen years of age, and many of the participants appeared to be between the ages of thirteen and eighteen. I was working with a research assistant in the summer, and I had her scour Wattpad to locate potential interview participants using three different selection criteria. First, she looked for participants who were eighteen or older.

Second, she looked for participants with more than forty-nine pages of writing uploaded to the site ("page," as defined by the Wattpad site architecture), since forty-nine pages is the number that UNESCO has decided is the minimum number of pages necessary to constitute a book.[5] The decision was also tied to the fact that participants with more than forty-nine pages uploaded had spent more time on the site and would thus be a richer source of data.

Third, the writers had to have had some sort of public contact information. My research assistant generated sixty names, and I assigned each a number and used a random number generator to randomize the sample. We contacted potential participants and stopped once we had received responses from twenty participants, which nearly exhausted the original list of sixty names.

In a process similar to the one I used with the memoirists, I studied the profiles of the romance writers with my research assistant and developed a semistructured interview protocol that shared questions with the first two protocols yet also included questions about romance writing and the Wattpad experience in particular. There were a total of eighteen interviews, the sample was entirely female, and most writers were between the ages of twenty and twenty-nine. Twelve of the writers lived in the United States, three lived in England, one in Norway, one in Canada, and one in the Philippines. Fifteen of the writers identified as white, two as African American, and one as Filipina. After we transcribed the interviews, my research assistant and I collaboratively open-coded them and generated four guiding categories that dominated the data, which I used to guide the second round of coding: (1) publishing and attention, (2) plagiarism, (3) quantitative data feedback, and (4) recursive writing and reading processes.

After coding the data from the poker players, memoirists, and romance writers individually, I developed a set of broader categories that were common to all three sets: (1) peer-to-peer production, (2) legacies of print authorship and books, (3) intellectual property, and (4) the process of learning to publish. I then recoded the three data sets using these categories as a way of comparing samples. When I finally interviewed the bestselling popular fiction writers in 2014, I did not open-code. I simply coded the sample using this categorical scheme.

Bestselling Popular Fiction (Indie) Authors

When I began the study in 2007, self-published books for sale were largely isolated to small niche topics and discussed in the corners of the web. By the time I concluded my analysis on the first three groups of writers, more and more self-published authors were earning a living from their writing, and more and more were hitting bestseller lists. In early 2014 I used a list from a reputable publishing industry website to compile a list of bestselling authors so I could include this perspective in the study. These authors had bestselling ebooks on Amazon in late 2013 and early 2014, and they represented a phenomenon so new that it would not have been possible to study them when I began in 2007. (Indeed, it might not have been possible to study them until sometime around 2012, when the number of indie authors who had bestsellers grew to such a critical mass that companies began to track them specifically.)

The bestseller lists I used yielded sixty-five names; I randomized them and contacted each author. This randomization process was something of a moot point, given that I had to exhaust the list simply to schedule ten interviews. I read samples of the authors' work and their websites and followed the same procedures to design the semistructured interview protocol, drawing common questions from previous protocols and developing new ones that seemed unique to the experiences of these writers. The sample resulted in eight women and two men, and all were American, all of whom were white.

All these authors wrote fiction. The sample included authors of science fiction, thrillers, fantasy, young adult novels, new adult novels, romance, and erotic romance. The discrepancy between men and women warrants future research. The conventional wisdom among indie authors is that female authors sell more books in many of the bestselling fiction genres. They attribute this to the fact that American women seem to read fiction almost twice as much as men do.[6] Given widespread accusations that the publishing industry is biased toward male authors, however, it is worth investigating in the future if more indie authors are female because they feel shut out from trade publishing. Because I had already used four established categories to code the other three sets of data, I did not open-code the interviews with the bestsellers. I simply coded the sample using this categorical scheme (documented above).

Mass Authorship and the Limits of Qualitative Internet Research

Qualitative methods function well to identify and theorize a range of emergent social phenomena. They do have significant limits, however. Although I tried to introduce some randomness into my sampling decisions, the process was ultimately nonprobability sampling and reveals a number of biases that were the result of access to participants, sites of research, geography, and linguistic barriers. Although the Internet affords the opportunity to conduct qualitative research on widely distributed populations, researchers—especially those in the humanities with little access to grant money—still face linguistic, material, and temporal constraints (e.g., difficulties of synchronizing schedules with an interviewee because of time zones) that make it difficult though not impossible to achieve international representation.

The knowledge claims I make in this book have been heavily inflected by the dominance of Americans and of participants who identified as white, which suggests that the diversity of practices surrounding books—the functions of books in people's lives, diverse routes of production and distribution, and plural forms of materiality—does not necessarily indicate diversity of content within them, nor does it necessarily indicate diversity of authorship. Overall, 10 percent of the sample participants lived in countries other than the United States, 14 percent identified as nonwhite,

74 percent had some sort of higher education, and 59 percent were male. At the moment there's no research that shows whether these numbers reflect the demographics of self-publishing as a whole; the dominance of participants who identify as white, however, does reflect the lack of diversity in the traditional publishing industry.[7]

To an extent, the lack of international representation is an outcome of the sites where I conducted my research. All the websites from which I drew samples were located in North America. The game of poker began in the United States, and American companies dominated the economy of instruction, although there have been instructional sites in Europe. Lulu.com, the site from which I drew the sample of memoirists, is an American print-on-demand company, and the sample reflects this. On a more cynical note, it might also reflect what has been said to be Americans' willingness to talk about themselves through autobiographical writing. The bestseller popular fiction lists came from US-based Amazon.com, and although there was significant international representation in my initial pool of potential interviewees, logistics and a lack of international volunteers created an American-dominated sample.

The sample from Wattpad was American dominated, which is curious, given the large international user base it draws. I believe this reflects questions about access to technologies and about the kinds of writers most likely to upload ebooks as user-generated content. Based in Canada, Wattpad draws only 40 percent of its users from the United States. It has a large international reach, with many visitors from Asia. The site was built primarily for mobile technologies, and 75 percent of Wattpad's traffic is mobile.[8] Yet in my interview sample, Americans still outnumbered international participants by a two-to-one margin. This could have to do with the sampling technique, which was criteria-based sampling and not random sampling.

There are some other possible explanations, however. Given that Wattpad is a site for long-form writing, it could also show that many of the writers who uploaded forty-nine pages of writing had access to computers and were not posting their writing on mobile technologies like smartphones. Despite the emerging popularity of short-form writing that culminates in long-form text—the so-called cell-phone novels that have been a popular form of writing in Japan—book writers still seem to prefer computers, and all the writers I interviewed from Wattpad reported writing their ebooks on computers.

The sample also skewed toward writers who were actively seeking audiences for their work and had public contact information. This means that *Mass Authorship* did not fully address enough writers who self-publish for personal reasons—for example, to produce a cookbook as a family heirloom or to give away as a Christmas gift. Although I did interview a number of writers who used pseudonyms on the books they authored, my sample could also not account for fiction writers who bent their identity (e.g., their sex, sexual identity, or age) under the mask of Internet anonymity. This is more likely to happen, I suspect, in fiction than in memoir or nonfiction, where the ethos of the writer is important.

In sum, my approach to this research project did not address the full potential of self-publishing to contribute to mass authorship. It did address writers whose books would probably never have been published in the twentieth century—that is, writers who would have otherwise been shut out of traditional publishing. However, it failed to address groups of writers, such as African American authors, who have historically been excluded from the publishing establishment, and whether members of diverse groups use self-publishing as a potential route around exclusion. This is clearly a gap in the study and an opportunity for future research.

Participant Anonymity

Finally, I would like to address the question of participant anonymity and explain the hybrid approach to it that I used in this study. Qualitative researchers have long anonymized participants for a number of reasons, not the least of which is the ethical obligation to do the subjects no harm. As I began this study, I realized that in some cases I would be unable to cite web data related to ebooks if I anonymized my participants. Readers would simply be able to search for the text online and in many cases determine the identities of the participants. Because the writers I interviewed all had public lives online, I indicated in my IRB applications that I would provide my participants with the option to forgo anonymity, and when I asked the authors if I could use their real names, eighty of the eighty-one writers agreed.

In some initial publications, I used the real names of my participants, but as I moved further into the research, I became less satisfied with the prospect of doing the same for everyone. I thus decided to employ a hybrid approach and use real names in some cases and pseudonyms in others. This decision hinged on two considerations. First, it is not immediately clear to me that we have a solid grasp of what the long-term consequences of the web and social media will be for privacy and surveillance. There have been some exaggerated claims that the "Internet doesn't forget," but some publicly available digital texts (especially those not circulated widely) are indeed deleted, and search engine optimization techniques make it possible to bury information deep in search results. I thought about this as I read a discussion forum post of a self-published author I did not interview. He had returned from serving in the military in Iraq and had subsequently published a scathing critique of the leadership in his unit. He had apparently experienced some negative consequences, and the discussion post indicated that he had spent considerable time trying to remove his book from the various databases that held it.

In one sense, this case serves as yet another hackneyed reminder that Internet users need to consider the possible consequences before writing in public. But as a researcher, I wondered how my research would have affected this writer's ability to recede from the public had I interviewed him and written about his experience, especially because databases that store academic articles are likely to be more durable than other kinds of texts available through the web. Had he managed to remove all traces of his book from the web (and he was already having limited success), his story would have still lingered in my text if I were to have published it through some sort of open-access journal.

Given the multiple concerns about digital privacy, it is not difficult, hypothetically speaking, to imagine a huge privacy blowback in the United States that results in European-style "right to be forgotten" legislation, which would make it easier for an author to "unpublish" a text, or to delete the search results that mention it. But it is unlikely that such legislation would extend to academic research, especially when the participant had signed a form consenting to his or her name being used. On the one hand, then, I wanted to respect the ability of my participants to choose whether I used their real names and then be able to trust that they would adapt their conversations with me accordingly. On the other hand, digital volatility makes it extremely difficult to understand how issues of privacy and digital memory will evolve. The more I considered all the hypothetical situations, the less I was inclined to use real names unless it was necessary.

There is, however, an important consideration beyond ethics when determining whether to anonymize participants. Annukka Vainio has questioned the extent to which using people's real names interferes with the researcher's independence when making claims about the participants. There have been a number of debates about whether participant anonymity leads to greater objectivity for the researcher's knowledge claims or to an unduly harsh analysis of the participants protected through the guise of anonymity.[9] Despite approaching this project from an emic perspective, which sought to examine how the participants understood their writing and publishing lives, my research inevitably required bringing the experiences of the participants into a dialogue with academic literature. I felt some minor distress during this process when writing about participants with their real names; the existence of the names tacitly shaped the claims I was making in what I ultimately thought were undesirable ways.

After deciding to employ a hybrid approach I used a number of factors to determine in each case whether I should anonymize the participant: (1) whether the participant wanted to have his or her real name used, (2) how potentially sensitive the interview information was and whether the author had revealed it in other web spaces or in his or her book, (3) whether I needed to quote any data about the case from the web, (4) the extent to which using the author's real name would impinge on my ability to make fair knowledge claims about his or her experience, and (5) the overall size of the participant's online presence. Although not ideal, the hybrid approach allowed me to negotiate what I still consider to be largely open questions about conducting Internet research.

Notes

Introduction

1. Umberto Eco, "Afterword," in *The Future of the Book*, ed. Geoffrey Nunberg (Berkeley: University of California Press, 1996), 301.

2. Although the contemporary publishing industry seems to have adopted *e-book* as the preferred spelling of the term, I use *ebook* for two reasons. As I will explain, many of the ebooks I studied would not meet industry standards for what counts as an e-book, and so industry terminology is not completely germane. Moreover, I think *e-book* will eventually be reduced to *ebook* through popular usage in the same way *e-mail* has shrunk to *email* in many places. I retain the hypen in *e-reader*, however, since *ereader* is visually awkward.

3. Raffaele Simone, "The Body of the Text," in *The Future of the Book*, ed. Geoffrey Nunberg (Berkeley: University of California Press, 1996), 239.

4. Jana Bradley et al., "Nontraditional Book Publishing," *First Monday* 16, no. 8 (2011): n.p. *Hyperabundance* is used by this source to describe the digital output of nontraditional publishing in an attempt to quantify the number of self-published books now being produced.

5. In the contemporary publishing industry, the claim that there are many more manuscripts than publishers want to print is largely conventional wisdom based on ubiquitous anecdote. But research on nineteenth-century publishing shows that manuscripts were already so abundant that even reputable publishers offered to print books at the authors' expense, either because they did not want to risk investment in the books or because they received more submissions than they could handle. See Leslie Howsam, *Kegan Paul: A Victorian Imprint; Publishers, Books and Cultural History* (New York: Routledge, 1998); see also Michael Winship, *American Literary Publishing in the Mid-Nineteenth Century: The Business of Ticknor and Fields* (New York: Cambridge University Press, 2003), 40–53.

6. Edward Uhlan, *The Rogue of Publishers' Row: Confessions of a Publisher* (New York: Exposition Press, 1968), 174.

7. Smashwords keeps a running counter of its words published on its website, https://www.smashwords.com. As of February 2016 the counter registered more than fourteen billion words.

8. "Self-Publishing in the United States, 2008–2013." Bowker, March, 16, 2016, http://www.bowker.com/documents/self-publishing-report-in-united-states-2008-2013.html. Bowker includes all texts published through certain ebook distributors as "self-published," and it could be the case that some small independent publishers are using these services, too.

9. Maria Cootauco, "Wattpad: A Way for Indie Authors to Build an Audience," *Publishers Weekly*, June 2, 2013, http://www.publishersweekly.com/pw/by-topic/authors/pw-select/article/57649-wattpad-a-way-for-indie-authors-to-build-an-audience.html.

10. Joel Waldfogel and Imke Reimers, "Storming the Gatekeepers: Digital Disintermediation in the Market for Books," *Information Economics and Policy* 31 (June 2015): 47–58.

11. Matthew G. Kirschenbaum, *Mechanisms: New Media and the Forensic Imagination* (Cambridge, MA: MIT Press, 2008).

12. Richard A. Grusin, "What Is an Electronic Author?: Theory and the Technological Fallacy." *Configurations* 2, no. 3 (1994): 469–83.

13. Shirky made this argument most explicitly in an interview entitled "How We Will Read," which was originally published on Findings.com, but all links to that site were dead as of this writing. The interview was widely reported in publishing industry news. Some of the ideas also appear in Clay Shirky, *Here Comes Everybody: The Power of Organizing without Organizations* (New York: Penguin Press, 2008).

14. Technological predictions about the book often function on the logic of supersessionism (that the new technology will surpass the old) and the logic of liberation (that the new technology will lead to greater human freedom). Paul Duguid, "Material Matters: The Past and Futurology of the Book," in *The Future of the Book*, ed. Geoffrey Nunberg (Berkeley: University of California Press, 1996), 65. For a number of anxieties about self-publishing decimating the eighteenth-century publishing industry, see Andrew Piper, *Book Was There: Reading in Electronic Times* (Chicago: University of Chicago Press, 2012), 160.

15. Timothy Laquintano, "Sustained Authorship: Digital Writing, Self-Publishing, and the Ebook," *Written Communication* 27, no. 4 (2010): 469–93; Michael Bhaskar, *The Content Machine: Towards a Theory of Publishing, from the Printing Press to the Digital Network* (New York: Anthem Press, 2013); Waldfogel and Reimers, "Storming the Gatekeepers"; Ann Haugland, "Opening the Gates: Print-on-Demand Publishing as Cultural Production," *Publishing Research Quarterly* 22, no. 3 (2006): 3–16.

16. Evgeny Morozov, *To Save Everything, Click Here: The Folly of Technological Solutionism* (New York: Public Affairs, 2013), 5–7.

17. Ibid., 165.

18. Laura J. Miller, "Whither the Professional Book Publisher in an Era of Distribution on Demand?", in *The International Encyclopedia of Media Studies*, vol. 2, ed. Angharad N. Valdivia and Vicki Mayer (Chichester, UK: Wiley-Blackwell, 2013), 173.

19. Shirky, *Here Comes Everybody*, 78.

20. Since its formalization as an academic discipline in the latter half of the twentieth century, writing studies has sought to explain the meaning of writing in people's lives and describe how people negotiate worlds saturated with writing—how it shapes their identities and sense of being, their economic and social opportunities, and their processes of learning and communicating. Largely supported with historical accounts of literacy and contemporary studies of literacy in natural settings, the field of writing studies has challenged the understanding that literacy is a technical skill, an act of decoding that one learns when one is young and then easily transfers to diverse kinds of practices that require symbolic interaction. Literacy learning has become understood as something that is lifelong and situated in multiple and overlapping discourse communities, each of which has its own conventions, values, genres, and assumptions that writers need to learn to succeed in it. Literacy is an ongoing and situated process of lifelong learning, then, rather than a binary of literate-illiterate.

21. Paul Prior, *Writing/Disciplinarity: A Sociohistoric Account of Literate Activity in the Academy* (Mahwah, NJ: Erlbaum, 1998), 3–13. There is one important note about the terms I use in this book, and that is the difference between the way literacy scholars and book professionals use the term *genre*. In the book industry, it is typically a marketing term that classifies books by one or more commonalities in content or form. In writing studies, a genre has been defined as a kind of recurrent social situation that represents "typified rhetorical action." Carolyn Miller, "Genre as Social Action," *Quarterly Journal of Speech* 70, no. 2 (1984): 151. Efforts have been made to reconcile this difference by synthesizing the term's two usages. See Julie Rak, *Boom!: Manufacturing Memoir for the American Public* (Waterloo, ON: Wilfrid Laurier University Press, 2013). I discuss this difference more extensively in chapter 6.

22. Charles Bazerman and David Russell, eds., "Introduction," in *Writing Selves/Writing Societies: Research from Activity Perspectives* (Fort Collins, CO: WAC Clearinghouse, 2002), 1.

23. Clay Spinuzzi, "Losing by Expanding: Corralling the Runaway Object," *Journal of Business and Technical Communication* 25, no. 4 (2011): 449–86. Spinuzzi argues that some of the purer strains of activity theory concentrate on how tools and systems of labor transform an object and, strictly speaking, have been less successful studying objects that circulate in the public sphere. However, to the

extent possible, I have used *literate activity* to highlight the kinds of labor, collaboration, media, and modes that participants engage in to transform writing into books that circulate on the Internet. This has enabled me to show how systems typically associated with publishing (e.g., preventing copyright infringement), become infused into the embodied and discursive work of writing as writers work with readers to create and circulate texts they value.

24. John B. Thompson, *Merchants of Culture* (Malden, MA: Polity, 2010), 10.

25. Michel Foucault, "What Is an Author?", in *The Foucault Reader*, ed. Paul Rabinow (New York: Pantheon Books, 1984), 101–20. For an extensive discussion of this contradiction, see Kathleen Fitzpatrick, *Planned Obsolescence: Publishing, Technology, and the Future of the Academy* (New York: New York University Press, 2011), 50–88.

26. Casey Boyle, "Low Fidelity in High Definition: Speculations on Rhetorical Editions," in *Rhetoric and the Digital Humanities*, ed. Jim Ridolfo and Bill Hart-Davidson (Chicago: University of Chicago Press, 2014), 127. Boyle discusses the relationship of rhetorical scholarship to what he calls traditional literary scholarship: "Rhetoricians are not as interested in what a text *is* as we are in what a text *does*."

27. Prior, *Writing/Disciplinarity*, 138.

28. Siva Vaidhyanathan, *Copyrights and Copywrongs: The Rise of Intellectual Property and How It Threatens Creativity* (New York: New York University Press, 2003), 8–11.

29. Foucault, "What Is an Author?", 107.

30. Of course, these are not the only two models of authorship that exist, nor are they the only two studied. Researchers have also explored collaborative models of authorship, work for hire, authorship in new media, and models afforded by digital technologies. See, e.g., Lisa Ede and Andrea Lunsford, *Singular Texts/Plural Authors: Perspectives on Collaborative Writing* (Carbondale: Southern Illinois University Press, 1992); and Lev Manovich, "Models of Authorship in New Media," 2002, http://manovich.net/content/04-projects/032-models-of-authorship-in-new-media/32_article_2002.pdf.

31. Vaidhyanathan, *Copyrights and Copywrongs*, 10.

32. Deborah Brandt, *Literacy in American Lives* (New York: Cambridge University Press, 2001); Harvey J. Graff, *The Legacies of Literacy: Continuities and Contradictions in Western Culture and Society* (Bloomington: Indiana University Press, 1987). When I talk about the legacies of books and authorship, I mean to resonate with Graff's term "legacies of literacy." Graff's work on the history of literacy emphasizes the traditions and continuities associated with literacy (like religion) that cling to it and become recontextualized to shape new scenes of mass literacy and literacy learning. But Graff also emphasizes the various contradictions that exist simultaneously with traditions. For example, although literacy has been inexorably linked to "development, growth, and progress," Graff finds many

instances in which economic development happened with surprisingly low levels of literacy (10–12). I use the term *legacy* to indicate the various traditions associated with books and authorship that appear at sites of literacy learning that include books, but with the caveat that these traditions manifest in sometimes chaotic and very inconsistent ways.

33. Ted Striphas, *The Late Age of Print: Everyday Book Culture from Consumerism to Control* (New York: Columbia University Press, 2009), 8.

34. Lawrence Lessig, *Remix: Making Art and Commerce Thrive in the Hybrid Economy* (New York: Penguin Press, 2008), 36–83.

35. For books, these complaints reach farther into the past than the twentieth century. A nineteenth-century English writer reviewed a book subsidized by an author and noted caustically: "There is something irresistibly pathetic in the spectacle of a learned man issuing a work in eight large volumes to illustrate a theory which will certainly not find acceptance by any mind but the author's." Quoted in Howsam, *Kegan Paul*, 131-32.

36. Media like zines and newsletters show that there is a long history of localized, recreational, and amateur publishing in print cultures, much of it underground and/or in niche areas. Stephen Duncombe, *Notes from Underground: Zines and the Politics of Alternative Culture* (Bloomington, IN: Microcosm, 2008); Henry Jenkins, Sam Ford, and Joshua Green, *Spreadable Media: Creating Value and Meaning in a Networked Culture* (New York: New York University Press, 2012), 107–9. However, I would argue that with notable exceptions, like African American street literature circulated by writers shut out of commercial publishing, little of this print culture made the medium of the book central to its mode of dissemination in the twentieth century. See Justin Gifford, *Pimping Fictions: African American Crime Literature and the Untold Story of Black Pulp Publishing* (Philadelphia: Temple Press, 2013), 8–9. Gifford looks at the African American street literature that circulated both through self-publishing avenues and small independent publishing houses. Likewise, we have historical examples of amateur book writers engaging in prolific book writing that very much resembles the practices I document in this book. Ronald J. Zboray and Mary Saracino Zboray, *Literary Dollars and Social Sense: A People's History of the Mass Market Book* (New York: Routledge, 2005). However, I would argue that digital practices tend to differ in their relationship to potential network effects. In other words, although I don't think that the practices I document in this book are radically new in every way, I also don't think that they are simply a continuation of vernacular print culture brought online.

37. Deborah Brandt, *The Rise of Writing: Redefining Mass Literacy* (New York: Cambridge University Press, 2015), 19. I develop this point further in the first chapter.

38. Patrick Bazin, "Toward Metareading," in *The Future of the Book*, ed. Geoffrey Nunberg (Berkeley: University of California Press, 1996), 153. Bazin accounts for

the way we read across multimedia with the term *metareading*, and he argues that the field of the book is "undergoing a reconfiguration centered no longer on a founding object but on the very process of reading." *Mass Authorship* will argue that this reconfiguration is happening in terms of both reading *and* writing.

39. This point has been made a number of times in cultural studies of reading. See, e.g., Joan Bessman Taylor, "Book Groups and the Social Contexts of Reading," in *From Codex to Hypertext: Reading at the Turn of the Twenty-First Century*, ed. Anouk Lang (Amherst: University of Massachusetts Press, 2012), 147. Taylor found that book group participants' discussions often focused on "creative processes," by which she means that members of the groups discussed how the book could have been different and what the readers wished would have happened in the narrative.

40. Jay David Bolter, *Writing Space: Computers, Hypertext, and the Remediation of Print*, 2nd ed. (Mahwah, NJ: Lea Press, 2001).

41. Henry Jenkins, *Convergence Culture: Where Old and New Media Collide* (New York: New York University Press, 2006); Yochai Benkler, *The Wealth of Networks: How Social Production Transforms Markets and Freedom* (New Haven, CT: Yale University Press, 2007), 59–90.

42. Anders Ekström et al., *History of Participatory Media: Politics and Publics, 1750–2000* (New York: Routledge, 2012).

43. Eszter Hargittai and Gina Walejko, "The Participation Divide: Content Creation and Sharing in the Digital Age," *Information, Communication & Society* 11, no. 2 (2008): 239–56.

44. Bradley et al., "Nontraditional Book Publishing," n.p.

45. For an example of this definition of independent publishing, see Bill Henderson, "The Small Book Press: A Cultural Essential," *Library Quarterly* 54, no. 1 (1984): 61–71.

46. Ian Bogost, *How to Do Things with Video Games* (Minneapolis: University of Minnesota Press, 2011), 7–9.

47. Janice A. Radway, *Reading the Romance: Women, Patriarchy, and Popular Literature* (Chapel Hill: University of North Carolina Press, 1991).

48. Barney Glaser and Anselm Strauss, *The Discovery of Grounded Theory: Strategies for Qualitative Research* (New Brunswick, NJ: Aldine, 2006).

Chapter 1: The Decline of Vanity and the Rise of Self-Publishing

1. Miller, "Whither the Professional Book Publisher?", 184.

2. James T. Macdonald, "Yog's Law," SFF [Science Fiction and Fantasy Writers] Net, http://www.sff.net/people/yog.

3. Michael R. Gabriel, "The Astonishing Growth of Small Publishers, 1958–1988," *Journal of Popular Culture* 24, no. 3 (1990): 61–68.

4. I recognize that taboos and stigmas are methodologically difficult to trace, because they often appear in hallway conversations, through embodied

microaggressions, or even in little asides in published writing. Yet I found the traces of evidence overwhelming enough in the sources I consulted to be convinced that the vanity stigma was widespread throughout the publishing industry in the twentieth century and certainly had an influence on self-published authors. For some of the most visible taboos on self-published authors, see Gérard Genette, *Paratexts: Thresholds of Interpretation* (New York: Cambridge University Press, 1997), 344–67.

5. Walter Besant, for example, worked constantly with the nascent Society of Authors to keep authors from being exploited by commission publishers. Robert Colby, "Harnessing Pegasus: Walter Besant, 'The Author' and the Profession of Authorship," *Victorian Periodicals Review* 23, no. 3 (1990): 111–20.

6. Michael Winship, "The Rise of a National Trade System in the United States," in *A History of the Book in America*, vol. 4, *Print in Motion: The Expansion of Publishing and Reading in the United States, 1880-1940*, ed. Carl Kaestle and Janice Radway (Chapel Hill: University of North Carolina Press, 2007), 56–77; Zboray and Zboray, *Literary Dollars*, xii.

7. Zboray and Zboray, *Literary Dollars*, xiv, 169.

8. Beth Luey, "Modernity and Print III: The United States, 1890–1970," in *A Companion to the History of the Book*, ed. Simon Eliot and Jonathan Rose (Malden, MA: Blackwell, 2007), 368–80.

9. Ann Fabian, "Amateur Authorship," in *A History of the Book in America*. vol. 3, *The Industrial Book, 1840–1880*, ed. Scott E. Casper, Jeffrey D. Groves, Stephen W. Nissenbaum, and Michael Winship (Chapel Hill: University of North Carolina Press, 2007), 407–16.

10. This does not mean that there was a lack of options for different kinds of royalty publishers. In addition to large publishing companies, there were almost fifty thousand independent presses by 2004 with revenues of less than $50,000, although many of these so-called independent publishers were self-publishing authors who had begun an imprint to publish their own work. Thompson, *Merchants*, 152; see also Gabriel, "Astonishing Growth."

11. Timothy Laquintano, "The Legacy of the Vanity Press and Digital Transitions," *Journal of Electronic Publishing* 16, no. 1 (2013): n.p.

12. Ibid.; see also Kenneth Davis, *Two-Bit Culture: The Paperbacking of America* (New York: Houghton Mifflin, 1984).

13. Brandt, *Rise of Writing*, 90.

14. Ibid., 5.

15. Haugland, "Opening the Gates," 15.

16. Ann Fabian, "Amateurism and Self-Publishing," in *American History through Literature*, vol. 1, *Abolitionist Writing to Gothic Fiction*, ed. Janet Gabler-Hover and Robert Sattelmeyer (Farmington Hills, MI: Charles Scribner's Sons, 2006), 19–20.

17. Alison Flood, "Self-Published Authors React with Anger to 'Laziness'

Charge," *Guardian*, August 29, 2012, http://www.theguardian.com/books/2012/aug/29/self-published-laziness-charge-sue-grafton.

18. Brandt, *Rise of Writing*, 91.

19. I support the open-access movement in academic publishing, and I support the idea of authors paying subventions to reputable journals and presses to have their peer-reviewed work published through open access. By predatory publishers I mean the open-access journals and presses that publish the work of academics without peer review and that use the author's ability to pay as the sole criterion for publication while promising the author that he or she will reap professional awards through the publication.

20. Thompson, *Merchants*, 312–13.

21. Waldfogel and Reimers, "Storming the Gatekeepers," 47–51, report that 43 percent of households owned an e-reader in 2013. See also "Report Two of Consumer Attitudes toward E-book Reading, Volume 4," *Book Industry Study Group*, October 29, 2013, http://ftp.bisg.org/news-5-861-now-available-report-two-of-consumer-attitudes-toward-e-book-reading-volume-4.php. According to this source, about 30 percent of the books sold in 2013 were ebooks. Conventional wisdom suggests that growth is not sustainable, and the percentage of ebooks might certainly regress depending on whether the users of e-readers replace their devices when they break or become obsolete. Regardless of the actual year-to-year numbers, however, screen culture has a central place in the immediate future, and I think it is safe to say that because of this, ebooks will also play an important role in publishing even if they do not surpass the popularity of print.

22. Strawberry Saroyan, "Storyseller," *New York Times*, June 17, 2011, http://www.nytimes.com/2011/06/19/magazine/amanda-hocking-storyseller.html?pagewanted=all&_r=0.

23. Leslie Kaufman, "New Publisher Authors Trust: Themselves," *New York Times*, April 16, 2013, http://www.nytimes.com/2013/04/17/business/media/david-mamet-and-other-big-authors-choose-to-self-publish.html?pagewanted=all.

24. Some libraries have already begun to engage, curate, buy, and lend self-published titles to patrons. An interesting example of this is the Illinois Author Project, which worked to find and then publicize the best self-published book that it could find from Illinois authors. Libraries might be able to use this model as leverage with corporate publishers if the libraries think these publishers are placing unfair restrictions and policies on ebook lending. David Vinjamur, "With Ebooks Still Pricey, Illinois Libraries Flex Their Marketing Muscle," *Forbes*, June 6, 2014, http://www.forbes.com/sites/davidvinjamuri/2014/06/06/with-ebooks-still-pricey-illinois-libraries-flex-their-marketing-muscle/?utm_content=buffer3613e&utm_medium=social&utm_source=linkedin.com&utm_campaign=buffer).

25. "SFWA Statement on Harlequin's Vanity Press Imprint," Science Fiction and Fantasy Writers of America, November 2009, http://www.sfwa.org/2009/11/sfwa-statement-on-harlequins-self-publishing-imprint/.

26. Lynn Andriani, "Harlequin Horizons Now DellArte Press," *Publishers Weekly*, November 25, 2009, http://www.publishersweekly.com/pw/by-topic/ industry-news/publisher-news/article/27076-harlequin-horizons-now-dellarte-press.html.

Chapter 2: Becoming an Author without a Publisher

1. Rebecca Moore Howard, *Standing in the Shadow of Giants: Plagiarists, Authors, Collaborators* (Stamford, CT: Ablex, 1999), 58.

2. Abigail Gibbs is one of the authors mentioned in this study whom I did not interview. This study has been constructed through media reports and an analysis of comments and discussions on Wattpad.

3. At the time of this writing, Wattpad's comment system worked in such a way that it did not number individual comments, and the time stamps were vague. This makes citing such data virtually impossible.

4. Michael H. Goldhaber, "The Attention Economy and the Net," *First Monday* 2, no. 4 (1997): n.p. For an extensive treatment of attention in the arts, see Richard Lanham, *The Economics of Attention: Style and Substance in the Age of Information* (Chicago: University of Chicago Press, 2006). Although Lanham's work has informed my thinking, I primarily rely on Goldhaber's article to provide a more succinct framework for interpreting the activity of my participants. Lanham provides an extensive discussion of electronic books in relation to attention, but we diverge somewhat in our points of emphasis. Whereas I concentrate intensely on how distribution and circulation patterns condition the work of authorship and publishing, Lanham attends more closely to the expressive potential of digital media and how it might manifest itself in electronic books. Lanham argues that electronic books have, to date, largely been remediated codices that fail to take advantage of the full expressive potential of digital media and the multiple modes of communication they enable (130–45). This has been a frequent complaint about ebooks: they are too conservative and resemble print books. My own position—and one reason for my emphasis on the importance of new patterns of circulation and distribution that ebooks enable—is that the expressive potential Lanham anticipates for the future electronic book has already been realized in video games. In other words, I think that video games have been offering the kind of semiotic experience Lanham speculates ebooks might provide in the future and that ebooks will continue to be largely dedicated to the written word even as they integrate various kinds of social communication and multimodal elements.

5. Goldhaber, "Attention Economy," n.p.

6. Ann M. Blair, *Too Much To Know: Managing Scholarly Information before the Modern Age* (New Haven, CT: Yale University Press, 2010).

7. Goldhaber, "Attention Economy," n.p.

8. Stephen Toulouse, "The Story of My Book, Part 2: The Publishening," *Stepto*

(blog), February 11, 2011, http://www.stepto.com/2011/02/the-story-of-my
-book-part-2-the-publishening/.

9. Ibid.

10. Duguid, "Material Matters," 65.

11. John Updike, "The End of Authorship," *New York Times*, June 25, 2006,
http://www.nytimes.com/2006/06/25/books/review/25updike.html?pagewanted
=all&_r=0.

12. Howard, *Standing in the Shadow*, 58.

13. Pierre Bourdieu, *Distinction: A Social Critique of the Judgment of Taste*
(Cambridge, MA: Harvard University Press, 1984), 5.

14. Paul W. Kingston, *The Wages of Writing: Per Word, Per Piece, or Perhaps*
(New York: Columbia University Press, 1986); Wiliiam Jackson Lord, *"How
Authors Make a Living* (New York: Scarecrow Press, 1962).

15. Goldhaber, "Attention Economy," n.p.

16. Alice E. Marwick and danah boyd, "I Tweet Honestly, I Tweet Passionately:
Twitter Users, Context Collapse, and the Imagined Audience," *New Media &
Society* 13, no. 1 (2011): 114–33.

17. Ibid. 114–15.

18. Finn Brunton, *Spam: A Shadow History of the Internet* (Cambridge, MA:
MIT Press, 2013).

19. Danielle DeVoss and James Porter, "Why Napster Matters to Writing:
Filesharing as a New Ethic of Digital Delivery," *Computers and Composition* 23, no.
2 (2006): 178–210.

20. This sentiment appeared most stridently with the writers I interviewed who
had formal training in English studies when they attended higher education.

21. This is a flashpoint of contention among indie authors. Many argue that
becoming a successful author on the royalty model requires just as much self-
marketing as becoming a successful indie author.

Chapter 3: The Birth of Independent Authorship

1. Thompson, *Merchants*, 100–187; Gabriel, "Astonishing Growth."

2. M. Thomas Inge, "Collaboration and Concepts of Authorship," *PMLA* 116, no.
3 (2001): 623–30, http://www.jstor.org/stable/463502. Inge provides a precise
example of this effacement while commenting on Maxwell Perkins, the famous
editor of modernist literature. Perkins minimized his contributions to venerate the
authors he helped produce. See also Adrian Johns, *The Nature of the Book: Print
and Knowledge in the Making* (Chicago: University of Chicago Press, 1998).

3. N. Katherine Hayles, *Writing Machines* (Cambridge, MA: MIT Press, 2002),
33, argues that early copyright debates about literary property concentrated on the
exclusion of materiality in favor of a purely intellectual construction: "With
significant exceptions, print literature was widely regarded as not having a body,

only a speaking mind." This ideology has contributed to the effacement of publishers.

4. "What Is the Difference between a Self-Publisher and an Indie Author?", Alliance of Independent Authors, http://allianceindependentauthors.org/faq/#what-is-the-difference-between-a-self-publisher-and-an-indie-author.

5. Mark Coker, "The Indie Author Manifesto," Smashwords, April 23, 2014, http://blog.smashwords.com/2014/04/indie-author-manifesto.html.

6. Orna Ross, "Introduction," in *Opening Up to Indie Authors*, by Debbie Young and Dan Holloway (n.p.: Font, 2014), Kindle edition.

7. Debbie Young and Dan Holloway, *Opening Up to Indie Authors* (n.p.: Font, 2014), Kindle edition, chap. 1.

8. Ibid.

9. Deborah Brandt, "Afterword: The Real and Fake Economies of Writing," *JAC* 34, no. 3–4 (2012): 769.

10. Teresa Mummert, *Indie Author Guide of Awesome* (n.p.: printed by author, 2013), Kindle edition, chap. 2.

11. Orna Ross, "Self-Publishing: The Basics," in *Choosing a Self-Publishing Service*, by Jim Giammatteo and Mick Rooney (n.p.: Font, 2013), Kindle edition, chap. 3.

12. "Final Thoughts," in *The Naked Truth about Self-Publishing*, ed. Jana DeLeon et al. (n.p.: Indie Voice, 2013), Kindle edition, chap. 30.

13. David Gaughran, *Let's Get Digital: How to Self-Publish and Why You Should* (n.p.: Arriba Arriba Books, 2011). Kindle edition. chap. 18.

Chapter 4: Amazon as a New Intermediary: Experimental Self-Publishing and Popular Fiction Writing

1. Johns, *Nature of the Book*; Jay David Bolter and Richard Grusin, *Remediation: Understanding New Media* (Cambridge, MA: MIT Press, 2000), 21–30.

2. The belief that one is communicating with an author and the belief that one is entering a world represent two different philosophies of reading that developed over the history of the West. Chad Wellmon, "Sacred Reading: From Augustine to the Digital Humanists," *Hedgehog Review* 17, no. 3 (Fall 2015): n.p. While I acknowledge the different genealogies, I also think they have in common a propensity to look beyond the material technology to something else: to wish or believe that the technology disappears. In that sense, different philosophies of reading nevertheless share a commitment to immediacy.

3. Steven Levy, "The Future of Reading," *Newsweek*, November 26, 2007.

4. Tarleton Gillespie, "Algorithm," Digital Keywords, June 2014, http://culturedigitally.org/2014/06/algorithm-draft-digitalkeyword/.

5. For a critique of how this data collection during the reading process threatens

privacy and the "right to read," see Ted Striphas, "The Abuses of Literacy: Amazon Kindle and the Right to Read," *Communication and Critical/Cultural Studies* 7, no. 3 (2010): 297–317.

6. Tarleton Gillespie, "The Relevance of Algorithms," in *Media Technologies: Essays on Communication, Materiality, and Society*, ed. Tarleton Gillespie, Pablo Botzkowski, and Kristen Foot (Cambridge, MA: MIT Press, 2014), 189, 192.

7. Ted Striphas, "Algorithmic Culture," *European Journal of Cultural Studies* 18, no. 4–5 (2015): 396.

8. Gillespie, "Relevance of Algorithms," 175, 179–82.

9. Hugh Howey, "Does Barnes and Noble Manipulate Its Rankings?" *Hughhowey* (blog), May 24, 2013, http://www.hughhowey.com/ does-bn-manipulate-its-bestseller-list/.

10. The term *paratext* comes from Genette, *Paratexts*. Paratexts are elements of a book other than the main text that nonetheless guide our interpretation of the book, such as the book cover, the table of contents, and interviews with the author.

11. Liliana Hart, "Taking It in the Back Door (Navigating Algorithms, Categories, and Keywords)," in *The Naked Truth about Self-Publishing*, ed. Jana DeLeon et al. (n.p.: Indie Voice, 2013), Kindle edition.

12. Gillespie, "Relevance of Algorithms," 184.

13. Laura J. Miller, "The Best-Seller List as Marketing Tool and Historical Fiction," *Book History* 3, no. 1 (2000): 289, 291, 293, 294, 297, 300, http://www. jstor.org/stable/30227320.

14. Jana DeLeon, "Keeping Score—AKA Notches in Your Bedpost," in *The Naked Truth about Self-Publishing*, ed. Jana DeLeon et al. (n.p.: Indie Voice, 2013), Kindle edition.

15. Ibid.

Chapter 5: Microclimates of Intellectual Property

1. The case has been made that the view of the Romantic Author as the dominant model of authorship underpinning contemporary copyright law has been overstated. Mark Lemley, "Romantic Authorship and the Rhetoric of Property," *Texas Law Review* 75, no. 4 (1997): 873–923. In eighteenth-century Germany, the lack of legal and economic arrangements, including a "fully developed concept of intellectual property," made it extremely difficult for writers to make a living. Martha Woodmansee, "The Genius and the Copyright: Economic and Legal Conditions of the Emergence of the 'Author,'" *Eighteenth-Century Studies* 17, no. 4 (1984): 433, http://www.jstor.org/stable/2738129.

2. Mark Rose, *Authors and Owners: The Invention of Copyright* (Cambridge, MA: Harvard University Press, 1993), 1–2. The extent to which the Romantic Author still influences copyright is the subject of much debate. Vaidhyanathan, *Copyrights and Copywrongs*, 101–2, thinks that little about authorship can be

considered "romantic" after the introduction of corporate authorship in 1909. Although I concur that corporations have a profound influence on copyright, I also think that Vaidhyanathan underestimates the Romantic Author's lingering power in everyday composition, especially when it comes to books.

3. Vaidhyanathan, *Copyrights and Copywrongs*, 97.

4. Ibid., 4–8; see also Lessig, *Remix*, 1–21.

5. Lessig, *Remix*, 143–45, gives an example of a "representative youth" who engages in the sharing economy that often violates copyright infringement. Although Lessig's work suggests that he defines *youth* as teenagers and college students, at other times he uses the term in a more polemical way, as a homogeneous rhetorical construct (common to debates about new technology) to lend force to his arguments against oppressive copyright regimes.

6. William St. Clair, "Metaphors of Intellectual Property," in *Privilege and Property: Essays on the History of Copyright*, ed. Martin Kretschmer, Lionel Bently, and Ronan Deazley (Cambridge, UK: Open Book, 2010), 370–73.

7. The term *microclimate* is from Laura J. Murray, "Plagiarism and Copyright Infringement: The Costs of Confusion," in *Originality, Imitation, and Plagiarism: Teaching Writing in the Digital Age*, ed. Caroline Eisner and Martha Vicinus (Ann Arbor: University of Michigan Press, 2009), 178–80. Murray uses it to describe the agency librarians are willing or able to exert over local IP practices for making fair use of copyrighted material.

8. Fitzpatrick, *Planned Obsolescence*, 65.

9. Mark Poster, *What's the Matter with the Internet?* (Minneapolis: University of Minnesota Press, 2001), 93.

10. Ibid., 89–90. In this chapter I will demonstrate the durability of the author function in everyday writing, but of course this is not the first time someone has argued that the individual author is more durable than some strains of theory have made it out to be. See Jonathan Gray, "When Is the Author?", in *A Companion to Media Authorship*, ed. Jonathan Gray and Derek Johnson (Malden, MA: Wiley Blackwell, 2013), 90. When discussing why the author has proved to be such an extremely durable "interface" between fan cultures and media production companies, Gray wryly notes that the difficulty of the prose that challenged the author was partly responsible for why the author remains such a popular construct.

11. Poster, *What's the Matter*, 93–97.

12. For a critique of hypertext theory from a material perspective, see Kirschenbaum, *Mechanisms*.

13. Fitzpatrick, *Planned Obsolescence*, 59.

14. Lawrence Lessig, *Code and Other Laws of Cyberspace* (New York: Basic Books, 2000). Lessig provides a broad overview of the relationship between code and IP on the Web. Writing database sites like Wattpad are interesting spaces in which to explore the way code helps regulate authorship because of the way the users, administrators, and code interact to initiate limited control over attribution

on a system primarily designed to foster free and open access to user-generated writing.

15. Ede and Lunsford, *Singular Texts*, provide a seminar study of the relationship between the individual author and practices of collaboration.

16. Martine Courant Rife, *Invention, Copyright, and Digital Writing* (Carbondale: Southern Illinois Press, 2013), 32–33.

17. Howard, *Standing in the Shadow*, 57–95.

18. Etienne Wenger, *Communities of Practice: Learning, Meaning, and Identity* (Cambridge, UK: Cambridge University Press, 1998), 58.

19. "The WattPad Writer's Rant," Wattpad, http://www.wattpad.com/story/247338-the-wattpad-writers-rant.

20. Brunton, *Spam*, 44, 47.

21. Ibid., 47, 94.

22. "The FictionPress Watchers: An Anti-Plagiarism Coalition," FictionPress Watchers, http://fpwatchers.livejournal.com/.

23. "StillKuukuu on AsianFanFics.com," FictionPress Watchers, April 13, 2013, http://fpwatchers.livejournal.com/70720.html.

24. Amy E. Robillard, "We Won't Get Fooled Again: On the Absence of Angry Responses to Plagiarism in Composition Studies," *College English* 70, no. 1 (2007): 19.

25. "Angelica L. on 4shared.com," FictionPress Watchers, July 16, 2013, http://fpwatchers.livejournal.com/66936.html?thread=239224.

26. Jan Fernback, "There Is a There There: Notes toward a Definition of Cybercommunity," in *Doing Internet Research: Critical Issues and Methods for Examining the Net,* ed. Steve Jones (London: Sage Press, 1999), 203–20; Lee Komito, "The Net as a Foraging Society: Flexible Communities," *Information Society* 14, no. 2 (1998): 97–106; Howard Rheingold, *The Virtual Community: Homesteading on the Electronic Frontier* (Cambridge, MA: MIT Press, 2000).

27. David Opderbeck, "Socially Rivalrous Information: Of Candles, Code, and Virtue." Social Science Research Network eLibrary, 2007, http://dx.doi.org/10.2139/ssrn.1008500.

28. "Idea protection" is adapted from Vaidhyanathan, *Copyrights and Copywrongs*, 17–21. He uses this term to describe a host of corporate practices like nondisclosure agreements to protect information that is not otherwise protectable through patents, copyrights, and trademarks.

29. It is possible that the romance writers also operated at this border, despite being in a mostly free economy. The platform they worked on was undoubtedly commercial, and the commercial nature of this platform influenced how they experienced the writing space and the dynamics of copyright. Yet they were not personally experiencing the border of the market and the nonmarket in the same way the poker players were, because most were not selling their work.

30. DeVoss and Porter, "Why Napster Matters to Writing," 189, 204.

31. Benkler, *Wealth of Networks*, 102.

32. David M. Hayano, *Poker Faces: The Life and Work of Professional Card Players* (Berkeley: University of California Press, 1982), 16.

33. Ibid.; David Sklansky, *The Theory of Poker*, 3rd ed. (Las Vegas, NV: Two Plus Two), 1994.

34. Eckstut reported that he was generally happy with how closely he was able to guard the text, but he was also realistic that it could not be completely protected. I saw reports not long after the publication of the text that it was for sale in Russian for $20.

35. Fitzpatrick, *Planned Obsolescence*, 50–88.

Chapter 6: Book Reviews and Credibility in a Nonfiction Niche Market

1. For myriad examples of the state's capricious attitude toward gambling as it negotiates questions of vice, revenue, and gambling's popularity, see David Schwartz, *Roll the Bones: The History of Gambling* (New York: Gotham Books, 2006).

2. Brandt, *Literacy in American Lives*, 170–72.

3. Pawel "verneer" Nazarewicz, "I Need Help with the Cover of My Book," Cardrunners, July 19, 2011, http://www.cardrunners.com/blog/verneer/i-need -help-with-the-cover-of-my-book.

4. These niche markets certainly existed in the twentieth century, but they were less accessible, and the distribution of material seemed to be more difficult. For some of the ways that fans in a niche market circulated media materials like newsletters and video without the aid of the Internet, see Jenkins et al., *Spreadable Media*, 106–12.

5. Ibid., 238–42; Chris Anderson, *The Long Tail: Why the Future of Business Is Selling Less of More* (New York: Hyperion Books, 2008). Anderson developed a theory about the relationship between niche media products and the ability of the Internet to help consumers locate them. He argued that the distribution mechanisms afforded by Web stores have driven the demand for niche content and that media industries will develop strategies to exploit an interest in niche products. Jenkins et al. survey some of the research that has debunked Anderson's most far-reaching claims, and they conclude that mass media and niche media will ultimately coexist because they play different roles in the lives of consumers, with mass media providing something of a common culture and niche media providing the means for consumers to differentiate themselves.

6. David Streitfeld, "The Best Book Reviews Money Can Buy," *New York Times*, August 25, 2012, http://www.nytimes.com/2012/08/26/business/book-reviewers- for-hire-meet-a-demand-for-online-raves.html.

7. Richard Lea and Matthew Taylor, "Historian Orlando Figes Admits Posting Amazon Reviews That Trashed Rivals," *Guardian*, April 23, 2010, http://www.theguardian.com/books/2010/apr/23/historian-orlando-figes-amazon-reviews-rivals.

8. Komito, "Net as a Foraging Society," 97, argues that Internet researchers have used *community* in nebulous ways, to indicate variously "a moral community, a normative community, a community of practice, an intentional community, or proximate community."

9. Mason Malmuth, "Re: PLO Book for 2500$," Two Plus Two, December 14, 2009, http://forumserver.twoplustwo.com/33/books-publications/plo-book-2500-learnedfromtvs-advanced-plo-theory-543219/index12.html.

10. Jenkins et al., 76–77.

11. Genette, *Paratexts*, 367, explains that autocommentary has long been taboo in Western book culture, regardless of whether the author meant to deceive readers. In the eighteenth century it was taboo because it violated propriety; in the Romantic period (the first half of the nineteenth century) it was taboo because it was "irrelevant"—the Romantics didn't believe that they could pinpoint the source of their creativity; and more recently autocommentary has been taboo because an author is not supposed to be "privileged" in the interpretation of his or her work.

12. Rak, *Boom!*, attempts to reconcile the two competing conceptions of genre.

13. Miller, "Genre as Social Action," 151.

14. Spaceball, "Re: Review of SSNLHE," Two Plus Two, June 19, 2009, http://forumserver.twoplustwo.com/33/books-publications/review-ssnlhe-510735/index4.html.

15. Isura, "Re: Bobbos Book," Leggo Poker, March 6, 2008, http://www.leggopoker.com/forums/general-online-poker-discussion/bobbos-book-149/8025-post48.html.

16. Brian Townsend, "Advanced PLO Theory, Volume 1," Cardrunners, 2010, http://www.cardrunners.com/blog/Brian/advanced-plo-theory-volume-one 2010.

17. Newman, "Review: CTS E-Book 'Let There be Range,'" Leggo Poker, January 16, 2009, http://www.leggopoker.com/blogs/clayton/review-cts-e-book-let-there-range-2926.html.

18. Cero_z, "Re: Review of Small Stakes," Two Plus Two, August 5, 2009, http://forumserver.twoplustwo.com/33/books-publications/review-small-stakes-no-limit-hold-em-ed-miller-sunny-mehta-matt-flynn-551065/index2.html.

19. Derrick Haynie, "SlowHabit's Unreleased PLO Book Review," Cardrunners, March 28, 2009, http://www.cardrunners.com/blog/SixPeppers/slowhabits-unreleased-plo-book-review

20. Irishman07, "Re: Bobbos Book, Post 257," Leggo Poker, December 9, 2008, http://www.leggopoker.com/forums/poker-discussion/bobbos-book-149-page26.html.

21. Squizzel, "Re: Bobbos Book, Post 260," Leggo Poker, December 14, 2008, http://www.leggopoker.com/forums/poker-discussion/bobbos-book-149-page26.html.

22. Andrew Brokos, "Transitioning from NLHE to PLO by Tri Nguyen," Thinking Poker, May 25, 2009, http://www.thinkingpoker.net/2009/05/book-review-transitioning-from-nlhe-to/.

23. Carla Hesse, "Books in Time," in *The Future of the Book*, ed. Geoffrey Nunberg (Berkeley: University of California Press, 1996), 27.

24. Shirky, *Here Comes Everybody*, 161.

25. Sir Neb, "Re: Bobbos Book . . . ?" Leggo Poker, March 1, 2008, http://www.leggopoker.com/forums/poker-discussion/bobbos-book-149-page4.html.

26. Gunther R. Kress, *Literacy in the New Media Age* (London: Routledge, 2003), 6.

Conclusion: Hyperabundance and the Future of Books

1. Blair, *Too Much to Know*, 58–60.

2. Gabriel Zaid, *So Many Books: Reading and Publishing in an Age of Abundance*, trans. Natasha Wimmer (Philadelphia: Paul Dry Books, 2003), 26, 29.

3. Ibid., 33.

4. Mikhail M. Bakhtin, *The Dialogic Imagination*, ed. Michael Holquist, trans. Caryl Emerson and Michael Holquist (Austin: University of Texas Press, 1981), 270.

5. Pierre Bourdieu, *Language and Symbolic Power* (Cambridge, MA: Harvard University Press, 1991), 48; John Guillory, *Cultural Capital: The Problem of Literary Canon Formation* (Chicago: University of Chicago Press, 1995), 38; Bill Readings, *The University in Ruins* (Cambridge, MA: Harvard University Press, 1996), 6–13.

6. "What Are Words Worth Now?", Authors Licensing and Collecting Society, 2014, http://www.alcs.co.uk/About-us/News/News/What-are-words-worth-now-not-much.aspx.

7. Alison Flood, "Traditional Publishing Is 'No Longer Fair or Sustainable', says Society of Authors," *Guardian*, July 11, 2014, http://www.theguardian.com/books/2014/jul/11/traditional-publishing-fair-sustainable-society-of-authors.

8. "What Are Words Worth Now?", Authors Licensing and Collecting Society.

9. Will Manley, "One Manley, One-Tenth of One Percent," *Booklist* 96 (1999): 485.

10. Laura J. Miller, *Reluctant Capitalists: Bookselling and the Culture of Consumption* (Chicago: University of Chicago Press, 2008), 23.

Appendix: Notes on Methods

1. Glaser and Strauss, *Discovery of Grounded Theory*, 32–33.

2. Christine Hine, *Virtual Ethnography* (London: Sage Press, 2000), 64–65.

3. Anselm Strauss, *Qualitative Analysis for Social Scientists* (New York: Cambridge University Press, 1987), 28–32.

4. Ibid., 38–39.

5. "Recommendation Concerning the International Standardization of Statistics Relating to Book Production and Periodicals," United Nations Educational, Scientific, and Cultural Organization, November 19, 1964. http://portal.unesco.org/en/ev.php-URL_ID=13068&URL_DO=DO_TOPIC&URL_SECTION=201.html.

6. Stephen Tepper, "Fiction Reading in America: Explaining the Gender Gap," *Poetics* 27, no. 4 (2000): 271.

7. Albert N. Greco, Clara E. Rodriguez, and Robert M. Wharton, *The Culture and Commerce of Publishing in the 21st Century* (Stanford, CA: Stanford University Press, 2007), 191–99. These authors found the US industry to be lacking in racial diversity and those in the industry recognized the lack of diversity to be an acute problem that ultimately limited the diversity of books published.

8. Grace Bello, "Wattpad Revolutionizes Online Storytelling," *Publishers Weekly*, December 21, 2012, http://www.publishersweekly.com/pw/by-topic/authors/pw-select/article/55231-pw-select-december-2012-wattpad-revolutionizes-online-storytelling.html.

9. Annukka Vainio, "Beyond Research Ethics: Anonymity as 'Ontology,' 'Analysis,' and 'Independence,'" *Qualitative Research* 13, no. 6 (2013): 685–89.

Bibliography

Anderson, Chris. *The Long Tail: Why the Future of Business Is Selling Less of More.* New York: Hyperion Books, 2008.

Bakhtin, Mikhail M. *The Dialogic Imagination.* Edited by Michael Holquist. Translated by Caryl Emerson and Michael Holquist. Austin: University of Texas Press, 1981.

Baron, Dennis. *A Better Pencil: Readers, Writers, and the Digital Revolution.* New York: Oxford University Press, 2009.

Barthes, Roland. "The Death of the Author." In *Image-Music-Text*, edited and translated by Stephen Heath, 142–48. New York: Hill, 1977. Reprinted in *Authorship: From Plato to the Postmodern*, edited by Sean Burke, 125–30. Edinburgh, UK: Edinburgh University Press, 1995.

Baverstock, Alison, and Jackie Steinitz. "Who Are the Self-Publishers?" *Learned Publishing* 26, no. 3 (2013): 211–23.

Bazerman, Charles. "Speech Acts, Genres, and Activity Systems: How Texts Organize Activity and People." In *What Writing Does and How It Does It*, edited by Charles Bazerman and Paul Prior, 309–39. New York: Lea Press, 2004.

Bazerman, Charles, and David Russell, eds. "Introduction." In *Writing Selves/Writing Societies: Research from Activity Perspectives*, 1–7. Fort Collins, CO: WAC [Writing across the Curriculum] Clearinghouse, 2002. http://wac.colostate.edu/books/selves_societies/selves_societies.pdf.

Bazin, Patrick. "Toward Metareading." In *The Future of the Book*, edited by Geoffrey Nunberg, 153–69. Berkeley: University of California Press, 1996.

Benkler, Yochai. *The Wealth of Networks: How Social Production Transforms Markets and Freedom.* New Haven, CT: Yale University Press, 2007.

Bhaskar, Michael. *The Content Machine: Towards a Theory of Publishing, from the Printing Press to the Digital Network.* New York: Anthem Press, 2013.

Blair, Ann M. *Too Much to Know: Managing Scholarly Information before the Modern Age*. New Haven, CT: Yale University Press, 2010.

Bogost, Ian. *How to Do Things with Videogames*. Minneapolis: University of Minnesota Press, 2011.

Bold, Melanie Ramdarshan. "The Sorry Tale of Contemporary Authorship: A Study of Scottish Authors." *Publishing Research Quarterly* 29, no. 1 (2013): 73–92.

Bolter, Jay David. *Writing Space: Computers, Hypertext, and the Remediation of Print*. 2nd ed. Mahwah, NJ: Lea Press, 2001.

Bolter, Jay David, and Richard Grusin. *Remediation: Understanding New Media*. Cambridge, MA: MIT [Massachusetts Institute of Technology] Press, 2000.

Bourdieu, Pierre. *Distinction: A Social Critique of the Judgment of Taste*. Cambridge, MA: Harvard University Press, 1984.

———. *Language and Symbolic Power*. Cambridge, MA: Harvard University Press, 1991.

Boyle, Casey. "Low Fidelity in High Definition: Speculations on Rhetorical Editions." In *Rhetoric and the Digital Humanities*, edited by Jim Ridolfo and Bill Hart-Davidson, 127–39. Chicago: University of Chicago Press, 2014.

Bradley, Jana, Bruce Fulton, Marlene Helm, and Katherine A. Pittner. "Nontraditional Book Publishing." *First Monday* 16, no. 8 (2011): n.p.

Brandt, Deborah. "Afterword: The Real and Fake Economies of Writing." *JAC* [*Journal of Advanced Composition*] 34, no. 3–4 (2012): 769–78.

———. *Literacy as Involvement: The Acts of Writers, Readers, and Texts*. Carbondale: Southern Illinois University Press, 2011.

———. *Literacy in American Lives*. New York: Cambridge University Press, 2001.

———. *The Rise of Writing: Redefining Mass Literacy*. New York: Cambridge University Press, 2015.

———. "Writing for a Living: Literacy and the Knowledge Economy." *Written Communication* 22, no. 2 (2005): 166–97.

Brunton, Finn. *Spam: A Shadow History of the Internet*. Cambridge, MA: MIT Press, 2013.

Carr, Nicholas. *The Shallows: What the Internet Is Doing to Our Brains*. New York: W. W. Norton, 2011.

Colby, Robert. "Harnessing Pegasus: Walter Besant, 'The Author' and the Profession of Authorship." *Victorian Periodicals Review* 23, no. 3 (1990): 111–20.

Currie, Susan, and Donna Lee Brien. "Mythbusting Publishing: Questioning the 'Runaway Popularity' of Published Biography and Other Life Writing." *M/C* [*Media & Culture*] *Journal* 11, no. 4 (2008): n.p. http://journal.mediaculture.org.au/index.php/mcjournal/article/viewArticle/43.

Davis, Kenneth. *Two-Bit Culture: The Paperbacking of America*. New York: Houghton Mifflin, 1984.

DeLeon, Jana. "Keeping Score—AKA Notches in Your Bedpost." *The Naked Truth about Self-Publishing*. Edited by Jana DeLeon et al. N.p.: Indie Voice, 2013.

DeVoss, Danielle, and James Porter. "Why Napster Matters to Writing: Filesharing as a New Ethic of Digital Delivery." *Computers and Composition* 23, no. 2 (2006): 178–210.

Duguid, Paul. "Material Matters: The Past and Futurology of the Book." In *The Future of the Book*, edited by Geoffrey Nunberg, 63–95. Berkeley: University of California Press, 1996.

Duncombe, Stephen. *Notes from Underground: Zines and the Politics of Alternative Culture*. Bloomington, IN: Microcosm, 2008.

Eco, Umberto. "Afterword." In *The Future of the Book*, edited by Geoffrey Nunberg, 295–306. Berkeley: University of California Press, 1996.

Ede, Lisa, and Andrea Lunsford. *Singular Texts/Plural Authors: Perspectives on Collaborative Writing*. Carbondale: Southern Illinois University Press, 1992.

Ekström, Anders, Solveig Jülich, Frans Lundgren, and Per Wisselgren, eds. *History of Participatory Media: Politics and Publics, 1750–2000*. New York: Routledge, 2012.

Ezell, Margaret J. M. *Social Authorship and the Advent of Print*. Baltimore: Johns Hopkins University Press, 2003.

Fabian, Ann. "Amateur Authorship." In *A History of the Book in America*. Vol. 3, *The Industrial Book, 1840–1880*, edited by Scott E. Casper, Jeffrey D. Groves, Stephen W. Nissenbaum, and Michael Winship, 407–16. Chapel Hill: University of North Carolina Press, 2007.

———. "Amateurism and Self-Publishing." In *American History through Literature*. Vol. 1, *Abolitionist Writing to Gothic Fiction*, edited by Janet Gabler-Hover and Robert Sattelmeyer, 19–21. Farmington Hills, MI: Charles Scribner's Sons, 2006.

Fernback, Jan. "There Is a There There: Notes toward a Definition of Cybercommunity." In *Doing Internet Research: Critical Issues and Methods for Examining the Net*, edited by Steve Jones, 203–20. London: Sage Press, 1999.

"Final Thoughts." In *The Naked Truth about Self-Publishing*. Edited by Jana DeLeon et al. N.p.: Indie Voice, 2013.

Fitzpatrick, Kathleen. "The Exhaustion of Literature: Novels, Computers, and the Threat of Obsolescence." *Contemporary Literature* 43, no. 3 (2002): 518–59.

———. *Planned Obsolescence: Publishing, Technology, and the Future of the Academy*. New York: New York University Press, 2011.

Foucault, Michel. "What Is an Author?" In *The Foucault Reader*, edited by Paul Rabinow, 101–20. New York: Pantheon Books, 1984.

Fraser, Nancy. "Rethinking the Public Sphere: A Contribution to the Critique of Actually Existing Democracy." *Social Text*, no. 25–26 (1990): 56–80.

Gabriel, Michael R. "The Astonishing Growth of Small Publishers, 1958–1988." *Journal of Popular Culture* 24, no. 3 (1990): 61–68.

Gaughran, David. *Let's Get Digital: How to Self-Publish and Why You Should*. N.p.: Arriba Arriba Books, 2011.

Gee, James Paul. *Situated Language and Learning: A Critique of Traditional Schooling*. New York: Routledge, 2004.

Genette, Gérard. *Paratexts: Thresholds of Interpretation*. New York: Cambridge University Press, 1997.

Gere, Anne Ruggles. *Writing Groups: History, Theory, and Implications*. Carbondale: Southern Illinois University Press, 1987.

Gifford, Justin. *Pimping Fictions: African American Crime Literature and the Untold Story of Black Pulp Publishing*. Philadelphia: Temple Press, 2013.

Gillespie, Tarleton. "Algorithm." Digital Keywords, June 2014. http://culturedigitally. org/2014/06/algorithm-draft-digitalkeyword/.

———. "The Relevance of Algorithms." In *Media Technologies: Essays on Communication, Materiality, and Society*, edited by Tarleton Gillespie, Pablo Botzkowski, and Kristen Foot, 167–93. Cambridge, MA: MIT Press: 2014.

Glaser, Barney, and Anselm Strauss. *The Discovery of Grounded Theory: Strategies for Qualitative Research*. New Brunswick, NJ: Aldine, 2006.

Goldhaber, Michael H. "The Attention Economy and the Net." *First Monday* 2, no. 4 (1997): n.p.

Graff, Harvey J. *The Legacies of Literacy: Continuities and Contradictions in Western Culture and Society*. Bloomington: Indiana University Press, 1987.

———. *The Literacy Myth: Literacy and Social Structure in the Nineteenth-Century City*. New York: Academic Press, 1979.

Gray, Jonathan. "When Is the Author?" In *A Companion to Media Authorship*, edited by Jonathan Gray and Derek Johnson, 88–111. Malden, MA: Wiley Blackwell, 2013.

Gray, Jonathan, and Derek Johnson, eds. "Introduction." In *A Companion to Media Authorship*, 1–22. Malden, MA: Wiley Blackwell, 2013.

Greco, Albert N., Clara E. Rodriguez, and Robert M. Wharton. *The Culture and Commerce of Publishing in the 21st Century*. Stanford, CA: Stanford University Press, 2007.

Grusin, Richard A. "What Is an Electronic Author?: Theory and the Technological Fallacy." *Configurations* 2, no. 3 (1994): 469–83. https://muse.jhu.edu/journals/configurations/v002/2.3grusin.html.

Guillory, John. *Cultural Capital: The Problem of Literary Canon Formation*. Chicago: University of Chicago Press, 1995.

Haas, Christina. *Writing Technology: Studies on the Materiality of Literacy*. Mahwah, NJ: Lea Press, 1996.

Habermas, Jürgen. *The Structural Transformation of the Public Sphere: An Inquiry into a Category of Bourgeois Society*. Translated by Thomas Burger with Frederick Lawrence. Cambridge, MA: MIT Press, 1991.

Hallinan, Blake, and Ted Striphas. "Recommended for You: The Netflix Prize and the Production of Algorithmic Culture." *New Media and Society* 16, no. 4 (2014): 1–21.

Hargittai, Eszter, and Gina Walejko. "The Participation Divide: Content Creation and Sharing in the Digital Age." *Information, Communication & Society* 11, no. 2 (2008): 239–56.

Hart, Liliana. "Taking It in the Back Door (Navigating Algorithms, Categories, and Keywords)." In *The Naked Truth about Self-Publishing*. Edited by Jana DeLeon et al. N.p.: Indie Voice, 2013.

Haugland, Ann. "Opening the Gates: Print-on-Demand Publishing as Cultural Production." *Publishing Research Quarterly* 22, no. 3 (2006): 3–16.

Hayano, David M. *Poker Faces: The Life and Work of Professional Card Players*. Berkeley: University of California Press, 1982.

Hayles, N. Katherine. *Writing Machines*. Cambridge, MA: MIT Press, 2002.

Hesse, Carla. "Books in Time." In *The Future of the Book*, edited by Geoffrey Nunberg, 21–36. Berkeley: University of California Press, 1996.

Heath, Shirley Brice. *Ways with Words: Language, Life, and Work in Communities and Classrooms*. New York: Cambridge University Press, 1983.

Henderson, Bill. "The Small Book Press: A Cultural Essential." *Library Quarterly* 54, no. 1 (1984): 61–71.

Hine, Christine. *Virtual Ethnography*. London: Sage Press, 2000.

Howard, Rebecca Moore. *Standing in the Shadow of Giants: Plagiarists, Authors, Collaborators*. Stamford, CT: Ablex, 1999.

Howsam, Leslie. *Kegan Paul: A Victorian Imprint; Publishers, Books and Cultural History*. New York: Routledge, 1998.

Inge, M. Thomas. "Collaboration and Concepts of Authorship." *PMLA* [*Publications of the Modern Language Association*] 116, no. 3 (2001): 623–30. http://www.jstor.org/stable/463502.

Jenkins, Henry. *Convergence Culture: Where Old and New Media Collide*. New York: New York University Press, 2006.

Jenkins, Henry, Sam Ford, and Joshua Green. *Spreadable Media: Creating Value and Meaning in a Networked Culture*. New York: New York University Press, 2012.

Johns, Adrian. *The Nature of the Book: Print and Knowledge in the Making*. Chicago: University of Chicago Press, 1998.

Kingston, Paul W. *The Wages of Writing: Per Word, Per Piece, or Perhaps*. New York: Columbia University Press, 1986.

Kirschenbaum, Matthew G. *Mechanisms: New Media and the Forensic Imagination*. Cambridge, MA: MIT Press, 2008.

Komito, Lee. "The Net as a Foraging Society: Flexible Communities." *Information Society* 14, no. 2 (1998): 97–106.

Kress, Gunther R. *Literacy in the New Media Age*. London: Routledge, 2003.

Landow, George, and Paul Delany. "Hypertext, Hypermedia, and Literary Studies: The State of the Art." In *Hypermedia and Literary Studies*, edited by George Landow and Paul Delany, 3–52. Cambridge, MA: MIT Press, 1984.

Lanham, Richard. *The Economics of Attention: Style and Substance in the Age of Information*. Chicago: University of Chicago Press, 2006.

Laquintano, Timothy. "The Legacy of the Vanity Press and Digital Transitions." *Journal of Electronic Publishing* 16, no. 1 (2013): n.p.

———. "Sustained Authorship: Digital Writing, Self-Publishing, and the Ebook." *Written Communication* 27, no. 4 (2010): 469–93.

Lemley, Mark. "Romantic Authorship and the Rhetoric of Property." *Texas Law Review* 75, no. 4 (1997): 873–923.

Lessig, Lawrence. *Code and Other Laws of Cyberspace.* New York: Basic Books, 2000.

———. *Remix: Making Art and Commerce Thrive in the Hybrid Economy.* New York: Penguin Press, 2008.

Lord, William Jackson. *How Authors Make a Living.* New York: Scarecrow Press, 1962.

Luey, Beth. "Modernity and Print III: The United States, 1890–1970." In *A Companion to the History of the Book,* edited by Simon Eliot and Jonathan Rose, 368–80. Malden, MA: Blackwell, 2007.

Manley, Will. "One Manley, One-Tenth of One Percent." *Booklist* 96 (1999): 485.

Manovich, Lev. "Models of Authorship in New Media." http://manovich.net/content/04-projects/032-models-of-authorship-in-new-media/32_article_2002.pdf.

Marwick, Alice E., and danah boyd. "I Tweet Honestly, I Tweet Passionately: Twitter Users, Context Collapse, and the Imagined Audience." *New Media & Society* 13, no. 1 (2011): 114–33.

McGill, Meredith. "The Matter of the Text: Commerce, Print Culture, and the Authority of the State in American Copyright Law." *American Literary History* 9, no. 1 (1997): 21–59.

Miller, Carolyn R. "Genre as Social Action." *Quarterly Journal of Speech* 70, no. 2 (1984): 151–67.

Miller, Laura J. "The Best-Seller List as Marketing Tool and Historical Fiction." *Book History* 3, no. 1 (2000): 286–304. http://www.jstor.org/stable/30227320.

———. *Reluctant Capitalists: Bookselling and the Culture of Consumption.* Chicago: University of Chicago Press, 2008.

———. "Whither the Professional Book Publisher in an Era of Distribution on Demand?" In *The International Encyclopedia of Media Studies.* Vol. 2, edited by Angharad N. Valdivia and Vicki Mayer, 171–91. Chichester, UK: Wiley-Blackwell, 2013.

Morozov, Evgeny. *To Save Everything, Click Here: The Folly of Technological Solutionism.* New York: Public Affairs, 2013.

Motta-Roth, Désirée. "Discourse Analysis and Academic Book Reviews: A Study of Text and Disciplinary Cultures." In *Genre Studies in English for Academic Purposes,* edited by Inmaculad Foranet, Santiago Posteguillo, Juan Carlos Palmer, and Juan Francisco Coll, 29–58. Castello de la Plana, Spain: Universitat Jaume, 1998.

Mummert, Teresa. *Indie Author Guide of Awesome.* N.p.: printed by author, 2013.

Murray, Laura J. "Plagiarism and Copyright Infringement: The Costs of Confusion." In *Originality, Imitation, and Plagiarism: Teaching Writing in the Digital Age,* edited by Caroline Eisner and Martha Vicinus, 173–83. Ann Arbor: University of Michigan Press, 2009.

Nunberg, Geoffrey, ed. "Farewell to the Information Age." In *The Future of the Book,* 103–38. Berkeley: University of California Press, 1996.

———. "Introduction." In *The Future of the Book*, 9–20. Berkeley: University of California Press, 1996.

Opderbeck, David W. "Socially Rivalrous Information: Of Candles, Code, and Virtue." Social Science Research Network eLibrary. 2007. http://dx.doi.org/10.2139/ssrn.1008500.

Piper, Andrew. *Book Was There: Reading in Electronic Times*. Chicago: University of Chicago Press, 2012.

Poster, Mark. *What's the Matter with the Internet?* Minneapolis: University of Minnesota Press, 2001.

Prior, Paul. "Tracing Process: How Texts Come into Being." In *What Writing Does and How It Does It*, edited by Charles Bazerman and Paul Prior, 167–200. New York: Lea Press, 2004.

———. *Writing/Disciplinarity: A Sociohistoric Account of Literate Activity in the Academy*. Mahwah, NJ: Erlbaum, 1998.

Prior, Paul, and Jody Shipka. "Chronotopic Laminations: Tracing the Contours of Literate Activity." In *Writing Selves, Writing Societies: Research from Activity Perspectives*, edited by Charles Bazerman and David Russell, 180–238. Fort Collins, CO: WAC Clearinghouse, 2007. http://wac.colostate.edu/books/selves_societies/.

Radway, Janice A. *Reading the Romance: Women, Patriarchy, and Popular Literature*. Chapel Hill: University of North Carolina Press, 1991.

Rak, Julie. *Boom!: Manufacturing Memoir for the American Public*. Waterloo, ON: Wilfrid Laurier University Press, 2013.

Readings, Bill. *The University in Ruins*. Cambridge, MA: Harvard University Press, 1996.

Rheingold, Howard. *The Virtual Community: Homesteading on the Electronic Frontier*. Cambridge, MA: MIT Press, 2000.

Rife, Martine Courant. *Invention, Copyright, and Digital Writing*. Carbondale: Southern Illinois Press, 2013.

Robillard, Amy E. "We Won't Get Fooled Again: On the Absence of Angry Responses to Plagiarism in Composition Studies." *College English* 70, no. 1 (2007): 10–31.

Rose, Mark. *Authors and Owners: The Invention of Copyright*. Cambridge, MA: Harvard University Press, 1993.

Ross, Orna. "Introduction." In *Opening Up to Indie Authors*, by Debbie Young and Dan Holloway. N.p.: Font, 2014.

———. "Self-Publishing: The Basics." In *Choosing a Self-Publishing Service*, by Jim Giammatteo and Mick Rooney, chap. 3. N.p.: Font, 2013.

Schwartz, David. *Roll the Bones: The History of Gambling*. New York: Gotham Books, 2006.

Shirky, Clay. *Here Comes Everybody: The Power of Organizing without Organizations*. New York: Penguin Press, 2008.

Simone, Raffaele. "The Body of the Text." In *The Future of the Book*, edited by Geoffrey Nunberg, 21–36. Berkeley: University of California Press, 1996.

Sklansky, David. *The Theory of Poker*. 3rd ed. Las Vegas, NV: Two Plus Two, 1994.

Spinuzzi, Clay. "Losing by Expanding: Corralling the Runaway Object." *Journal of Business and Technical Communication* 25, no. 4 (2011): 449–86.

———. *Network: Theorizing Knowledge Work in Telecommunications*. New York: Cambridge University Press, 2008.

St. Clair, William. "Metaphors of Intellectual Property." In *Privilege and Property: Essays on the History of Copyright*, edited by Martin Kretschmer, Lionel Bently, and Ronan Deazley, 369–95. Cambridge, UK: Open Book, 2010.

Strauss, Anselm. *Qualitative Analysis for Social Scientists*. New York: Cambridge University Press, 1987.

Street, Brian V. *Literacy in Theory and Practice*. New York: Cambridge University Press, 1984.

Striphas, Ted. "The Abuses of Literacy: Amazon Kindle and the Right to Read." *Communication and Critical/Cultural Studies* 7, no. 3 (2010): 297–317.

———. "Algorithmic Culture." *European Journal of Cultural Studies* 18, no. 4–5 (2015): 395–412.

———. *The Late Age of Print: Everyday Book Culture from Consumerism to Control*. New York: Columbia University Press, 2009.

Taylor, Joan Bessman. "Book Groups and the Social Contexts of Reading." In *From Codex to Hypertext: Reading at the Turn of the Twenty-First Century*, edited by Anouk Lang, 142–58. Amherst: University of Massachusetts Press, 2012.

Tepper, Steven J. "Fiction Reading in America: Explaining the Gender Gap." *Poetics* 27, no. 4 (2000): 255–75.

Thompson, John B. *Merchants of Culture*. Malden, MA: Polity, 2010.

Uhlan, Edward. *The Rogue of Publishers' Row: Confessions of a Publisher*. New York: Exposition Press, 1968.

Vaidhyanathan, Siva. *Copyrights and Copywrongs: The Rise of Intellectual Property and How It Threatens Creativity*. New York: New York University Press, 2003.

Vainio, Annukka. "Beyond Research Ethics: Anonymity as 'Ontology,' 'Analysis,' and 'Independence.'" *Qualitative Research* 13, no. 6 (2013): 685–98.

Waldfogel, Joel, and Imke Reimers. "Storming the Gatekeepers: Digital Disintermediation in the Market for Books." *Information Economics and Policy* 31 (June 2015): 47–58.

Wellmon, Chad. "Sacred Reading: From Augustine to the Digital Humanists." *Hedgehog Review* 17, no. 3 (Fall 2015): n.p.

Wenger, Etienne. *Communities of Practice: Learning, Meaning, and Identity*. Cambridge, UK: Cambridge University Press, 1998.

Winship, Michael. *American Literary Publishing in the Mid-Nineteenth Century: The Business of Ticknor and Fields*. New York: Cambridge University Press, 2003.

———. "The Rise of a National Trade System in the United States." In *A History of the Book in America*. Vol. 4, *Print in Motion: The Expansion of Publishing and*

Reading in the United States, 1880-1940, edited by Carl F. Kaestle and Janice A. Radway, 56–77. Chapel Hill: University of North Carolina Press, 2007.

Wirtén, Eva Hemmungs. "The Global Market, 1970–2000: Producers." In *A Companion to the History of the Book*, edited by Simon Eliot and Jonathan Rose, 395–405. Malden, MA: Blackwell, 2007.

Woodmansee, Martha. "The Genius and the Copyright: Economic and Legal Conditions of the Emergence of the 'Author.'" *Eighteenth-Century Studies* 17, no. 4 (1984): 425–48. http://www.jstor.org/stable/2738129.

Yagoda, Ben. *Memoir: A History*. New York: Penguin, 2009.

Young, Debbie, and Dan Holloway. *Opening Up to Indie Authors*. N.p.: Font, 2014.

Zaid, Gabriel. *So Many Books: Reading and Publishing in an Age of Abundance*. Translated by Natasha Wimmer. Philadelphia: Paul Dry Books, 2003.

Zboray, Ronald J., and Mary Saracino Zboray. *Literary Dollars and Social Sense: A People's History of the Mass Market Book*. New York: Routledge, 2005.

Index

abundance/hyperabundance of books, 180–84, 187–89; and Amazon, 187; and digital technologies, 2–3, 34; Eco on, 1; everyday readers' approach to, 181; and mass education/literacy, 2, 20, 184; of self-published books, 2–3, 205n4; and writing-oriented literacy, 34

academic humanism, 123–24

academic publishing, 42, 154–55

accessibility of publications, 57, 59

agents, 36, 44, 88

algorithmic culture, 98

algorithms (ranking and recommendation systems), 97–101; and authors' emphasis on content, 115–16; belief in objectivity of, 116; and bestseller lists, 109; and experimentation of authors, 94; and free reading material, 104; and new releases, 106; and shelf-life of books, 103; texts revised in response to, 95; and updates to books, 106

Alliance of Independent Authors (ALLi), 45, 80–81, 82–85

amateurs and amateur tradition in writing: in antebellum America, 36; and antiamateurism, 36; and publishers, 8, 41; and quality of books, 39; and reading-oriented literacy, 39; respect for, 33; in twentieth-century America, 36

Amazon, 93–117; abundant selection of, 187; algorithms (ranking and recommendation system) of, 94, 95, 97–101, 109, 115–16; analytics of, 101–7; CreateSpace service of, 49; dubious business practices of, 187; e-readers of (*see* Kindles and Kindle eBook store); and independent ("indie") author movement, 82; influence of, 49, 50, 179, 188; and prices of ebooks, 102–3, 105; readers' policing of intellectual property on, 134, 135; regulations for self-publishers, 49–50; review system of, 159, 163; royalty system of, 105; and sales data, 113–14; and stealth tactics of writers, 107–11; storage capacity of, 59; support services provided by, 46

analytics, 101–7

Anderson, Chris, 219n5

antebellum America, social authorship in, 36

Apple, 43, 46

argument of supersession, 66

astroturfing, 166

attention economies, 58–59

attribution, 125, 126, 140, 154

audiences, 28–29. *See also* readers and reading

Author Solutions, 47

authors and authorship: and antiamateurism, 36; as audience members of reviews, 170–72; authority and credibility of, 175–77; autonomy of, 75; characteristics of, 53; definition of, 18; democratization of, 5; earnings of, 44, 59, 184–85; effect of digital technologies on, 4–5; emergence of professional, 36; freedom of, 4; genius/celebrity image of, 78; and hierarchies of value, 53; as identity, 8, 39, 54, 62, 75; and intermediary support services, 97; mass authorship, 9, 17–19; microclimates' effect on, 154; plagiarism as threat to, 126, 128–29; and pressure from fans, 107; and prestige, 53; and reading-oriented literacy, 39, 40; relationships of readers with, 94–95, 215n2; respect for, 122–23; sponsorship of, 186; status of, 127–29, 140; tactics of, 107–11; and urge to create, 187; and vanity stigma, 40. *See also* amateurs and amateur tradition in writing

Authors Licensing and Collecting Society (ALCS), 184–85

Bakhtin, Mikhail, 182–83

Barnes and Noble, 99–100

Bazerman, Charles, 12–13

Bazin, Patrick, 209n38

"being published," 57, 58, 60, 63

Benkler, Yochai, 21, 143

bestseller titles and lists, 3, 36, 99–100, 108–11

Bezos, Jeff, 96

bibliometrics, 101, 102

bibliophiles, 181

BitTorrents, 150, 152

Blair, Ann, 180

Bogost, Ian, 25

Bolter, Jay, 21, 95

book culture: accessible publishing as threat to, 4, 7; Amazon's influence on, 50, 93, 188; analytic framework for, 8–13; and autocommentary, 220n11; and golden age ideal, 187–88; and history of the codex, 180; and hyperabundance, 180, 187; and immediacy, 95; and indie authorship, 80; isolation of, 63; and quality of books, 113; and reading-oriented literacy, 39; and Romantic Authors, 18; and self-published reviews, 159; and standards in publishing, 7; and value of books, 179; and vanity stigma, 42

book launches, 113–14

books, number of, 1–2

bookstores, 1, 46, 113

Bourdieu, Pierre, 68

Bowker, 3, 206n8

boyd, danah, 69

Boyle, Casey, 14

brachylogy of the book, 2, 16, 188

Bradley, Jana, 23–29

Brandt, Deborah, 20, 34, 38–40, 41, 184

Brunton, Finn, 69, 131, 136

business aspects of self-publishing, 71–72

canon, literary, 36

capital investments, 24, 85

Carr, Nicholas, 186

charivari, 131, 136, 138

China, self-publishing culture in, 28

Coker, Mark, 50, 82

commerce, writing associated with, 38

commission publishing, 35

communal resources, 141–42, 144, 146–48

Communities of Practice (Wenger), 129

control in publishing, 94, 140, 153–55

copyrights: and Amazon's Kindle store, 94; applied to digital works, 120; attention prompted by infringements of, 139–140; conflation of plagiarism with, 125, 140; copyright creep, 121; and experimentation of authors, 103; extreme perspectives on, 121, 154; and identity of the author, 121; misunderstandings of, 125; and poker authors/texts, 126–27, 141, 149, 158; priority of, for authors, 120; readers' policing of, 123, 134–35, 150; and Romantic Authors, 216nn1–2; and status of authors, 140; technological means of protecting, 132–33; and unauthorized translations, 141; violated by youth, 121, 217n5. *See also* intellectual property (IP)

costs of publishing: and print-on-demand (POD) companies, 37; subsidized by the author, 35, 36 (*see also* vanity publishing)

covers of books, 100

CreateSpace, 49

creativity, 186, 220n11

credibility: and forum discussions, 166; and reviews, 162–64, 166, 167, 170, 177

cultural studies, 15–16

curated book collections, 36, 39

The Dark Heroine (Gibbs), 56–60

definition of self-publishing, 23–29

DeLeon, Jana, 109–11

delivery systems, 96

Dellarte Press, 46–47

democratization, 5, 57

desktop publishing, 42

determinism, technological, 5

DeVoss, Danielle, 69, 142–43

digital attention model of authorship, 67, 68

digital economies, 58, 59

digital media, 68

digital responsivity, 172–73

digital technologies: effect of, on authorship, 4–5; and perceptions of self-publishing, 33; print-on-demand (POD) companies, 24, 37, 40, 42, 49; and production responsibilities, 42; and standards in publishing, 18; and stigma of self-publishing, 41–42. *See also* ebooks

Dinner with a Vampire (Gibbs), 55–60

disintermediation, 9–10; and algorithmic objectivity, 116; development of, 5; and new intermediaries, 7–8, 48; and reader-writer communication, 96; and solutionism, 10

distribution: and ebooks/e-readers, 43; and emergence of professional authors, 36; and immediacy, 96; and independent ("indie") author movement, 82; intermediaries providing, 46, 48; and traditional publishers, 6

dot-com bubble, 42

Duguid, Paul, 66

earnings of authors, 44, 59, 184–85

ebooks: back-channel sharing of, 140; and brachylogy of the book,

2; and digital technologies, 42; and e-readers, 42–43, 49, 205n2, 212n21 (*see also* Kindles and Kindle eBook store); and intellectual property issues, 148–152; potential future of, 213n4; prevalence of, in self-publishing, 24; pricing of, 102–3, 104–5, 150, 160, 161–62; and print readership, 44; revisions to (*see* revisions to books); sales of, 212n21; term, 205n2; and threat of BitTorrent, 152

Eco, Umberto, 4

editing and editorial services, 85–86

education, 2, 38

email, 1

"The End of Authorship" (Updike), 67

English, standardized: and expectations of readers, 17, 87; and feedback from readers, 175; and standards in publishing, 16–17, 85

ephemeral engagement with books, 183

expectations of readers, 17, 86–87, 167–68

experimentation: and analytics of Amazon, 101, 102; experimental publishing environments, 93–94; with prices of ebooks, 104–5

Fabian, Ann, 39

Facebook, 135

fair-use doctrine, 125

fan production, 111–13. *See also* readers and reading

feedback loops in web publishing: and authority of authors, 175–77; and developing writing skills, 61; and engagement with readers, 62; impact of, 127–28; and quality of books, 175–76; and revisions to books, 171, 175; and volume of feedback, 174, 175. *See also* reviews

Fictionpress Watchers, 134, 135–36

Fitzpatrick, Kathleen, 123–24, 154–55

forums: and credibility of self-published authors, 163; and intellectual property issues, 144–46, 147–48, 149–51, 152, 153; and prices of ebooks, 161–62; and reviews/feedback, 160, 163, 165, 166, 172, 175, 177; of Two Plus Two, 162, 164, 165–66, 192, 194; of Wattpad, 70

Foucault, Michel, 14, 17–18

free reading material, 87, 104

Galloway, Alexander, 98

gatekeepers in publishing world: in digital authorship, 65; and disintermediation, 5, 10; and expectations of readers, 87; fall of, 4; and independent ("indie") author movement, 79; and independent publishing, 78; as metaphor for publishing, 11; and production standards, 79; as regulators of abundance and quality, 180–81; reviews' role in, 159; roles functioning as, 11; and vanity publishing, 36; and vanity stigma, 40. *See also* intermediaries

genre (term), 167, 207n21

Gibbs, Abigail, 55–60, 213n2

Gillespie, Tarleton, 97, 98–99, 107

Goldhaber, Michael, 58, 59, 68, 213n4

Google, 98–99

GoogleBooks, 135

Graff, Harvey J., 208n32

Grafton, Sue, 39

Gray, Jonathan, 217n10

grounded theory approach to qualitative research, 191, 192

Grusin, Richard, 5, 95

7; displacement of, 10; forms of, 27, 181; four models of, 46–50; and immediacy, 94–97; importance of, minimized by authors, 97; and independent ("indie") authors, 82, 111; and ranking systems of online bookstores, 94, 95; reviews as, 159; and vanity stigma, 46, 48, 50; and Wattpad, 48. *See also* Amazon; gatekeepers in publishing world

International Standard Book Numbers (ISBNs), 3

Internet, 21, 123–24

Internet ethnography, 191, 192

intertextuality of books, 14, 138, 182

Jenkins, Henry, 21, 219n5

Johns, Adrian, 94

journalists, 185

Kindles and Kindle eBook store: and Amazon's algorithms, 97, 98; bestseller list of, 108; and intellectual property issues, 134; and new releases, 106; and popular fiction writers, 27; potential audience with, 93; readers' adoption of, 43; regulation of, 49

Kirschenbaum, Matthew, 5

Kress, Gunther, 176

Lanham, Richard, 213n4

learning modalities, 168–69

Leibniz, Gottfried Wilhelm, 180

lemons, 129

Lessig, Lawrence, 20, 121, 154, 217n5, 217n14

libraries, public: collection development standards of, 41, 46; community-based publishing programs in, 40; and fan production, 113; and modernization of book industry,

36; self-published titles offered in, 212n24

literacy, mass, 20, 38, 40, 184, 208n32

literacy practice, publishing as, 9, 12–17

"literate activity," 12

Livejournal, 135

Macdonald, James D., 34–35

Malmuth, Mason, 162, 163

Manley, Will, 187

manufacturing scarcity, 123, 127, 142–43

marketing, 94, 108, 113, 116

Marwick, Alice, 69

mass production, 19

memoirists, 25; ages of, 27; audiences of, 29; and barriers to production, 187; motives of, 73–75; rejection of, by publishers, 26; and research methods, 195–96; of Toulouse, 63–67

microcelebrity, 69

microclimates, 122, 123–27, 154, 217n7. *See also* poker players/authors; romance fiction writers

Miller, Carolyn, 167

Miller, Laura J., 10–11, 33, 108–9, 187

modern authors, 17–18

Morozov, Evgeny, 10–11

Murray, Laura J., 217n7

Napster music-copyrighting phenomenon, 142–43

narcissism, digital, 69

National Novel Writing Month, 40

networked participants, 9, 21–23, 174. *See also* readers and reading

new releases, 106

New York Times, 44, 90, 159

New York Times E-Book Fiction List, 108–11

niche media products, 219n5

nonfiction niche markets, 25, 158–160, 193–95. *See also* poker players/authors

nontraditional publishing, 23

Nook, 82

online communities: and book production, 50; and credibility of self-published authors, 163, 166; and fan production, 112; and feedback loops in web publishing, 175; influence of, 168; reviews posted to, 165–66; and self-promotion, 69; and *self-publishing* misnomer, 178; Two Plus Two online community, 162, 164, 165–66, 192, 194; and value of ebooks, 163. *See also* forums; Wattpad.com

open-access publishers/movement, 42, 143, 212n19

Opening Up to Indie Authors (Young and Holloway), 83–84

originality, 141

paratexts, 102, 105, 216n10

payment systems, 43

peer pressure, 131, 152

peer production, 111, 143–44

peer review, 42, 159, 160, 163

peer-to-peer file sharing, 142–43, 163

Penguin, 47

perceptions of self-publishing, 33. *See also* vanity stigma

Perkins, Maxwell, 214n2

personal narratives, 25

piracy, 106, 121, 152, 153

plagiarism: and antiplagiarism efforts, 125–26, 128, 129–32; attention prompted by accusations of, 137–38; coalitions organized to fight, 134–36; communal responses to, 129–32; conflation of copyright with, 125,

140; and fair-use doctrine, 125; practices of, 128, 137; priority of, for authors, 120; readers' policing of, 128; as spam, 137; technological means of fighting, 132–34; as threat to authorship, 126, 128–29; and Wattpad participants, 128–29, 131–32. *See also* intellectual property (IP)

Poker Faces (Hayano), 144

poker players/authors: ages of, 27; audiences of, 28; authority and credibility of, 141, 151, 161, 162–64; and back-channel sharing of ebooks, 140; coaching programs and practices of, 143, 144–48, 149–51, 160; and communal resources, 141–42, 144, 146–48; and digital responsivity, 172–73; and economy of instruction, 143, 154, 155, 157–58, 161, 200; and ethic of sharing, 147; and idea protection, 126–27, 141; and increasing difficulty of poker, 144; and modalities of learning, 168–69; and nonfiction niche market, 25; and peer production, 111, 143–44, 146; and prices of ebooks, 150, 160, 161–62, 174, 177; and proprietorship, 143, 147; readers' policing of intellectual property, 150, 151; and research methods, 193–95; and reviews of ebooks, 159–61, 165–66, 167–74, 174–77; and shutdown of online poker companies, 26, 157–58; and value of ebooks, 173–74, 177–78

popular fiction writers, 25, 27; audiences of, 29; ephemerality of, 183; and hybrid model, 91; and new authors, 103; and peer production, 111; and research methods, 198–99

Porter, James, 69, 142–43

Poster, Mark, 123–24

poststructuralism, 14–15, 17